Mexico's Oil

Westview Replica Editions

The concept of Westview Replica Editions is a response to the continuing crisis in academic and informational publishing. Library budgets for books have been severely curtailed. Ever larger portions of general library budgets are being diverted from the purchase of books and used for data banks, computers, micromedia, and other methods of information retrieval. Interlibrary loan structures further reduce the edition sizes required to satisfy the needs of the scholarly community. Economic pressures (particularly inflation and high interest rates) on the university presses and the few private scholarly publishing companies have severely limited the capacity of the industry to properly serve the academic and research communities. As a result, many manuscripts dealing with important subjects, often representing the highest level of scholarship, are no longer economically viable publishing projects--or, if accepted for publication, are typically subject to lead times ranging from one to three years.

Westview Replica Editions are our practical solution to the problem. We accept a manuscript in camera-ready form, typed according to our specifications, and move it immediately into the production process. As always, the selection criteria include the importance of the subject, the work's contribution to scholarship, and its insight, originality of thought, and excellence of exposition. The responsiblity for editing and proofreading lies with the author or sponsoring institution. We prepare chapter headings and display pages, file for copyright, and obtain Library of Congress Cataloging in Publication Data. A detailed manual contains simple instructions for preparing the final typescript, and our editorial staff is always available to answer questions.

The end result is a book printed on acid-free paper and bound in sturdy library-quality soft covers. We manufacture these books ourselves using equipment that does not require a lengthy make-ready process and that allows us to publish first editions of 300 to 600 copies and to reprint even smaller quantities as needed. Thus, we can produce Replica Editions quickly and can keep even very specialized books in print as long as there is a demand for them.

About the Book and Author

Mexico's Oil: Catalyst for a New Relationship with the U.S.?
Manuel R. Millor

Analyzing the effects of Mexico's newly flourishing petroleum industry, Dr. Millor first traces the evolution of Mexico's oil development and provides a detailed assessment of its socioeconomic, political, and ecological consequences and of the Mexican government's current energy policies. In his subsequent examination of U.S.-Mexican relations, he emphasizes that, aside from the issues directly related to Mexico's petroleum, a complex assortment of concerns remain unresolved between the two nations--illegal immigration, drug traffic, terms of technical and scientific cooperation, restrictions on Mexican exports in the U.S. market, and the more assertive foreign policy stance recently taken by Mexico.

Dr. Millor argues that, far from representing a clear case of positive growth for Mexico, petroleum could bring about distorted development and increased dependency, as well as a difficult period of relations with the U.S. If a stable association between the two governments is to emerge, he concludes, U.S. policymakers must understand the changes taking place in Mexico and accept its emergence as a middle power with autonomous goals. Representing both the Mexican and the U.S. point of view, this study contributes much to a better understanding of the significance of oil for Mexican development and to a balanced assessment of present and future U.S.-Mexican relations.

Manuel Millor is professor of public administration at the National University of Mexico.

Mexico's Oil

Catalyst for a
New Relationship
with the U.S.?

Manuel R. Millor

Westview Press / Boulder, Colorado

A Westview Replica Edition

Copyright © 1982 by Westview Press, Inc.

Published in 1982 in the United States of America by
    Westview Press, Inc.
    5500 Central Avenue
    Boulder, Colorado 80301
    Frederick A. Praeger, President and Publisher

Library of Congress Cataloging in Publication Data
Millor, Manuel R.
    Mexico's oil.
    (A Westview replica edition)
    Bibliography: p.
    Includes index.
    1. Petroleum industry and trade--Mexico. 2. Mexico--Foreign economic
relations--United States. 3. United States--Foreign economic relations--
Mexico. 4. Mexico--Dependency on the United States. I. Title.
HD9574.M6M647 1982   338.2'7282'0972   82-10849
ISBN 0-86531-923-5

Printed and bound in the United States of America

For my family

And with gratitude to my professor and friend,
Howard J. Wiarda,
for his encouragement and guidance

Contents

1
Theoretical Framework

CULTURAL HERITAGE AND DEPENDENCY

The understanding of the Latin American region has often been impaired by ethnocentrism. Scholars and public officials have tended to view the area with preconceived values and notions about development derived from the historical experiences of the United States and Western Europe. And the result has usually been misconceptions about Latin American society and politics, and frustration with policy failures.

Perhaps the most relevant example of the ethnocentric North American interpretation of Latin America is the Diffusion Model.[1] This model assumes a continuum whose two poles are tradition and modernity. The concept of tradition implies backward, archaic, and static structures. Modernity is viewed in terms of social and political mobility, the complexity of the social structure, the degree of specialization of roles and institutions in the political and social spheres, "democratic" forms of government, and indicators such as urbanization. According to the Diffusion Model, underdevelopment is a condition which has been experienced by all nations at one time or another. The concept of "progress," usually seen in terms of economic growth and industrialization, involves the passage from the traditional to the modernity end of the continuum. Obviously, this process is of a teleological character.

In North American social science, structural-functionalism in the writings of Gabriel Almond and G. Brigham Powell[2] exemplifies this emphasis on development as a linear progression from traditionalism to modernity. Likewise, Walt W. Rostow[3] applies the same conceptualization to the stages of economic development. Other theoretical levels of the Diffusion Model include: a preoccupation with stability and orderly change; the decline of ideology as modernization and technology advance; and the notion of development through the spread of knowledge

1

and benefits from the developed to the underdeveloped areas.[4]

According to the Diffusion Model, "...the solutions to the problems and conditions of underdevelopment must originate from beyond the borders of Latin America."[5] This notion triggered during the 1950s and 1960s a substantial amount of literature that praised investments in capital and technology from the United States to Latin America, as decidedly beneficial to the development of the latter.[6] Social and political stability in Latin America was, of course, a precondition for a greater participation of foreign enterprise.

By the end of the 1960s the Diffusion Model was in crisis. The Cuban Revolution proved to be a profoundly disturbing event for U.S. policymakers. The answer by the American government to the challenges posed by the Cuban Revolution was the Alliance for Progress. But the Alliance failed to promote consistent socioeconomic development and political democracy.[7] Throughout the 1960s, in response to real and imaginary constitutional and socioeconomic crisis, and to the fear of communism, many Latin American governments were successively taken over by the military, as it happened in Brazil in 1964, in Argentina in 1966, and in Peru in 1968.[8] In less than a decade, scholars switched their appreciations of Latin America in reaction to these various events. As the forebodings about violent upheavals to come, publicized in the "scare" literature of the early 1960s,[9] failed to materialize, the scholarly pendulum swung to a vision of an "unrevolutionary society,"[10] where the structural and institutional obstacles to change were quite resilient.[11]

As the previous expectations of orderly democratic progress have subsided, as well as the immediate fear of revolution, shrouded by the ascent of the military, various observers have undertaken the analysis of authoritarian-corporatist regimes as a possible dominant model for understanding Latin America. Among the main contributors to this approach are Howard Wiarda, James Malloy, Philippe Schmitter, Ronald Newton, and Frederick Pike.

James Malloy sees corporatism as an authoritarian mode of organizing state and society in Latin America. Regimes such as those of Brazil, Argentina, Peru, and Mexico would seem to share certain basic elements of the corporatist model, such as: no competition; interest representation based on enforced limited pluralism; statism; ex officio membership; and co-optation. The recognized groups in the corporate regime are organized in vertical functional categories rather than horizontal class categories, and interact with the state through the designated leaders of authoritatively sanctioned interest associations.[12]

However, there are variations in the corporatist
model. For example, Guillermo O'Donnell differentiates
between the populist authoritarianism of Juan Perón in
Argentina and Getulio Vargas in Brazil, the military-
populism of Peru after 1968, and the bureaucratic-
authoritarianism of Brazil since 1964.[13] Alfred Stepan
makes a distinction between "inclusionary" corporatism,
which would correspond to the populist regimes, and
"exclusionary" corporatism, which would conform with the
characteristics of the bureaucratic-authoritarian
period.[14] Philippe Schmitter approaches the question by
referring to two types of corporatism, state and
societal, that would discern the relative power of
governments and pressure groups.[15]

The theoretical perspective of corporatism in
regards to the role of the state in Latin America, as
well as the relationship between state and society is
heavily indebted to those who stress the cultural heritage of Latin American countries as the key factor in
understanding the region. From this perspective, the
corporate tradition, since the conquest and colonization
of the area by Spain and Portugal, has consisted of a
complex amalgam of social, cultural, religious, legal,
philosophical, and moral principles which support the
notion of a functional social hierarchy.

The explanation for current manifestations of corporatism in Latin America can be derived from historical
and cultural antecedents. Cultural relativism affords an
apparently logical perspective for contemporary authoritarianism. Howard Wiarda argues that Latin America has
taken shape along distinct lines of societal structure,
organization, and functions. The Latin American colonies
were established during the 1500s, on the basis of
feudal and medieval institutions very much in force in
Spain at the time. This fact gave rise to political,
economic, and social constants that, to a varying degree,
are still present in the area, including: absolutist,
hierarchical, elitist, and bureaucratic-patrimonial
political bases; semifeudal, mercantilist, and monopolistic economic policies; a rigid, stratified, closed
social system; and a religious tradition of Catholic
hegemony and absolutism.[16]

Glen Dealy maintains that Latin American society is
structured according to a monistic tradition, just as the
United States has followed a liberal, pluralistic tradition. Expressed in other terms, this would mean that
while North American institutions tend to reflect a
Lockean prospect, Spanish American institutions share a
Thomist outlook.[17] Two of the central principles of
Thomist political thought are organicism and patri-
archalism. First, society is based on hierarchy;
casuistry plays a more important role than law or
rational behavior. Second, there are inequalities

inherent in society, which imply the acquiescence of its members; thus, conflict is resolved by "public acceptance of the supreme power."[18]

Wiarda would seem to agree with John Mander in referring to Latin America as a historically conservative and nonrevolutionary area, "in the sense of having been cut off and only marginally affected by the great transformations that molded our modern world."[19] In the view of Stein and Stein, Latin America has never been able to escape its colonial legacy.[20] Louis Hartz has added insight to this stance with his concepts on the fragmentation of European culture and ideology. Detached from the originating center, says Hartz, that part of the European nation "loses the stimulus toward change that the whole provides...(and)...lapses into a kind of immobility."[21] Robert Adie and Guy Poitras develop a notion of the "politics of immobility" by stressing the resistance to change and to effective government by the politically predominant groups in Latin American society.[22] According to Wiarda, the distinctively Iberic-Latin tradition has proven to be quite resilient. Through its corporate-organic mold it blended "the traditional regard for order and hierarchy with the newer imperative of change and modernization." Thus, positivism was assimilated within the prevailing tradition, and liberalism was seldom successful.[23]

The historical cultural explanations suffer from the "fallacy of the single factor." Undoubtedly, cultural heritage is an important factor in understanding Latin America, but not the only one. Douglas Chalmers warns against the temptation to conclude too soon that authoritarian-corporatist regimes are here to stay. Change may be the enduring quality of contemporary Latin American politics.[24] In what may be considered as a supplement to historical-cultural explanations, O'Donnell sees the bureaucratic-authoritarian state as a response to modernizing pressures, including the "extended political activation of the popular sector."[25]

The ideas of these authors constitute a link between the cultural heritage approach and the imperative of the developmental process. Malloy sees the emergence of authoritarian-corporatist regimes as "responses to a general crisis of public authority brought about by the multiple effects of delayed dependent development."[26] An attempt to understand the nature and shortcomings of this process of development is the dependency model.

Most "dependentistas" seem to agree on four basic themes:

    1.   Underdevelopment is the result of a certain type of relationships between expanding industrial capitalist nations and peripheral countries.

2. Development and underdevelopment are two components of the same system, two simultaneous and intimately related faces of the same global process.
3. Underdevelopment is not a temporary, evolutionary stage, but a persistent, natural condition.
4. There are external and internal factors that determine dependency. The interaction between internal domination and external dependency, is deeply embedded in the structures, institutions, and processes of each Latin American national system.

There are differences between "dependentistas" in regards to the analytical approach and the solutions perceived to the problems of underdevelopment. The conservative approach[27] includes scholars such as Raul Prebisch, Miguel Wionczek, and Aníbal Pinto. The "Prebisch thesis"[28] took as its starting point the deteriorating terms of trade for Latin America, as a result of low income elasticities of demand in its exports, and high income elasticities in its imports. From there it evolved into recommendations to push import-substitution industrialisation, encourage economic integration among Latin American countries and obtain a higher reciprocity in dealing with developed nations. Prebisch and Wionczek have no abiding fears of foreign investments, although these should be more selective and controlled. Wionczek emphasizes the possibility of solutions to the economic problems born out of Latin America's own initiatives.[29] Some Marxist "dependentistas" such as Ronald H. Chilcote view this conservative approach as a mere variant of the Diffusion Model, and dismiss the expectations of attaining economic independence and national development within the capitalist framework.[30]

The moderate dependency current tends to place the blame for underdevelopment on internal as well as on external factors. They differ from Prebisch in believing that foreign aid investments, as well as trade negotiations, constitute policy weapons used consciously by the center against the peripheral economies.[31] Some of the members of this group are Helio Jaguaribe, Osvaldo Sunkel, Fernando Henrique Cardoso, Enzo Faletto, Celso Furtado, and Theotonio dos Santos. Sunkel sees development as a deliberate process which must have as its final consequence the equalization of social, political, and economic opportunities, internally as well as in relation to more developed societies.[32] In a historical analysis of development in Latin America, Cardoso and Faletto perceive as the basic problem the fact that political power has never been able to overcome the contradiction between national society and dependent

economy.[33] Jaguaribe analyzes the structural problems of
Latin America according to three main aspects: economic,
political, social and cultural stagnation; marginality,
internal as well as in relation to the developed nations;
and economic, cultural, and political-military denation-
alization.[34] These three categories define the interaction between internal domination and external dependency. Jaguaribe sees a basic alternative between dependency and autonomy.[35] In general, however, the moderates
are rather vague about policy prescriptions.

The radical dependency approach includes Andre
Gunder Frank, Octavio Ianni, James Cockcroft, and James
Petras, among others. This group sees the interests of
Latin America and those of the center powers, especially
the United States, as intrinsically contradictory.
According to Frank, the colonial and neocolonial relationship to the capitalist metropolis has shaped the
economic and class structure, as well as the culture, of
Latin American society. In this context, there are well
defined class interests for the dominant sector of the
bourgeoisie. These class interests of the local capi-
talists perpetuate the imbalance of the economy, as well
as the repressive central governments. National capitalism and the national bourgeoisie do not and cannot
offer any way out of underdevelopment.[36] Octavio Ianni
elaborates further on the historical and structural
conditions, internal and external, that generate repression and bourgeois violence.[37] It is clear that the
radicals pay much closer attention to class conflicts
than the other dependency currents. Radicals favor
social revolution as the only way out of underdevelopment.

As can be easily seen from above, there is no
unified theory of dependency. However, by necessity a
dependency approach to politics must be historical: the
axis of Latin America dependency has changed, from Spain
and Portugal, to Great Britain, and to the United States.
Likewise, the structural and historical arguments central
to the dependency approach imply a theory of conflict.
"Dependentistas" could be spread along most points of the
political spectrum, in regards to their attitudes towards
the role of the state and of social classes in national
development.

The controversy between the cultural relativists and
the "dependentistas" is more apparent than real. To be
sure, there are differences between them. Whereas the
first emphasize culture and tradition, many "dependentistas" share the assumption that economic arrangements
are the primary determinants of political, social, and
cultural forms.[38] On the other hand, the corporatist
model seems to share with the moderate and the conservative conceptions of dependency an appreciation of the
role of the state as the protagonist in Latin America's
societal transactions. In various ways the cultural-

corporatist and the dependency approaches are not exclusive, but complementary. Both cultural and economic factors must be taken into account to understand Latin America. However, the dependency approach would seem to have an advantage, that is, the fact that it affords a more dynamic analysis of both the external influences and internal changes that, through time, have contributed to shape Latin American society.

DEVELOPMENT

The distinctive cultural and developmental patterns of Latin America have given rise to the idea that the region represents a "Fourth World of Development," that corresponds neither to the earlier capitalist or socialist models, nor to the "new nation" model of Africa and Asia.[39] Indeed, Latin American countries are still in search of models of development appropriate to their own reality. Since their inception as independent republics they have tried to copy models such as liberalism and positivism, that are inadequate to deal with the problems of the area and result in distortions. At the same time, most of the prominent development theorists, such as Gabriel Almond, Cyril Black, Karl Deutsch, and W.W. Rostow, have tended to omit Latin America from their "universal" models.

The contemporary definitions of development that tend to reflect the bias of foreign schemes and solutions are not of much benefit for the study of Latin America. The Diffusion Model falls within this group. Latin American countries are not following the same "progressive" trajectory or stages that the developed nations went through, because the conditions are simply different. By this time it seems clear that the future of most Latin American political systems will not be the "ideal" type of Anglo-Saxon democracy. Likewise, Marxism does not lend itself easily to the analysis of Latin American society and politics, as Wiarda points out:

> The categories of Marxian analysis apply to the area at best imperfectly and through some elaborate stretching that at times leaves them all but unrecognizable.[40]

The radical dependency approach which pretends to fit all facets of dependency neatly into Marxist theory usually relies more on ideology than factual analysis. On the other hand, the moderate dependency and the corporatist-cultural approaches, even though not all-inclusive, provide useful insights to understand Latin American reality.

In the history of the Latin American countries, since the middle of the nineteenth century, there have been three vital objectives that emerge once and again, as imperatives in the process of consolidation of their respective societies: national unity; modernization and development; and regional integration. It is indispensable to arrive at a general definition of what development must mean for Latin America, in the context of these three goals. And it means, basically, the conjunction of economic, social, and political advancement. The relationship between these aspects is crucial. A true process of development would tend to spread in an equitable way through all the sectors in society the benefits obtained by economic growth, thereby promoting the social welfare of the population. Implicit in this definition is the assumption that Latin American governments would uphold sovereignty as an essential element of the state, to be either maintained or achieved by all means.[41]

Still pending would be the necessity to conceptualize what is meant by "advancement." And this task is unavoidably qualified by value judgments. Perhaps the best way to proceed would be through the analysis of some key elements in each of the three broad categories of development: economic, social, and political.

With respect to economic development, three basic groups of indicators should be mentioned:

- Rate of economic growth.
- Relative weight of primary, secondary, and tertiary sectors.
- Infrastructure.

These economic indicators must be qualified by two additional considerations:

- Penetration of foreign capital, especially through multinationals.
- Distribution of income.

In regards to economic performance, economic growth in Latin American countries has been accompanied by a disturbing phenomenon: the increasing control by foreign capital of the most dynamic sectors of their economies. Likewise, in most cases national income is distributed very unevenly.

With respect to social development, most of Latin America suffers the effects of a structural dichotomy: a small, modern, developed, industrialized, urban sector, and a sizeable backward, archaic, rural, and static sector. This division hinders an effective national integration. However, there is a process of social change all throughout the region, in varying degrees of intensity. In this context, development must be measured

in terms of social change: a society is developed to the
extent that it guarantees equality, effectiveness, and
accessibility of social benefits to all of its members.

The third great category of development, i.e.
political, confronts us with contradictory views on the
nature of political change. Kalman Silvert maintains
that asymmetry, clashes and conflicts characterize Latin
America's politics; there is no time for peaceful adjustments of political relationships.[42] Martin Needler distinguishes among three states of stability of the Latin
American polity, "stable," "evolving" (i.e. changes
towards increasing harmony among the members of the
polity), and "permanent instability" (i.e persistent
inconsistency among the elements), and concludes that the
patterns of "permanent instability" accurately describe
the political life of most of Latin American countries
since independence.[43] Fred W. Riggs suggests that instability may be a permanent feature of developing countries. Riggs' conception of the "prismatic society"
revolves around what he denominates as the "clect,"
a ruling group that reflects the social cleavages and is,
thus, incapable of compromise.[44]

Opposite to the previous view is the idea that
development must be understood in Latin America's own
terms. Howard Wiarda maintains that "...the question has
been not so much one of 'development' or 'modernization'
but of reconciling...the static and vegetative features
of the older, patrimonial-corporate state with the imperative of a modern, urban, industrial order."[45] It is a
matter of "blending the traditional regard for order and
hierarchy with the newer imperative of change and
modernization."[46] Another scholar, Albert Hirschman,
points out that "the very forces that are responsible for
stagnation in one period can make for progressive change
in the next."[47] In this context, Charles Anderson has
characterized Latin American politics as a "living
museum," where old as well as new power contenders find
accommodation and continue to exist, operate and interact
with each other.[48]

In dealing with political changes one must keep in
mind the transplantation and adaptation of exogenous
political categories to Latin America. In his theory of
"secondary development," Richard Adams talks about this
phenomenon in terms of assimilation and reorganization,
not of innovation.[49] But, it should be added, there must
always be frictions in this process, and the end product
will not be the same as any of its components. The
contemporary political crisis in Latin America must be
defined in terms of the necessity to create new models
of development, which do not ignore those already exist-
ent under different historical settings, but attempt to
adapt, readjust, and incorporate some of their features
with a view towards new results.[50] This constitutes the
scenario for Latin America's political process.

Pressure groups constitute one of the fundamental channels of political action in Latin America. In the comparative setting of the region, specific government policies are not extrapolative, but would rather reflect the constantly changing conformation of pressure groups in society. A useful approach to pressure groups is Abraham Lowenthal's "bureaucratic politics model." Lowenthal argues against the "rational policy model" of decision-making, and suggests that the policies of any given country are not the result of a single or even a few policymakers, but the product of a series of inter-locking bargaining within the system among different agencies, groups, and individuals. The outcome of this political process would depend on the relationship of forces at the time.[51]

At the vertex of action by the politically relevant groups in Latin American countries in the state. Regard-less of the various ideological orientations, the state is today the protagonist of the process of development in most of the region. Only the state can face the enormous task of gearing development within the framework of sovereignty. It must confront the challenges of internal antagonisms, foreign penetration, and clientelism.

The process of socioeconomic development in Latin American countries is fostering an ever higher degree of political awareness among all sectors of the population. This phenomenon galvanizes political action towards the expansion of the existing levels of participation. Legitimacy, in the end, rests "on the possibility of identifying the locality with the center."[52] Development must lead to equitable economic, social, and political advancement. Only in this context can the categories of political freedom have definite meaning. However, at present, political achievement in the Latin American nations seems to be a measure of the relative portion of the population who enjoy economic and social preroga-tives, and these are, to a varying degree, always a minority.

MEXICO AS A CASE STUDY

A pertinent means to study the previous approaches and variables related to dependency and development, would be the consideration of specific Latin American cases. A framework for analysis is needed that takes fully into account both domestic development and foreign relations, especially with the United States. At pre-sent, Mexico constitutes an ideal case to illustrate these areas: the context, cause, and effects of depend-ency, vis a vis the process of national development; and the impact of this amalgam on U.S.-Mexican relations. Mexico's petroleum boom deeply permeates these issues.

If a factor were to be singled out as a useful means to understand U.S.-Mexico relations during the twentieth century, that factor most likely would be petroleum. Ownership, exploitation, and commercialization of the Mexican petroleum industry have been at the fore of some of the most intense episodes of conflict and cooperation between the two countries since the beginning of the century. At stake have been issues such as Mexico's economic and political independence, the reach of U.S. power in its sphere of influence, and the friction between national and private interests in the United States.

The primary objective of the present study will be to analyze the overall impact of Mexico's newly flourishing petroleum industry on Mexican development and on the relations between the United States and Mexico. Since the mid-1970s, the existence of huge reserves of oil and natural gas in Mexico has brought about a radical reassessment of these relations, in terms of: a new delineation of the goals and expectations of both countries vis a vis each other; and a new perception, by both, of the national capabilities of Mexico.

The operational context is complex. At present, Mexico's petroleum circumscribes the intricate assortment of issues as yet unresolved between the United States and Mexico, including: migrant workers, the terms of technical and scientific cooperation, restrictions in U.S. markets to Mexican exports, and Mexico's assertive foreign policy. Petroleum may be the catalyst for better and more amicable relations, or for a recrudescence of misunderstanding and conflict. The result will be contingent upon the conduct of the respective governments, and of all the various pressure groups that compete for attention and for the enactment of specific policies in both nations.

NOTES

1. Ronald H. Chilcote and Joel C. Edelstein, _Latin America: The Struggle with Dependency and Beyond_ (New York: John Wiley & Sons, 1974), pp. 3-26.

2. Gabriel A. Almond and G. Brigham Powell, _Comparative Politics: A Developmental Approach_ (Boston: Little, Brown & Co., 1966).

3. Walt W. Rostow, _The Stages of Economic Development: A Noncommunist Manifesto_ (Cambridge: University Press, 1971).

4. Chilcote, _op. cit._, p. 25.

5. _Ibid._, p. 14.

6. For example, Adolph Berle, _Latin America: Diplomacy and Reality_ (New York: Harper and Row, Inc., 1962); and John Lloyd Mecham, _A Survey of U.S.-Latin_

12

American Relations (Boston: Houghton Mifflin Co., 1965).
7. See Jerome Levinson and Juan de Onis, The Alliance That Lost its Way (Chicago: Quadrangle Books, 1970).
8. For a discussion of military takeovers in Latin America during the first half of the 1960s, see Edwin Lieuwen, Generals vs. Presidents (New York: Frederick A. Praeger, 1964)..
9. For example, James Petras and Maurice Zeitlin, Latin America: Reform or Revolution? (New York: Fawcett Publications, Inc., 1968). For a later version of this type of literature, see Gary McEoin, Revolution Next Door (New York: Holt, Rinehart, and Winston, 1971).
10. For example, John Mander, The Unrevolutionary Society: The Power of Latin American Conservatism in a Changing World (New York: Knopf, 1969).
11. For example, Claudio Veliz, The Politics of Conformity in Latin America (London: Oxford University Press, 1967), and Obstacles to Change in Latin America, by the same publisher, 1965.
12. James M. Malloy, "Authoritarianism and Corporatism in Latin America: The Modal Pattern," in Malloy (ed.), Authoritarianism and Corporatism in Latin America (Pittsburgh: University of Pittsburgh Press, 1977).
13. Guillermo O'Donnell, Modernization and Bureaucratic-Authoritarianism: Studies in South American Politics (Berkeley: Institute of International Studies, University of California, 1973).
14. Alfred Stepan, The State and Society: Peru in Comparative Perspective (Princeton: Princeton University Press, 1978).
15. Philippe Schmitter, "Still the Century of Corporatism?" in Frederick B. Pike and Thomas Stritch (eds.), The New Corporatism (University of Notre Dame Press, 1974).
16. Wiarda, Howard J., "Social Change, Political Development and the Latin American Tradition," in Wiarda (ed.), Politics and Social Change in Latin America: The Distinct Tradition (The University of Massachusetts Press, 1974), p. 12.
17. Glen Dealy, "The Tradition of Monistic Democracy in Latin America," in Wiarda, p. 74.
18. Richard M. Morse, "The Heritage of Latin America," in Wiarda, p. 51.
19. Wiarda, p. 12.
20. Stanley J. and Barbara H. Stein, La Herencia Colonial de America Latina (Mexico: Siglo XXI Editores, 1975).
21. Louis Hartz, The Founding of New Societies (New York: Harcourt, Brace & World, Inc., 1964), p. 3.
22. Robert F. Adie and Guy E. Poitras, Latin America: The Politics of Immobility (New Jersey: Prentice Hall, Inc., 1974).

23. Howard J. Wiarda, "Toward a Framework for the Study of Political Change in the Iberic-Latin Tradition: The Corporative Model," World Politics, Vol. XXV, No. 2 (January 1973), pp. 214-215.

24. Douglas A. Chalmers, "The Politicized State in Latin America," in Malloy.

25. Guillermo O'Donnell, "Reflections on the Patterns of Change in the Bureaucratic-Authoritarian State," Latin American Research Review, Vol. XIII, No. 1 (1978), pp. 6-7.

26. Malloy, op. cit., p. 5.

27. Richard C. Bath and Dilmus D. James use the taxonomy "Conservative Approach, Moderates, and Radicals," in referring to the various groups of dependentistas, in "Dependency Analysis of Latin America: Some Criticisms, Some Suggestions," Latin American Research Review, Vol. XI, No. 3 (1976). I will follow this categorization, supplementing it with the views of other authors, as well as my own.

28. Prebisch has published numerous studies and reports in the publications of the Economic Commission for Latin America: Economic Bulletin for Latin America and Economic Survey of Latin America.

29. For further development of this position, see Miguel Wionczek, Inversión y tecnología extranjera en América Latina (Mexico: Editorial Joaquín Mortiz, S.A., 1971).

30. Ronald H. Chilcote, "A Question of Dependency," Latin American Research Review, Vol. XIII, No. 2 (1978), pp. 57-58.

31. Bath and James, p. 10.

32. Osvaldo Sunkel, El Subdesarrollo Latinoamericano y la Teoría del Desarrollo (Mexico: Siglo XXI Editores S.A., 1971), p. 39.

33. Fernando Henrique Cardoso and Enzo Faletto, Dependencia y Desarrollo en América Latina (Mexico: Siglo XXI Editores, S.A., 1976).

34. Helio Jaguaribe, "Dependencia y Autonomía en América Latina," in Jaguaribe et al. (eds.), La Dependencia Político-Económica de América Latina (Mexico: Siglo XXI Editores, S.A., 1971).

35. Ibid., pp. 56-80.

36. Andre Gunder Frank, Lumperburguesia: Lumpendesarrollo (Mexico: Serie Popular, Era, 1971), and Capitalism and Underdevelopment in Latin America (New York: Monthly Review Press, 1967).

37. Octavio Ianni, Imperialismo y Cultura de la violencia en América Latina (Mexico: Siglo XXI Editores, S.A., 1976).

38. Richard R. Fagen, "Studying Latin American Politics: Some Implications of a Dependency Approach," Latin American Research Review, Vol. XII, No. 2 (1977), pp. 9-10.

14

39. Howard J. Wiarda, "Social Change, Political Development, and the Latin American Tradition," in Wiarda (ed.), p. 7.

40. Ibid., p. 9.

41. By sovereignty is understood "the supremacy of the state over all individuals and associations within it and the independence of the state from external control." Raymond Garfield Gettell, Political Science (Boston: Ginn & Co., 1949), p. 20.

42. Kalman H. Silvert, The Conflict Society: Reaction and Revolution in Latin America (New York: American Universities Field Staff, Inc., 1966).

43. Martin C. Needler, Political Development in Latin America: Instability, Violence and Evolutionary Change (New York: Random House, Inc., 1966).

44. Fred W. Riggs, Administration in Developing Countries: The Theory of Prismatic Society (Boston: Houghton Mifflin Co., 1964).

45. Howard J. Wiarda, "Toward a Framework...", op. cit., p. 226.

46. Ibid., p. 215.

47. Albert O. Hirschman, Journeys Toward Progress (New York: Doubleday & Co., Inc., 1965), p. 24.

48. Charles W. Anderson, Politics and Economic Change in Latin America (Princeton: D. Van Nostrand Co., 1967), p. 104.

49. Richard N. Adams, The Second Sowing: Power and Secondary Development in Latin America (San Francisco: Chandler Publishing Co., 1967).

50. Samuel P. Huntington is one of the few major Western development theorists who acknowledges the possibility of the process of development leading to results other than "ideal" liberal democracy, in Political Order in Changing Societies (New Haven: Yale University Press, 1968).

51. See, for example, Abraham F. Lowenthal, The Peruvian Experiment: Continuity and Change Under Military Rule (Princeton: Princeton University Press, 1975).

52. Frank Tannenbaum, Ten Keys to Latin America (New York: Random House, Inc., 1962), p. 159.

2
Evolution of the Mexican Petroleum Industry

A HISTORICAL PERSPECTIVE ON U.S.-MEXICO RELATIONS

The nature and reach of Mexico's development, and its relations with the United States, are two closely related phenomena in Mexican history, and both have followed unsteady courses. Because of a situation of political impasse at home during a good part of the nineteenth century, Mexico was in a comparatively defenseless position to safeguard its territorial integrity. The result of the lack of even a modicum of national political consensus was the loss of more than half of its territory to the United States in 1848.

Even though U.S. historians have tended to consider "Manifest Destiny" as a non-imperialistic course of demographic expansion, as compared with the more clearly imperialist era of Theodore Roosevelt,[1] it is indeed difficult, from the perspective of Mexico's territorial dismemberment, not to regard the episode as part of an imperialistic design. The recollection of the Mexican-American War is still deeply embedded in Mexico's national conscience: the official name for the conflict of 1846-1848, "the war of the North American invasion," is a reflection of public sensitivities in Mexico.

Geopolitical accommodations between the two countries during the nineteenth century effectively established, for purposes of future economic exchanges, the predominance of the United States. The takeover of its territory deprived Mexico of aspirations to great power status, which were by that act transferred to the United States, and left Mexico prostrated and subject to the will of its northern neighbor. The war between Mexico and the United States, and its fateful climax, were not isolated actions. They must be considered within the context of the Monroe Doctrine, proclaimed in 1824, the Gadsden Purchase of 1853, and the McLane-Ocampo Treaty of 1859; the latter, among various dispositions, gave the United States the right of transit through the Isthmus of Tehuantepec.[2]

The Civil War in the United States meant a pause in the expansionist action towards Mexico. However, those were bitter years for Mexico, too, during which the efforts of Juárez's Reform Movement at national reconstruction had to be channeled into a desperate struggle against French imperialism, allied with Mexico's conservative elements.

In short, the period between 1830 and the 1860s in Mexico, characterized internally by political chaos and economic stagnation, and externally by the loss of half of the national territory to the United States and a series of punitive expeditions staged by European powers, effectively turned Mexico into an appendage of rapidly expanding foreign industrial economies.

The period after the Civil War in the United States, one of rapid industrial growth, coincided with the era of Porfirio Díaz in Mexico, during which "peace" and "progress" were catchwords. Towards the end of the nineteenth century, accordingly, U.S. policies with regards to Mexico shifted to a significant degree from a political to an economic motivation. Throughout 30 years, from 1880 to 1910, Díaz and his "positivist" advisers opened the doors of Mexico to foreign capital and technology. American companies invested heavily in Mexican railroads, mining operations, and petroleum exploitation. U.S. trade with Mexico had amounted to seven million dollars in 1860. It doubled to fifteen million by 1880, doubled again to thirty-six million by 1890, and nearly doubled again to sixty-three million by 1900. During the early 1890s, Mexico imported 56 percent and exported 67 percent of the total of its foreign trade, from and to the United States; by 1910 these figures had risen, respectively, to 63 percent and 76.4 percent. U.S. direct foreign investment rose from 200.2 million in 1897 to 672 million in 1908. Of the total investment of the United States in other countries in 1908, 26.62 percent was located in Mexico.[3]

By 1910-1911, foreign capital had controlling interests in 130 of the 170 biggest corporations in Mexico; this represented 77.7 percent of the total capital of the 170 firms. Foreign investment came mainly from three countries: the United States, Great Britain, and France. U.S. companies controlled 44 percent of the total capital investment, that is, they had by far the preponderant share. Some of the most important U.S. corporations were: in mining, the American Smelting and Refining Company; in oil, the Mexican Petroleum; in railroads, National Railroads of Mexico and Kansas City Railroad. By contrast, Mexican capital had a share of only 23 percent of the total capital of the biggest 170 corporations.[4]

Representative of some of the views about Mexico prevalent in the United States during those years is

the following statement by William J. Bryan, which dates
from 1908:

> Before twenty years, North America will have
> swallowed Mexico. The absorption of that country
> by ours is necessary and inevitable, for economic
> as well as political reasons. It will take place
> in a natural and peaceful way, and will mean the
> perfection of our natural accommodation...[5]

Previously, U.S. pressures had affected Mexican
territory; now, U.S. business and commercial interests
began to affect Mexico's national resources and communi-
cations, both of which passed increasingly into foreign
concerns, mainly American. In this process of penetration, Díaz's government sponsored the activities of
foreign capital, while the nascent Mexican bourgeoisie
was clearly subordinated to them. The peaceful conquest
of Mexico, i.e. dollar diplomacy, economic conquest
through growing ownership of natural resources, by means
of sales and concessions of lands and mining interests,
continued unabated during this period. Internally, the
price was excessively high. The Díaz's regime meant the
denial of elementary justice to the majority of the population. The accumulation of social discontent, and the
increasing political awareness of a small middle class,
were the main factors that led to the upheaval of 1910.

The regime of Porfirio Díaz came to an end with the
Mexican Revolution of 1910, which also marks the birth
of modern Mexico. The Mexican movement of 1910 was an
authentic revolution. It altered completly the social
structures and destroyed the old aristocracy, established
the instruments for an economic transformation of the
country, and eliminated the oligarchy which had monop-
olized political power. The Mexican Revolution was a
far reaching effort in a process dating back to the
struggle for independence, to create an entity which
could be properly called the Mexican nation. It was not
a simple, clearly defined movement: the revolution did
not have a monolithic character, nor did it evolve in a
single direction. It was a tentative, experimental and
pragmatic movement absent, to a great extent, of a prior
ideology.

The period between 1910 and 1940 could be characterized as an intense struggle to achieve structural
changes in the economic, social, and political spheres.
The actors were, on the one hand, newly mobilized social
groups, such as the small middle class, organized labor,
and peasants. On the opposite side stood conservative
groups that had survived the onslaught of the revolution
and wanted to restore the old status quo, and external
forces, represented largely by U.S. business interests,

which persisted in their efforts to preserve and
strengthen their controlling position in Mexico.

To a varying degree, from 1910 until the government
of Franklin D. Roosevelt, U.S. administrations repeatedly
intervened in the Mexican revolutionary process, in
defense of American business corporations. These interventions ranged from subtle campaigns of destabilization
to outright military invasions. The following cases
illustrate U.S. interference in Mexico during this
period:

- Mexican President Francisco Madero, who was no
  radical, in 1910 made clear his intentions to
  pursue certain nationalistic policies and to
  deny privileges to foreign capital; for example,
  he established the first tax on petroleum. As
  a result, U.S. President William H. Taft, acting
  on behalf of American companies, alternatively
  stationed sizable contingents of troops along
  the Mexican border and sent ultimatums to Madero,
  threatening with military intervention.[6]
- U.S. ambassador to Mexico, Henry Lane Wilson,
  incensed by Madero's refusal to acquiesce in
  the activities of foreign capital, by 1912 began
  to show the symptoms of a phobia against Madero.
  Apparently following orders from President Taft's
  State Department, Wilson plotted to bring about
  the downfall of Madero's government, and turned
  the American embassy in Mexico City into a center
  of intrigues and conspiracy against the Mexican
  leader. Finally, through an alliance with
  General Victoriano Huerta, known as the "Pact of
  the Ciudadela," Wilson succeeded: in February
  1913, Madero was first overthrown and then
  murdered, together with his vice president.[7]
- Under the administration of President Woodrow
  Wilson, several grave incidents took place, such
  as the armed occupation by U.S. marines of the
  Mexican ports of Tampico and Veracruz in 1914,
  and General Pershing's punitive expedition from
  mid-1916 until early 1917 in pursuit of Mexican
  revolutionist Francisco Villa, who had previously
  raided the American border town of Columbus, in
  New Mexico.
- Warren G. Harding's government extended strong
  official support to the claims of U.S. corporations, and pressured the Mexican government in
  1922 to accede to the payment of what the Mexicans
  thought to be an exorbitant foreign debt, in
  return for U.S. recognition. During the Bucareli
  Conferences of 1923, the U.S. government pressured
  Mexico's Obregon administration to recognize

the unaffectability of the holdings of U.S.
petroleum corporations in Mexico.[8]

In spite of U.S. interventions and pressures, the
Mexican Revolution fulfilled significant goals. Above
all, it become a rallying point for Mexican nationalism
and a symbol of national unity. In more concrete terms,
the highest point of achievement was reached with the
Constitution of 1917, which stands as the most radical
document of its time. It embodied the revolutionary
doctrine that the common welfare takes precedence over
the parochial rights of the individual. And, pertinent
to future relations with the United States, the Constitution of 1917 gave ample flexibility and power to the
Mexican state to define, modify, and extend its authority
in a wide variety of functions.

THE TRAVAILS OF THE MEXICAN PETROLEUM INDUSTRY: 1901-1938

According to Lorenzo Meyer, the development of the
Mexican oil industry, between the years 1901 and 1938,
could be divided into four stages.[9] The first stage is
the period from 1901 to 1910 when, under Porfirio Díaz,
production increased at a modest but steady rate; during
these years the industry was for the first time economically important. The second stage runs from 1911 to
1921, when the highest level of production was reached:
Mexico was responsible for up to 25 percent of the
world's supply; only the United States produced more oil.
During the third stage, from 1922 to 1933, production
suffered a dramatic drop. And the fourth stage, from
1933 to the expropriation in 1938, was a period of relative improvement in the levels of production.
Traditionally, Mexican oil exploration followed the
practices inherited from colonial times: ownership
regulations established that property of the subsoil was
never separated from the crown, which held it for the
"public good;" the owner of the surface rights never
acquired property rights over the resources in the subsoil. This precedent was reinforced during the Reform
Movement in Mexico in the 1860s, when the Juárez's
administration made clear in 1863 that "...coal and
petroleum constitute part of the dominion of the
nation."[10]
In a series of laws, Porfirio Díaz altered the concept of national ownership over subsoil deposits. The
Mining Law of 1884 made petroleum and other minerals the
exclusive property of the owner of the land. The Mining
Law of 1892 restricted the surface owner's right to
exploit fully certain minerals, but permitted free
exploitation of combustible minerals, including petroleum, without need for concessions.[11] The Petroleum Law

of 1901, concerned itself with concessions rather than
titles to the land, and gave the executive branch the
power to grant permits to explore certain lands and
waters under federal jurisdiction. This law extended to
the companies which discovered successful oil wells, the
privilege of exclusive rights to surrounding lands.
Finally, the Mining Law of 1909 reaffirmed the ownership
of deposits of mineral fuels by the owner of the
surface.[12]

As a result of these laws, by 1910 landowners had
all rights to the subsoil. Foreign purchasers of Mexican
lands acquired subsoil as well as surface rights, a
practice which was actually the Anglo-American system,
and contrary to the Mexican tradition. Through these
laws foreign oil companies bought large holdings, in the
hope that they would prove to have a rich subsoil. In
the case of federal lands, the executive could issue
permits for unrestricted exploitation, which were tanta-
mount to ownership. Besides subsoil rights, Díaz granted
foreign oil companies other privileges. Exempt from
import taxes was the machinery brought into the country
for the development of the oil fields. By-products of
oil were not taxed, and neither was the capital invested
in oil. While Díaz was in power, there was no export
tax on oil. The oil fields themselves were taxed, but
at the rate of cheap agricultural lands, with no considerations given to their subsoil wealth.[13]

In this way, large petroleum properties passed into
the hands of American and British corporations. The
aforementioned laws would later be the cause of many
problems between foreign oil companies and the post-
revolutionary governments of Mexico.

Incipient exploration had taken place before 1900,
but steady exploration and exploitation did not come
until after the turn of the century. Two Americans,
Edward L. Doheny and Charles A. Garfield, and two
British, Weetman Pearson and Lord Cowdray, established
themselves as the leaders of the Mexican petroleum
industry during this period; together they controlled
98 percent of the oil production.[14] Doheny founded the
Mexican Petroleum Company, which would later be sold to
Standard Oil; Pearson founded the Pearson and Son Ltd.,
which would be sold to the Royal Dutch-Shell. Production during the first decade of the century was about
thirteen million barrels of oil a year.[15]

Around 1910 huge new reserves were discovered in
the Mexican state of Veracruz, which rapidly raised the
level of production. By 1917, Mexico occupied the third
place in the world as an oil-producing nation, with
55,292,767 barrels annually; oil became the principal
Mexican export. By 1921, foreign producers were pumping
out and exporting 193,397,586 barrels per year, about
25 percent of the entire world output at the time, which

gave Mexico the second place as an oil-producing country. The companies based in Mexico supplied most of the oil imports by the United States.[16]

There are several reasons that help explain the fact that, while the Revolution brought havoc on the Mexican economy, the oil industry was actually enjoying a boom. The oil industry was located mostly along the coast of the Gulf of Mexico, far from the main battlegrounds, and did not rely on inland transportation. Besides, the most important oil-producing area at the time, Tuxpan and Tampico, enjoyed "revolutionary protection" by the troops of General Peláez.[17] On the other hand, the world demand due to increasing industrialization and to the First World War promised high profits.

The Constitution of 1917 was a direct challenge to the established practices and activities related to the petroleum industry in Mexico. The land reforms which had attracted the foreign oil companies were repealed, and restrictions to their investments were added. The subsoil became again the inalienable property of the nation. In Article 27 of the Constitution, all resources lying in a natural state in the national subsoil, such as petroleum and minerals, were thereby declared to be the property of the nation and not of the person or corporation that owned the surface above it. This was a reversion back to the old system of land ownership that had existed prior to the regime of Porfirio Díaz. Article 27 enunciated the following:

> The ownership of lands and waters...is vested
> originally in the nation which...has the right
> to transmit title thereto private persons...
> (however) the nation shall have at all times
> the right to impose upon private property such
> restrictions as the public interest may require...
> in order to conserve and equitably distribute
> the public wealth....In the nation is vested
> direct ownership of all minerals or substances
> (in the subsoil)...solid mineral fuels; petro-
> leum and all hydrocarbons, solid, liquid or
> gaseous....The ownership of the nation is
> inalienable and imprescriptible...[18]

The same article specified that concessions to own or exploit natural resources could be granted only to Mexican citizens or companies. The state could grant similar rights to foreigners, as long as they agreed to be regarded juridically as Mexicans in their operations, and to waive all right of appeal to foreign nations for protection. Foreigners were forbidden to acquire owner-ship of lands and waters within a one-hundred kilometer zone from the national boundaries, or within fifty kilometers from the seacoast.[19]

The general consensus was that Mexico had the right to nationalize those petroleum deposits not already in private hands. However, the crucial point was whether Article 27 of the Constitution was retroactive or not. The reach of the doctrine of property set forth in Article 27 was limited somehow to a provision to the effect that no measure would be applied retroactively, but there was a qualifying clause that permitted revisions of past concessions which were deemed to be harmful to the public interest. Thus, in reality, it was left up to the Mexican president to determine the path to follow in reasserting national ownership of natural resources.

Mexican President Carranza had at first privately promised that Article 27 would not be applied retroactively, but in 1918, as a facet of his running confrontation with the United States government, he proceeded to decree that, after all, it was indeed retroactive. The issue remained unresolved for the next two years. In 1920, Carranza was overthrown by General Obregón, who then became president of Mexico. Obregon reaffirmed the promise of not applying Article 27 retroactively, but refused the request of U.S. Secretary of State Hughes to put it into a formal treaty. It was for this reason that Hughes effectively blocked U.S. recognition of Obregón's government. Obviously, there was a degree of correspondence between the actions of the U.S. government, and those of U.S. private companies with interests in the Mexican economy.

In a series of legal cases dealing with the rights of the foreign oil companies, the Mexican Supreme Court, in apparent contradiction with the Constitution, stated the "positive acts" principle. This meant that Article 27 was not retroactive on lands where "positive acts," such as drilling a well, had been performed by owners before 1917; if this was the case, then full ownership could not be questioned. However, if no such act had been performed, then the owner forfeited subsoil rights.[20]

This compromise would have been acceptable to the U.S. State Department if its permanency could have been guaranteed. But Obregón was fearful that if he yielded too much to the U.S. government, domestic repercussions might ensue; therefore, he still refused to make a treaty with the United States. However, Obregón did enter into an "extra official" pact, known as the "Bucareli Agreement, " which embodied the "positive acts" principle. This agreement led to the official recognition of Obregón by the U.S. government on August 31, 1923.[21]

Obregón's successor, Plutarco Elías Calles (1924-1928), adopted at first a tough stance in the continuing negotiations with the U.S. oil companies. In 1925 the Mexican Congress passed a petroleum law limiting the

ownership of oil rights acquired before 1917 to fifty
years. Thus, the Bucareli Agreement was considered to be
no longer in effect. The foreign oil companies protested
accordingly, expressing their dissatisfaction, and bringing about new negotiations.[22]

After a long process of bargaining, in December,
1927, the Mexican Congress adopted a new petroleum code,
which embodied the terms of the Bucareli Agreement. This
new code satisfied the U.S. State Department, as American
concerns could now rely upon the Mexican courts for
protection. Based on this code, shortly thereafter, in
1928, the Morrow-Calles Act went into effect, under which
U.S. oil companies could no longer look forward to
expanding their activities in Mexico. On the other hand,
those properties on which they had performed "positive
acts" before 1917 were tacitly theirs for intensive
development to perpetuity. The oil companies had, in
exchange, implicitly agreed that subsoil deposits were
nationally, and not privately owned resources.[23]

If the Mexican petroleum industry gained importance
during the period 1911-1921, its decline between 1925
and 1927 was equally drastic. As a result of unstable
conditions in Mexico regarding property rights in the oil
industry, foreign oil companies started turning their
attention to Venezuela, which at the time was far more
"cooperative" than Mexico, and appeared to have more
petroleum, anyway. Large discoveries of oil in Oklahoma
and Texas also made operations in Mexico less important.
In any case, the length of time during which Mexico
could continue to supply new reserves for exploitation
seemed to be uncertain. The decline in production in the
Tampico fields appeared to be directly related to the
controversy over the Mexican legislation of 1925. But
there were other, more ominous reasons, for the decline
and for Mexico's future as an oil-producing nation. In
the rich fields of Tuxpan, for example, the foreign oil
companies had exploited the wells irrationally, at full
capacity, bringing about the filtering of salt water
into the oil deposits and their subsequent destruction.[24]

The oil companies had been steadily losing importance in the Mexican economy since 1921. In that year,
when the highest peak in production was reached, the
industry accounted for 6.92 percent of Mexico's GNP;
by 1936 it had slipped to only 1.83 percent of the total
GNP. During the period of peak production, the petroleum industry employed between 30,000 and 50,000 workers,
or about 0.7-0.8 percent of the Mexican labor force. By
1936, only 14,000 workers were employed, that is, approximately 0.23 percent of the work force.[25] In 1922, the
Mexican treasury had received eighty-eight million pesos
in taxes from the oil companies; this figure dropped to
nineteen million pesos by 1927.[26]

Foreign investments in the petroleum industry fell from a total of 862 million pesos in 1923 to a mere 107 million at the time of the expropriation in 1938.[27] Towards the end of 1924, capital investment in the Mexican oil industry was estimated to be around 800 million pesos. Of this sum, American capital represented 57.46 percent; the British controlled 26.16 percent; and the Dutch had 11.37 percent. Only 3.02 percent of the invested capital was Mexican. From these investments, foreign companies had obtained, by 1924, almost 2,000 million pesos, from the sale of a little over one billion barrels.[28]

There was a clear drop in operations after 1926. By 1927, refineries had cut down their activities by 40 percent, in relation to the year 1924. In 1927 the Royal Dutch Shell suspended its drilling and pumping operations, and cut down to a third its refining operations.[29] The companies stated several reasons for their declining operations, including the arguments over the implementation of Article 27 of the Mexican Constitution, the denial of new drilling permits, less productive wells, and high taxation.[30]

Even though by 1928 the legal controversy seemed to be solved, the entrance of Venezuelan exports in the oil market, and the increase in production in the United States proper, lessened the interest of foreign companies in Mexican oil. During the following years there was a relative improvement in production, but never to the levels of the early 1920s.

THE OIL EXPROPRIATION OF 1938

In 1934, when Lázaro Cárdenas took over the presidency of Mexico, the Mexican economy was still very much under the control of foreign corporations, this in spite of the fact that eighteen years had elapsed since the enactment of the Constitution of 1917. Total foreign investments reached a value of 3,900 million pesos in 1935. The importance of this figure is easily ascertained by the fact that in the same year the GNP of Mexico was barely 4,500 million pesos.[31]

In many ways, Cárdenas symbolized the climax of the Mexican Revolution. He adopted a policy of profound structural changes. From the beginning of his government, Cárdenas accelerated agrarian reform. By 1936, this policy was affecting properties that belonged to important American concerns, such as the Chihuahua Cattle Company and the Cunningham Investment Company. Additional lands that belonged to U.S. companies were also taken over in Baja California and the Yaqui Valley of northwest Mexico. Under the administration of Franklin D. Roosevelt, the U.S. State Department recognized the right of Mexico to expropriate those lands, but asked the Mexican government to offer a just compensation. By 1938 Mexico had started paying these indemnities. This time the U.S. government was showing patience in something that affected the interests of its business corporations; there were no notes with threats or ultimatums, as had been the case before for much minor causes. In June 1937, the Cárdenas government proceeded to expropriate the railroads. The Mexican state assumed the direct obligations of the railroads' debt, and reached an agreement with the International Committee of Bankers; the final settlement for the compensation would be reached under the following administration of Manuel Avila Camacho.[32]

But the issue that brought to a head all the past conflicts between the United States and Mexico was the expropriation of the petroleum industry in 1938. Since 1917 the various Mexican administrations had tried, unsuccessfully, to apply effectively Article 27 of the Mexican Constitution and to carry out the nationalization of the subsoil. In the end, foreign corporations, often backed by the U.S. government, had held their ground; for example, the Mexican government had not been able to make foreign petroleum companies comply with Mexican tax laws.[33] By 1938, however, Lazaro Cárdenas had consolidated his political position firmly enough so that he felt confident to challenge the power of the foreign oil companies, natural targets of the resurgent revolution.

At the outset of the disputes, it was the question of labor relations that brought matters to a standstill. What the issue finally came down to was whether the foreign oil companies would conform to the conditions and restrictions of Article 123 of the Mexican Constitution, dealing with the rights of the workers, and backed not only by Mexican labor unions, but by the Cárdenas' government. Article 123 granted Mexican workers guarantees such as the eight-hour day, equal pay for equal work, control of wages, and the abolition of child labor, and established the responsibility of employers in protecting the workers against occupational accidents and diseases. On the other hand, Article 123 guaranteed the right of the workers to organize and bargain for the defense of their common interests through unions, and to strike. Strikes were considered to be licit when their objective was to achieve the equilibrium among the various factors of production.[34]

In 1934, during his presidential campaign, Cárdenas had asked the Mexican workers to organize themselves in order to pressure him to satisfy the needs of the people. In his annual presidential message of 1935, Cárdenas criticized the oil legislation of 1925, because it did not comply with the fundamental principles of Article 27 of the Constitution. In that same message, Cárdenas

pointed out that, while oil taxes in Mexico were just
1.82 pesos per barrel, in the United States they amounted
to 4.10 pesos per barrel. Shortly afterwards, Cárdenas
consolidated the twenty-one Mexican oil unions into the
National Petroleum Workers' Union. In 1936, the Mexican
Confederation of Workers (CTM) was organized, which
included the most important Mexican labor unions; the
National Petroleum Workers' Union merged into the CTM.
The CTM had in 1938 a total of 600,000 affiliated
workers, of whom 15,000 worked for the foreign oil companies.[35]

Late in 1936, the Petroleum Union struck for the
adoption of a new nationwide contract, based on the guarantees stipulated in Article 123 of the Constitution.
All bargaining failed. After a six-month cooling-off
period of discussions between union and company leaders,
which ended with no results in sight, the union called
for binding arbitration, reinforcing its demands with a
strike in May 1937. On August 3, 1937, the Board of
Conciliation and Arbitration delivered a report in which
it criticized the foreign oil companies for their responsibility in the decline of production and for reselling
oil back to Mexico at a higher price. The board found
the workers' demands justifiable, and ordered an increase
in wages of 27 percent, as well as social benefits and
better working conditions.[36]

The foreign companies refused to comply, and
appealed to the Mexican Supreme Court. Their appeal was
denied on March 1, 1938, but they still refused to accept
the ruling of the Board. The companies then tried delay-
ing tactics, which only helped Cárdenas in rallying
public opinion against them. The impasse in the oil
industry took the form of an "economic conflict" which
threatened Mexico's very viability; thus the matter
passed into federal channels. The companies now faced
the government, rather than the union. Bribery failed.
As Cárdenas took steps towards expropriation, the stunned
foreign corporations finally agreed to pay the additional
benefits for the workers on March 16, but by then it was
too late. On March 18, 1938, Cárdenas issued the decree
of expropriation.[37]

The conjunction of internal and external conditions
in the late 1930s made possible the expropriation.
Internally, by 1938 Mexico had achieved a considerable
degree of national unity, higher than ever before in its
history. The central government under Cárdenas had
managed, to a significant extent, to neutralize cen-
trifugal forces deeply embedded in Mexico's social
fabric. The revolution seemed to have come to fruition,
through government actions such as the agrarian reform
and the nationalization of the railroads. Under these
circumstances, the protracted dealings between the
foreign oil corporations and, in succession, the

petroleum workers' union and the Mexican government, served to incense and rally public opinion behind the nationalization.

Externally, Roosevelt's "Good Neighbor Policy" (and its impact in Mexico through the good offices of U.S. Ambassador Josephus Daniels), and his affirmation of the policy of nonintervention, as well as the forebodings of the European conflict, made possible a healthy differentiation between the interests of the United States as a nation, and those of some of its private companies. President Roosevelt acknowledged the principle of international law that underlines the right of a sovereign nation to expropriate holdings with the objective of public utility, as long as an immediate and fair indemnity takes place. Thus, in spite of a strong worldwide campaign by the petroleum companies against Mexico, finally they had to settle their differences through negotiations.

In the end, Mexico paid a sizeable indemnity. After long and difficult diplomatic negotiations, the two countries signed a pact on November 19, 1941, called the Mexican-American General Agreement, that settled in a global way all U.S. claims against Mexico, agrarian as well as those related to petroleum. On April 17, 1942, the Commission in charge of the negotiations concluded its mission and presented a report on the value of the expropriated American holdings; these were estimated to be worth 23,995,991 dollars, of which Standard Oil was assigned 18,300,000 dollars. Mexico paid a third of the debt by July of that same year, and the rest in five equal yearly payments.[38] The indemnity to the British oil companies, which owned a greater share of the industry, was much more substantial.

The oil expropriation was the apex of nationalistic fervor during the Cárdenas' years. Afterwards, extenuated by the struggle with the foreign oil corporations and their international campaign against Mexican exports, Cárdenas was not able, or willing, to proceed to nationalize the mining industry. For his successors, as we will see, it was a matter of attracting, not fending off, foreign investments.

FLUCTUATIONS OF THE NATIONALIZED OIL INDUSTRY: 1938-1976

The nationalization of the oil industry did not start a series of expropriations by the Mexican government. The expropriation of the railroads had already taken place, and the cases in which the agrarian reform affected U.S. interests were solved peacefully through the Mexican-American General Agreement. It could be argued that Cárdenas did not have a preconceived intention of nationalizing the oil industry. According to

this point of view, events themselves would have precipi-
tated the takeover in 1938. In any case, Cárdenas'
administration pushed ahead with the reorganization of
the industry, and on June 7, 1938, Mexican Petroleum
(PEMEX) was created as a public institution. By August
1940, PEMEX had in effect centralized all the oil-
related activities in Mexico.[39]

After the nationalization, Mexico's role as an oil
exporter declined sharply, mainly as a result of the
international boycott imposed by the expropriated oil
companies, Standard Oil of New Jersey and Royal Dutch
Shell. Whereas in February 1938, Mexico had exported
two million barrels of oil, this figure dropped dramatically to only 311,000 barrels by April of that same
year.[40] After 1938,, and until the mid-1970s, oil production was channeled almost entirely towards the domestic market. Indeed, the nationalization of the oil
industry was a crucial factor in Mexico's impressive rate
of economic growth beginning with the late 1940s. It
also contributed significantly to stabilize the country
politically, rallying substantial sectors of the population around a revived nationalistic mystique.

According to Antonio J. Bermúdez, former director
of PEMEX, the overall objectives of the expropriation
and nationalization of the oil industry could be placed
in two categories: to provide sufficient energy for
the general progress of Mexico; and to turn the oil
industry into the key element for achieving Mexico's
independent economic development.[41] It could be effectively argued that the first purpose was adequately
accomplished. The oil industry radically changed its
structure: it shifted its orientation from the exports
market to the satisfaction of Mexico's internal needs.
Petroleum and natural gas became the overwhelming source
of energy for Mexico's development.

However, there are indications that point to the
fact that the second objective of the nationalization of
the oil industry, for Mexico's state-owned oil company to
become the key to the country's independent economic
development, was never attained. To present this argument Bermudez charts the evolution of Mexico's oil
industry since 1938 through three periods: the "golden
epoch" of PEMEX, which lasted until around 1952; a
transition period from 1952 to 1958; and a third period
characterized by the deterioration of the mystique of the
petroleum industry, as it had been nurtured by the
nationalization.[42]

The "golden epoch" (1938-1952) was a period of
scarce financial resources and strong international pressures. In spite of these obstacles, the oil industry
underwent a radical transformation. Through ingenuity
and a rational distribution of the available resources,
the industry continued to function normally after the

nationalization; workers and administrators of PEMEX were imbued with a sense of determination to operate the company successfully. Its structure was geared to the domestic market, parallel to the gradual increment in production and the construction of new refineries and ducts. All this was made possible, in part, because of a prevailing mystique, defined in terms of a spirit of service to national goals, and in which group and personal interests were minimal.[43]

During the administrations of Presidents Avila Camacho (1940-1946) and Alemán (1946-1952), the Mexican government invested considerable sums in PEMEX.[44] Nevertheless, to enhance production and the possibilities of financing and acquisition of capital equipment, from 1949 to 1951 PEMEX signed five drilling contracts with private foreign oil companies. These drilling contracts included guarantees to the foreign companies for expenses and investments, as well as a percentage of the value of the oil production in the new wells. However, PEMEX reserved for itself all rights over any newly discovered deposits.[45]

During the period from 1952 to 1958, PEMEX increased its refining capacity by 50 percent. However, after the 1954 devaluation of the Mexican peso, the administration of President Ruiz Cortines followed a policy of restraint with respect to public investment, and as a result the rate of growth of PEMEX diminished appreciably. Oil production increased by 28.7 percent, barely half the figure of 59.3 percent obtained during the previous six-year period. By 1958 public investment in PEMEX had increased again, and in that year it represented 26 percent of the total public investment. However, another factor, the relative poorness of the new oil fields, kept increases in output at a low level. Although investments were geared to modernization of equipment and installation of new ducts, the increment in processed products could not keep up with demand, and substantial imports were necessary; meanwhile, exports increased only moderately. As a result of the general situation, PEMEX's finances were seriously affected and, since overall governnment investments were not sufficient it had to resort to internal and external credits to defray expenses.[46]

In November 1958, a clause was added to Article 27 of the Mexican Constitution, precluding contracts in the terms that had been agreed to from 1949 to 1951 by PEMEX and several foreign oil companies; with this new regulation, by 1965 all foreign participation in PEMEX came to an end. In any case, these drilling contracts had not significantly contributed to increased production or technological improvement in PEMEX. PEMEX paid the corresponding compensation to the foreign firms. The new petroleum regulatory law reaffirmed that all oil-related

resources and activities belonged to the exclusive realm
of action of the Mexican state.[47]
        After 1958, PEMEX seemed to lose momentum. Para-
doxically, or perhaps correspondingly, once international
pressures ceased and Mexican control over its petroleum
resources was unquestionable, nationalistic motivations
were significantly discarded, and instead of the goal of
service to the nation, mercantilistic criteria prevailed.
From 1959 to the mid-1970s, the level of administrative
corruption seemed to be rising. Some of the conditions
that characterized this period were: improper financing,
including the maintenance of excessively low prices for
derived products; lack of planning, which relegated the
search for new reserves; a significant increase in the
debt of the oil industry, brought about by credit-
financing; interference by the political sphere in the
management of the oil industry. All these factors made
impossible the attainment of the second main objective
of the nationalization of 1938: Mexico's independent
economic development through its oil industry. And they
also brought about the oil crisis of 1973 in Mexico.[48]
        In 1973, oil reserves in Mexico were at an all-
time low. There was a radical disequilibrium between
reserves, on the one hand, and production and growth in
consumption, on the other. The apparent lack of a
sustained and appropriate energy policy since 1959 meant
that Mexico had to import increasing amounts of oil.
Thus, even the first objective of the nationalization, to
provide enough petroleum and natural gas for internal
energy needs, was in danger of retrogression. If the
situation had continued much longer, it would have
spelled financial disaster for Mexico, for towards the
end of 1973 international oil prices quadrupled.
The discovery and exploitation of the new fields in the
states of Tabasco and Chiapas ameliorated what could
have been an economic crisis of major proportions, with
its corresponding political implications.
        By the mid-1970s, as stepped-up exploration and
exploitation of the new oil fields in southeastern
Mexico revealed an enormous potential, old expectations
came to the fore again. The question, once more, dealt
with a renewed opportunity for PEMEX to become effectively the key to Mexico's independent economic development. It remained to be seen whether the new petroleum
wealth might not be just a much wider scenario for a
repetition of past pitfalls.

NOTES

        1. See, for an example of this view, Ernest R. May,
American Imperialism (New York: Atheneum, 1968).

2. The McLane-Ocampo Treaty was not ratified by the American Congress, because of the opposition of the northern antislavery faction.

3. Gastón García Cantú, Las Invasiones Norteameri-canas en Mexico (Mexico: Ediciones Era S.A., 1971), pp. 233-234.

4. Jose Luis Ceceña, Mexico en la orbita imperial (Mexico: Ediciones El Caballito, 1970), pp. 51-62.

5. Quoted in García Cantú, op. cit., p. 238.

6. Ibid., pp. 272-275.

7. Ceceña, op. cit., p. 104.

8. Ibid., pp. 114-115.

9. Lorenzo Meyer, Mexico y Estados Unidos en el conflicto petrolero (Mexico: El Colegio de Mexico, 1968), p. 20.

10. Jose López Portillo y Weber, El Petróleo de Mexico (Mexico: Editorial Fondo de Cultura Economica, 1975), p. 10.

11. J. Richard Powell, The Mexican Petroleum Industry: 1938-1950 (Berkeley: University of California Press, 1956), p. 8.

12. El Petróleo (Mexico: Petroleos Mexicanos, XV Edicion, 1976), pp. 56-57.

13. Karl M. Schmitt, Mexico and the United States, 1821 1973: Conflict and Coexistence (New York: John Wiley and Sons, Inc., 1974), pp. 103-105.

14. Howard F. Cline, The United States and Mexico (New York: Atheneum, 1971), p. 230.

15. Meyer, op. cit., p. 14.

16. El Petróleo, op. cit., p. 66.

17. Enrique Krauze, Historia de la Revolución Mexicana, Vol. 10, Período 1924-1928: La Reconstrucción Económica (Mexico: El Colegio de Mexico, 1977), p. 239.

18. Constitución Política de los Estados Unidos Mexicanos, Article 27 (Mexico: Editorial Porrua, S.A., 48th Ed., 1971), pp. 18-21.

19. Ibid., pp. 21-22.

20. Powell, op. cit., p. 14.

21. Schmitt, op. cit., pp. 163-164.

22. Ibid., pp. 165-166.

23. Ibid., p. 167.

24. Joseph Edmund Sterrett and Joseph Stancliffe Davis, The Fiscal and Economic Condition of Mexico. Report submitted to the International Committee of Bankers on Mexico, May 1928, pp. 199-200.

25. Meyer, op. cit., p. 30.

26. Krauze, op. cit., pp. 239-240.

27. Meyer, op. cit., p. 25.

28. Merrill Rippy, Oil and the Mexican Revolution (Ball State University, 1972), p. 167.

29. Sterrett and Davis, op. cit., pp. 200-201.

30. Ibid., pp. 205-207.

31. Ceceña, op. cit., pp. 117-118.

32.   Luis G. Zorrilla, Historia de las Relaciones entre Mexico y los Estados Unidos de America, Vol. II (Mexico: Editorial Porrúa, 1966), p. 459.

33.   Ibid., p. 467.

34.   Constitución Político de los Estados Unidos Mexicanos, Article 123, op. cit., pp. 91-99.

35.   Gonzalo Martínez Corbalá, "Lázaro Cárdenas y la Expropriación Petrolera," Conference given at the Workers' University on May 13, 1975, El Dia, Mexico, May 29, 1975, p. 15.

36.   Cline, op. cit., p. 230.

37.   Ibid., pp. 235-236.

38.   Meyer, op. cit., pp. 258-262.

39.   El Petróleo, op. cit., p. 74.

40.   Powell, op. cit., pp. 97-98.

41.   Antonio J. Bermúdez, La Política Petrolera Mexicana (Mexico: Editorial Joaquín Mortiz, 1976), p. 13.

42.   Ibid., p. 35.

43.   Ibid., pp. 36-43.

44.   Raymond Vernon, The Dilemma of Mexico's Development (Cambridge: Harvard University Press, 1965), pp. 96 & 103.

45.   Rescisión de los Contratos CIMA (Mexico: Petróleos Mexicanos, 1969), pp. 5-11.

46.   Olga Pellicer de Brody, and Esteban L. Mancilla, Historia de la Revolución Mexicana, Vol. 23, Período 1952-1960; El Entendimiento con los Estados Unidos y la gestación del desarrollo estabilizador (Mexico: El Colegio de Mexico, 1978), p. 242.

47.   Rescisión de los Contratos CIMA, op. cit., pp. 12-67.

48.   Bermúdez, op. cit., pp. 52-61.

3
Modernization and Dependency in Mexico: 1940–1976

TENDENCIES IN MEXICO'S DEVELOPMENT

The expropriation of the petroleum industry has been a crucial factor in Mexico's impressive rate of economic growth since the 1940s. As the nationalized industry achieved viability, it became the basis for state intervention in the economy. However, this did not mean a prolonged halt to foreign investments; it just set the stage for their new manifestations: away from extractive activities, and fully and increasingly into manufacturing. Paradoxically, as Lorenzo Meyer has noted, oil would come to be the main source of energy for the expansion of a manufacturing sector controlled to a great extent by foreign capital. In other words, beginning in 1938 petroleum was the propelling force of the Mexican economy to higher levels of specialization and complexity, albeit not along lines of self-sufficiency and autonomy. In the end, the economic axis of dependency was merely displaced, from agriculture and raw materials to the industrial sector.[1]

By the late 1940s, Mexico had adhered to the postwar U.S. policy of fostering economic growth, mainly through industrialization, as a primary means to achieve political stability and social progress. As it was the case in the United States and other Western countries, this model of development led to higher levels of concentration of wealth. In Mexico these discrepancies would turn out to be far more acute, since the less advanced economic base and fiscal mechanisms cause the "trickle down" of wealth to be a much slower and less socially satisfying process. Moreover, some of the main beneficiaries of Mexico's development policies were to be foreign multinational corporations.

The industrial sector gained the greatest advantages in Mexico's process of development, and a key role was played by foreign capital. Starting in 1940, total foreign investments rose from the lowest levels of the twentieth century, 449 million dollars to 2,822 million

by 1970.[2] Foreign investments increasingly centered in
the manufacturing sector, from 147 million dollars in
1950 to 2,082 million in 1970. In this latter year, the
figure represented more than 70 percent of total foreign
investments. In addition, more than 80 percent of the
foreign capital invested in the manufacturing sector, the
predominant share, was American. The emphasis on industrialization came to mean, by the early 1970s, a growing
Mexican public and private foreign debt of more than
twenty-four billion dollars; more than 50 percent of this
impressive debt was contracted with totally or predominantly U.S. financial institutions.[3]

What were the reasons befind the new wave of foreign
investments? As one of the possible alternatives to
develop a country economically, foreign investments
constitute, apparently, a way "to have your cake and eat
it, too." That is, foreign investments can result in
significant contributions to economic growth, without
precluding present consumption. Many governments are
reluctant, for political as well as economic reasons, to
deal with the complex and difficult issues involved in
reforming the fiscal structure (a measure that, to be
effective, would imply progressive taxation), as a means
of securing domestic funds for development. Thus,
foreign investments are sometimes viewed as a panacea
for the ills of underdevelopment. It could be argued
that, especially since the 1950s, Mexico has been a clear
example of the previous assessment. In spite of still
ongoing, though mostly ineffective, attempts to shift
the tax burden to the more prosperous sectors of the
population, and to increase revenues, Mexico until the
early 1980s has consistently relied on foreign investments and credits as a practically indispensable factor
in its strategy for development.

The criticisms of this policy are obvious, such as
the often voiced radical indictments that foreign investments have been responsible for the postponement of
urgently needed, deep-seated changes in the social and
political spheres. On the other hand, an economic
counterargument would assert that, no matter how substantial domestic savings might have been, they would not
have been sufficient by themselves to sustain the high
indices of economic growth of the postwar era in Mexico.
In effect, foreign investments have filled this gap.
Furthermore, and mainly during the 1950s and 1960s, by
concentrating on "hard" projects, foreign investments
have resulted in a highly favorable "multiplying effect"
for the Mexican economy. Other areas of reference, in
any comparative assessment of the benefits and/or
liabilities of foreign investments in Mexico, would be
their effects on unemployment, on domestic savings, and
on income distribution.

The study of foreign investments in Mexico seems to
confirm the tendency of Latin American countries to

embark upon quick development schemes that are but an
extralogical imitation of the economic conditions prevalent in developed, industrialized nations. Since the
recipient society, in this case Mexico, usually does not
conform to the preordained formulas for development, the
results are not too attractive, from a global perspective: high unemployment; rising foreign debt; and
control of the industrial sector by foreign companies,
which have a comparative economic advantage over domestic
concerns.

During the late 1940s and early 1950s, Mexico was
achieving significant economic goals (for example, sustained progress in key industries such as steel), mainly
through national efforts, i.e. those of private domestic
investors and of the government. However, as the 1950s
wore on, international conditions ceased to favor Mexican
exports, and the scarce buying power of the popular
sectors of the population weakened the growth of basic
consumer-oriented industries. As a result of these
factors, private domestic investment declined. There was
a reticence on the part of investors to expand the industrial plant at an adequate pace. Some observers
detected, during the late 1950s and early 1960s, a loss
of momentum in the Mexican economy.4 The impasse was
related to the ever present political question in Mexico
of the roles and domains of the private and public
sectors of the economy. The possibility of stagnation,
then as well as now, might threaten the fabric of Mexican
society. Mexico's political leadership seemed to be
faced with a choice of risks. As Raymond Vernon posed
the issues: "Which risks will they prefer to accept:
the risks associated with inadequate economic performance
or the risks associated with change in the national
decision making machinery."5

Mexico's leaders opted for the latter, albeit within
the existing institutional framework. The Mexican
government returned to a more orthodox economic approach,
that is, a willingness to deal on an equal basis with
Mexico's domestic private capital. Nevertheless, to a
great extent, the crisis was resolved by the substantial
entrance of foreign capital: starting during the mid-
1950s, foreign investments mostly from multinational
corporations made possible the significant growth of the
industrial sector, on an average of more than 9 percent
annually between the mid-1950s and the late 1960s.6 For
Mexico it was a Faustian bargain: during this new
economic stage the most dynamic sectors of its economy
fell under the control of foreign entrepreneurs.

However, it would be unfair to single out the multinational corporations as responsible for the alienation
of the industrial sector of the Mexican economy. The
entrance and growing power of foreign investments in
Mexico were not just the result of a fortuitous and

favorable economic juncture. On the contrary, the
Mexican government and, seemingly strange, the prevailing
groups in the Mexican private sector, propitiated and
encouraged the entry of large amounts of foreign capital. The reasons behind this attitude are not hard to
discern. For the Mexican government, the economic
crisis augured a social impasse; it could not afford to
contract public expenditures, for the price in terms of
political instability might have been too high. In
other words, the ruling political circles needed a growing economy, as well as sources of external credit. As
for the private sector, their sympathy towards foreign
investors derived from their mutual economic, political,
and ideological ties. Of course, all these circumstances
coincided with a period when U.S. corporations were looking for promising foreign outlets.[7]

The decision of Mexico's governing elites to indus-
trialize the country no matter what the price was the
key to the massive entrance of foreign capital. This
conscious encouragement of the industrialization process
by the Mexican government brought about painful implications, among them: the promotion of capital-intensive
industry and technology, which have had a detrimental
effect on the unemployment level; and a tremendous
increase in the foreign debt.

A subtle and contrasting parallel could be traced
between the attitude of the Mexican government towards
the oil and the manufacturing industries. In the case
of the petroleum industry, the negotiations were directly
held between governments, which allowed the Mexican
government to chart the course for the industry, ultimately a nationalistic one. In contrast, in the case of
the manufacturing sector, foreign investors dealt
directly with Mexican entrepreneurs, who were primarily
concerned with private gains and profits, and the result
was the alienation of that economic sector.[8]

Finally, another very important determining factor
of Mexico's postwar magnet-like qualities in regard to
foreign investments, was the so-called "clima de
inversión," i.e. "investment climate." Since the late
1940s Mexico had offered a combination of economic
growth, an expanding domestic market, and a stable
political system, which proved to be an irresistible
target for the expansion of U.S.-based multinational
corporations.[9]

Thus, the stage was set for the period of "desarrollo estabilizador," i.e. "stabilizing development,"
in effect, roughly from the late 1950s until 1970.
According to Mexican critic Olga Pellicer, there were
three basic objectives in the strategy of "stabilizing
development." The first was to keep price stability,
i.e., an equal level of investments and expenditures.
This first goal was achieved basically through external

financing. The second objective, closely related to the
first, was to prevent a rise in prices of the goods and
services produced by state-related enterprises. However,
since the need for public investments was greater than
the available funds, once again the Mexican government
had to resort to credit financing. Finally, the third
objective was to promote capital accumulation and rein-
vestment of profits, through a series of fiscal incentives. This encouragement of the role of the private
sector represented a weakening of the financial capacity
of the government which, together with a drop in export
taxes, again made inevitable an increase in the public
debt. Thus, the objectives of the model of "stabilizing
development" were all contingent upon the utilization of
external credits.[10]

Within the general framework of the strategy of
"stabilizing development," the recourse to external
credit financing was a means to avoid other more extreme
measures which, if implemented at the time, might have
prevented a later reckoning during the 1970s. These
dreaded remedies were related to the need for a devaluation and a deep-seated fiscal reform.[11] The willingness
of the Mexican government to enter into new foreign debts
was coupled at the time with the inordinate availability
of funds in various international sources of capital.
In any case, Mexico's public foreign debt, which had
stood at 1,327 million dollars during the early 1960s,
reached the figure of 4,200 million in 1970. During this
last year, 22.5 percent of the income of the public
sector was destined to cover the debt service, basically
interests. External credit financing was nothing new,
but now its utilization was increasing and deliberate.[12]
Some of the additional characteristics of these credits
were: a marked tendency towards "privatization;" an
increasing reliance of private Mexican borrowers on
giant foreign banking enterprises; and a growing reliance of the Mexican public sector on U.S. banks.[13]

The development of the industrial sector was one of
the key priorities in the schemes of Mexico's "stabilizing development." But foreign capital retained a dominant position in much of the expanded manufacturing
activities. In this context, it could be argued that the
protectionist measures put into effect by the Mexican
government have often served to encourage the activities
of foreign corporations, since these are already located
in the most dynamic sectors of the economy, whose
further growth the government wants to foster. The
internal dynamism of the Mexican economy itself then
contributes to enhance the role of the foreign corporation.

At the same time, protectionism and fiscal incentives accounted for a strengthening of the political
position of native entrepreneurs. The renewed

assertiveness of Mexico's private sector would play a key
role later on, in the failure and demise of President
Echeverría's model of "shared development." Finally,
to complete the vicious circle, public economic policy
geared excessive funds as subsidies for urban infrastructure, accentuating tendencies towards centralization, whose momentum brought about larger increases in
public spending.[14] Meanwhile, the agricultural sector
was neglected.

Mexico followed one policy for industry, and just
the opposite for the agricultural sector. Agriculture,
which had previously been the mainstay of Mexico's
process of development, suffered from decreasing public
outlays: its share of total public investment dropped
from 20 percent in 1950 to barely 8 percent by 1960. In
this latter year, the agricultural sector registered a
growth of 5 percent, which meant a participation of 15
percent in Mexico's total domestic product; by the second
half of the 1960s, these figures had appreciably
declined, to 1.2 percent and 11 percent, respectively.
Moreover, a good portion of the growth in agricultural
output took place in products not destined to
domestic consumption but to the exports market. In
general terms, during the 1960s the situation of the
agricultural sector deteriorated sharply, as it was
totally subordinated to the objective of industrialization.[15] The neglect of the agricultural sector, with its
detrimental effects on rural employment, and the failure
of production to keep up with increasing demand due to
population growth, would have severe consequences for
Mexico by the late 1970s and early 1980s.

Indiscriminate industrialization brought about grave
structural imbalances in Mexico, and it tended to
polarize the social sectors along sharply contrasting
levels of income and consumption. In fact, it could be
argued that the overall model of "stabilizing development" actually undermined the capacity of the state as
the promoter par excellence of Mexico's development, and
the acknowledged arbiter of social pressures. As the
import of the state in gearing Mexico's development
declined, dependency vis a vis the United States became
more clear.

> By the early 1960s, the new pattern for Mexico's
> foreign economic relations was clearly established,
> which implied a new form of dependency, suffi-
> ciently pronounced, but with distinct modalities
> to those present during the first years of the
> Mexican Revolution. This scheme is similar to
> that which governs the foreign relations of other
> Latin American countries...(but) in the case of
> Mexico, the proximity of the United States gives
> a special character to its foreign relations;
> because of geographical vicinity there are

between both countries particular ties which have
a very decisive influence in Mexico's internal
life and contribute significantly to the complexity of its dependence vis a vis the United
States.[16]

In appearance, the decade of the 1960s was one of
uninterrupted growth for Mexico. This was reflected in
the literature on Mexican development during those
years.[17] In retrospect, the administrations of
Presidents López Mateos (1958-1964), and Díaz Ordaz
(1964-1970), especially the latter, favored relatively
conservative economic policies that enhanced the role
of the private sector and the maintenance of a high
growth index. However, there were deep problems, such
as: a high and rising level of unemployment, due to
increases in productivity; rapid demographic growth, and
urbanization; pressures for the distribution of land,
related to the stagnation of the rural sector; a deterioration in income distribution; labor pressures for wage
increases; a chronic and growing commercial deficit; and
an insufficient basis of income for the public sector.[18]
    In December 1970, the new administration of Presi-
dent Luis Echeverria marked the beginning of an attempt
to break with the priorities of the model of "stabilizing development," and to address some of its shortcomings, with respect to categories such as employment,
income distribution, and external financial dependency.
The new strategy would be called "shared development."[19]
The main objectives of Echeverría's economic policies
were the following:

- Economic growth with income distribution;
- Strengthening of public finances;
- Reorganization of international transactions;
- Modernization of the agricultural sector;
- Rationalization of industrial development.[20]

In the sociopolitical sphere, the policies of
Echeverría's administration attempted to face a dangerous
legitimacy crisis, partly a result of the social costs
implicit in the model of "stabilizing development" and,
more specifically, of the domestic unrest which had
culminated in the bloody confrontation between soldiers
and students in Tlatelolco in 1968.[21] The process of
political reform from 1970 to 1973 was meant to
strengthen the institutional and legal opposition to the
ruling party, "Partido Revolucionario Institucional"
(PRI), and to allow new means of expression to the
diverse ideological tendencies present in Mexico. These
reforms were introduced through constitutional amendments
and the promulgation of a new electoral law. Of course,
it was evident that these measures also purported to

channel and control social conflicts through legally
recognized political parties.[22]

The objectives of the model of "shared development"
made necessary a vigorous public sector, in order to
recover the initiative that had been partly lost to the
private sector, and to give the economy a new orientation. This gave rise to a conflict between the government and the private sector, which became a permanent
fixture of Echeverría's administration. President
Echeverría adopted a policy that strongly favored a
greater intervention of the state in Mexico's process of
development, and changes in the patterns of distribution
of income. On the other hand, the private sector opposed
this emphasis on state participation; instead, it sought
a continuation of the policies of the 1960s, which, to
a great extent, had placed the political and economic
resources of the state at its service.[23]

President Echeverría's administration considered
"stabilizing development" responsible for the relegation
of the social aspects of development. Therefore, public
investments would now be channeled towards the creation
of new jobs, an increase in productivity and efficiency
in basic industries, and the reinvigoration of the
agricultural sector. And indeed, the public sector
increased its participation in Mexico's domestic product,
from 11 percent in 1970 to 17.2 percent in 1975 and,
respectively, from 38 percent to 45 percent of the total
gross domestic investments.[24]

However, in the end, the model of "shared development" did not bring about the expected results. The
series of domestic measures undertaken by Echeverría
showed the critical interrelationship of social, political, and economic factors. Echeverría's attempt to tilt
the ideological orientation of the government to the
left, and to side with the poorer sectors of the population, brought about a break with the private sector of
the economy. As huge sums of capital left the country
and investments collapsed, Echeverría resorted to foreign loans to finance his government's social programs.
The growing debt, increased public spending, and the
diminishing production of basic articles of consumption
generated a strong inflationary spiral. In the end, the
worse-hit sectors of the population were those that
Echeverría had originally meant to help. And this, finally, brought about renewed social unrest, manifest in
the peasant land invasions of 1976,[25] and the general
anxiety over the presidential succession that same year.

During Echeverría's government, the attempts at
administrative reform failed. The expansion of public
spending stimulated economic growth indices: 7.3 percent
in 1972; 7.6 percent in 1973; 5.9 percent in 1974.
However, there were no perceptible changes in the distribution of income. And, by 1976, inflation had reached

a level of 16.5 percent annually. A new surge in imports
cancelled out the increments in exports: the deficit in
the balance of payments increased from 703 million dollars in 1971 to 3,643.4 million in 1976. Tourism as a
source of revenue was affected by Mexico's vote in the
United Nations on the "Zionist" resolution, which caused
a Jewish travel boycott to Mexico.[26]

During the period 1973-1976, Mexico's foreign debt
grew by leaps and bounds. By 1976, the total external
public debt had reached the figure of 15.845 billion
dollars, which represented 32.8 percent of Mexico's
GNP.[27] At the same time that private domestic investment
contracted, foreign investment increased its participation in the Mexican economy: from 2.373 billion dollars
in 1972 to close to five billion in 1975.[28] Obviously,
foreign investors did not share the lack of confidence
prevalent among Mexican private investors at the time.
"Shared development," if for different reasons, had fallen into the same trap as "stabilizing development:"
an overwhelming reliance on foreign credits and investments. According to Clark W. Reynolds, it would seem
that the years between 1971 and 1976 "...can be considered rather a period of 'destabilizing development'
than of 'shared development.'"[29]

Petroleum, although a crucial element in the Mexican
developmental equation, was only a part of the general
scenario of economic imbalance that persisted throughout
the first half of the 1970s. The normalization of the
petroleum supply lessened what could have been radical
political repercussions, but the economic crisis came
anyhow, climaxing in 1976. On August 30 of that year,
the Mexican peso was devalued. This action marked the
end of the transition period of "shared development,"
and seemed to settle the internal conflict in Mexico in
favor of the schemes of the private sector. It appeared
that, "with the devaluation the last conditions were
given for the reproduction of the accumulation process
on the basis of industrial exports controlled by dependent capital."[30]

Apparently, except that petroleum would take the
place of industrial exports. By the time Mexico's new
President, José López Portillo, took over in December
1976, the situation of the country was darkened by
dreadful economic indicators, which included: a trade
deficit of 3.2 billion dollars by February 1977; inflation running at a rate of 30 percent; high levels of
unemployment and subemployment; a high rate of demographic growth; uncontrolled urbanization; and a decline
in tourism.[31] To generate the resources necessary to
grapple with this multifaceted crisis, and to restore
confidence, the answer would be found in petroleum.

PRESENCE AND IMPACT OF U.S.-BASED
MULTINATIONAL CORPORATIONS IN MEXICO

Multinational corporations could be broadly defined
as "those economic enterprises -manufacturing, extractive, service and financial- that are headquarted in
one country and that pursue business activities in one
or more foreign countries."[32] This basic definition
could be widened or restricted, in relation to the number
of countries where a corporation operates, or to the
amount of their investments. In order to better understand the role of multinational corporations in Mexico,
it would be useful to mention some fundamental characteristics of their structure and behavior.

Global corporations are not only multinational, but
multifunctional, that is, they are involved in the different stages of the productive process through vertical
integration.[33] The distribution of different productive
capabilities throughout various countries gives the
corporation heaquarters an edge in determining volume
and prices. Multinational corporations share a conception of the world as one big integrated economic unit,
in which they exert an increasing control through the
technology of production, finance capital, and market-
ing.[34] The cosmopolitan vision of the multinationals
constitutes, indeed, a challenge to nationalism. In a
way, the upsurge of the global corporations has been
based on the beliefs in "progress" and "growth," i.e.
the "cult of bigness," and in the tendencies towards
centralization.[35]

Beginning after World War II, the development of
multinational enterprises and their presence in the
fields of investment, international commerce, and technology, have been steadily increasing. The sheer
economic weight of multinational corporations is impressive. In 1970, it was estimated that the total value of
all foreign investment was around 250 billion dollars,
with a rate of expansion of between 10 and 20 percent
yearly.[36] By the beginning of the 1970s, U.S.-based
multinational corporations made up 55.6 percent of the
total; European firms, 37.5 percent; Japan, 2.6 percent;
Canada, 3.9 percent; and Australia, 0.4 percent.[37] In
1970, the annual production by foreign enterprises in
the world surpassed the volume of world exports; from
another perspective, the volume of international production doubled that of exports by western countries.[38]

There are opposing views with respect to the activities of multinational corporations. Those who favor
them point out the increasing anachronism of the nation-
state in an age of expanding and complex interdependence,
when efficiency and rationality are key objectives to
suit the needs of the world. Instead of the old-
fashioned relative gains of particular states, multinational corporations would open the door for absolute

gains for all.[39] The adherents of the "sovereignty-
at-bay" theory "...regard the multinational corporation as the embodiment par excellence of the liberal
ideal of an interdependent world economy."[40] The global
corporations consider themselves as vehicles for peace
and better understanding among nations, as a step beyond
the narrow and confining allegiances of nationalism. In
short, centralized and integrated production is the best
way to run the world economy.

The opposing view is equally emphatic. Some theorists point out that in economic development there are
two basic laws: the law of increasing firm size, and the
law of uneven development. Parallel to the concentration
of economic wealth, there is a process of division of the
world between regions of development, and regions of
poverty. Thus, underdevelopment and development are but
two elements of the same phenomenon: the inability to
achieve balanced growth.[41] To the argument of efficiency
proclaimed by the promoters of the international division of labor, critics reply that top management continues to be recruited from rich countries, while workers
increasingly come from low-wage areas.[42] Furthermore,
the activities of multinationals often result in clashes
between the corporations themselves and/or their parent-
states, and the host countries. Finally, all these considerations implicitly question the ultimate compatibility of the profit motif with appeals to the issues of
morality and justice.

Other views of the subject emphasize that, even
though the multinationals have an international or trans-
national character, their matrix and decision centers are
located in the central metropolis, especially the United
States. Multinationals would appear to be controlled
by self-perpetuating elites that establish a symbiotic
relationship with the national state where they originate, in a process that conditions and mutually reinforces the two actors.[43] Even though their pursuits
and behavior may vary, both multinationals and the
states where they are headquartered share the same basis
of sustenance: economic growth. As such, their perception of the world is common more often then not.

The predominance of U.S. management in the big U.S.-
based corporations would seem to substantiate the previous assessment. Richard J. Barnet and Ronald E. Muller
avoid the use of the term "multinational," because
"...it suggest a degree of internationalization of management,to say nothing of stock ownership, which is not
accurate." In their analysis of global corporations, it
was found that of 1,851 top managers of leading U.S.
companies with large foreign sales, only 1.6 percent were
non-American. Besides, non-Americans have but an insig-
nificant amount of the stock of these corporations.[44]

What would have been the causes of the apparent confluence of interests of U.S. foreign policy and U.S.-
based multinationals? Some researchers have suggested
that after World War II, U.S. foreign policy was a
reflection of the objectives of U.S. domestic policy:
economic growth and productivity, as a way of resolving
political conflicts. The idea behind this emphasis on
economic development was that if scarcity could be overcome, then political stability would follow. In this
context, new wealth would make it unnecessary to radically redistribute economic benefits and power. As
international tensions and ideological rifts arose during
the late 1940s and 1950s, the attempt to ensure the
primacy of economics over politics led into higher levels
of concentration of economic power in multinational
corporations as engines of growth. In Germany and Japan,
as mainstays against communism, but mainly in the United
States, large corporations eventually managed to ascend
to the fore of the production process, weakening the concern over monopolistic power.[45] However, the economic
solution for political disequilibriums would seem to work
only under conditions of shared prosperity. Present day
tensions over U.S. foreign policy and the role of the
multinationals arise from the fact that

> Hegemony remains successful, however, only when
> it achieves advances for the whole international
> structure within which it is exercised. Hegemony
> imposed in a zero-sum cockpit, that is, at the
> expense of the secondary members of the system,
> must finally prove less durable.[46]

To a considerably degree, the phenomenon of the
growth of the multinationals since World War II has been
related to the dynamism of the U.S. economy. Between
1950 and 1968, U.S. private investments in foreign countries increased from nineteen billion dollars to more
than 101 billion.[47] The most important 187 U.S. corporations increased the number of their foreign subsidiaries
from 250 at the end of World War I to more than 5,500 in
1967.[48] Even though the relative importance of U.S.-
based corporations tended to diminish somewhat during the
1970's with the increasing participation of countries
such as Japan and West Germany, U.S. capital remained
predominant among the leading multinationals. By the
1970s it was estimated that close to 75 percent of world
commerce and industrial production was under the control
of 300 multinational corporations, based mainly, although
not exclusively, in the United States.[49]
The presence and impact of U.S.-based multinationals
in Mexico must be understood in light of these worldwide
tendencies. Because of its proximity to the United

States, its political stability, and its growing domestic
market, Mexico has been a much-favored target for the
expansion of the multinational corporations. The
increasing relevance of the role of the U.S.-based multinationals in Mexico coincides with the worldwide enlarge-
ment of these corporations; geographical, economic, and
political reasons explain the degree of the phenomenon
in Mexico.

Mexico is among the top five recipients of foreign
investments. By 1970, multinational corporations were
responsible for 23 percent of the total production in
manufacturing, up from the 18 percent they produced in
1962. Whereas in 1962 multinational corporations had
been responsible for 20 percent of all Mexican sales, in
1972 they accounted for 28 percent of the total.[50] Foreign investments are concentrated in the largest firms
and in certain key industries. For example, in 1972,
50 percent of the largest 300 Mexican industrial firms,
and 61 percent of the overall largest firms, were controlled by foreign interests. The predominance of foreign capital is a fact in the most technologically
advanced and capital-intensive industries in Mexico: in
non-electrical machinery, 95 percent; in transportation,
79 percent; and in chemicals, 68 percent.[51] Also, foreign investments find a favorite field for expansion in
the highly concentrated industries, where they accounted
for 71 percent of all manufacturing sales.[52]

In 1970, there were in Mexico 1,915 foreign owned
companies. Of these, 242 were subsidiaries of 170 U.S.-
based multinational corporations that have an undisputed
importance in their home country, in terms of their
volumes of production and sales, and technological development. These 242 subsidiaries represented more than a
third of the total foreign investments in Mexico, and
more than a third of the total sales income; they were
predominantly involved in manufacturing activities.[53]
Fully 166 of the 242 subsidiaries (or 68.6 percent) were
totally owned by some of the 170 aforesaid multinationals. In forty-one subsidiaries (17 percent), the
multinationals had a controlling share. Only in 14.4
percent of the 242 subsidiaries was there a participation
of less than 50 percent by the multinationals.[54]

In 1970, out of the total value of direct foreign
investments in Mexico, 80 percent came from U.S.-based
corporations. In mining, U.S. investments represented
91 percent of the total, and in commerce, 77 percent of
the total. But the clearest case of predominance of U.S.
firrms was in the manufacturing activities: 90 percent
of the activities of the U.S.-based multinational corporations were concentrated in industry and manufacturing.[55] From the perspective of a Mexican observer:

In conclusion, almost all foreign investment
in Mexico is Northamerican, and is located,
fundamentally, in the activities that are
cause and effect of a more dynamic development: manufacturing and commerce.[56]

In general terms, foreign-owned firms in Mexico are
highly integrated with their corresponding global corporations. Local subsidiaries are owned directly by the
parent corporation, rely on the corporation for financing, and do most of their trading with it.[57] In 1976,
foreign-owned corporations brought into Mexico 330 million dollars in new investments; during that same year,
they took out of the country 781 million in profits.
Thus, the negative balance for Mexico on this account
was -451 million dollars. The negative balance, i.e.
profits sent out of Mexico in excess of new investments,
reached between 1971 and 1976 a total of -1,900 million
dollars. This negative balance for Mexico, the difference between new investments entering the national
economy, and profits from their operations that are sent
to the headquarters of the multinationals, would seem
to indicate that it is Mexico which is financing the
development of the United States, and not the opposite.[58]
It has been documented that multinationals tend to
displace native entrepreneurs, and make use of native
capital, whenever that course of action is possible,
rather than to contribute new capital. In Mexico,
between 1965 and 1971, there was an increase of 74,542
million dollars in the total active capital of foreign
multinationals; of this sum, 62.6 percent was financed
with national resources.[59] By 1967, of the 412 subsidiaries which belonged to the 162 U.S.-based multinational
corporations operating in Mexico, only 143 subsidiaries
had been established as new companies; 112 subsidiares
were set up as acquisitions of already-existing firms,
and 109 as a result of branching out of already-
established subsidiaries.[60]
In regard to external credits to finance Mexico's
development, U.S. banking institutions have also been
predominant. In 1976, the total public and private
external debt of Mexico amounted to twenty-four billion
dollars. Of this figure, 15,830,000 million were contracted with private foreign firms, of which 11,540,000
million (72.9 percent) were credits from U.S. private
banking institutions. In 1976, the public external
debt of Mexico, 15,845,000 million dollars, amounted to
32.8 percent of the country's GNP.[61]
According to the market orientation of U.S.-based
corporations operating in Mexico, a general classification would show two main areas of investments: the
first, and by far most important, consists of direct
investments geared to produce for the Mexican market;

the second comprises the industrial plants established
in Mexico within a short distance of the U.S. border,
geared to sales in the U.S. market.

The Mexican government, by the beginning of the
1970s, offered tax concessions to foreign companies
interested in setting up industrial plants within twenty
kilometers of the U.S. border, as long as all finished
products were exported to the United States. By 1972,
there were 333 of these plants operating along the border
zone, employing 40,000 Mexican workers, and producing
electronic, textile, and other kinds of products with
a value of 500 million dollars annually.[62]

By mid-1974 the number of companies had increased
to more than 500, which employed more than 70,000 Mexican
workers. In effect, these were an exception to the
predominantly capital-intensive activities of U.S. corporations in Mexico. However, by 1975 the program began
to slow down, for a couple of important reasons. On the
one hand, the Mexican government had doubled the minimum
wage level towards the end of 1974. On the other hand,
and most important, under the U.S. Act of Commerce of
1974, all cotton articles finished in Mexico and exported
to the United States would now be included in the
American export quotas for Mexican cotton; fully 25
percent of the border plants were producing textiles.
These facts, coupled by the U.S. recession of 1974-1975,
had brought about by mid-1975 a reduction in the number
of plants down to 430 and in the number of Mexican
workers, down to 60,000.[63]

The picture that emerges out of the presence and
impact of the U.S.-based multinational corporations in
Mexico is a complex and often contradicting one. On
the one hand, the beneficial effects of foreign investments are considerable. They include a steady infusion
of capital and techniques, the promotion of modernization and industrialization, a more efficient utilization
of resources, employment creation, and a rise in productivity. Perhaps the most visible and tangible effect of
foreign investments is their contribution to fiscal
revenues, thus helping to cover the "gaps" between
domestic savings and public investment; that is, the
taxation of foreign capital helps to eliminate budgetary
deficits. Foreign corporations are important tax contributors: their participation in the federal budget
until recently has been around 20 percent of the total.
These taxes represent almost a fourth of the aggregate
value of their production, and their fiscal burden is
higher than the average in Mexico. These facts are the
result of their high rate of profits and the strict supervision of their activities by Mexican fiscal authorities.
Also, their usually large size makes them keep a more
careful accountability than small and medium-sized
Mexican firms. Finally, some foreign corporations prefer

not to enjoy the fiscal exemptions allowed to mixed
enterprises, as long as they keep absolute control of
the firms.[64]
   On the other hand, the detrimental effects for
Mexico's development from the activities of foreign corporations are also numerous. As it has been stated, an
overwhelming proportion of foreign investments comes from
the United States, a fact which underlines the dependence
of Mexico on its northern neighbor. Furthermore, foreign
corporations prefer to have total control of their firms
in Mexico, their rate of profit is considerably high,
they take advantage primarily of the Mexican domestic
market, and do not constitute a significant source of
exports. In spite of their fiscal contributions, it is
assumed that tax evasion takes place at substantial
levels, through "transfer-pricing" and other means.
Foreign investments are concentrated in the industrial
sector, and make use mainly of capital-intensive techniques, thus rendering its effect on employment creation
to a much lower level than might be expected from the
value of their investments. The technological dependence of Mexico on foreign patents continues to increase.
Finally, the activities of foreign corporations take
place primarily in or around the metropolitan area of
Mexico City and a few other major urban centers, contributing to regional imbalances.[65]
   In conclusion, the following could be said to be
some of the main characteristics of foreign corporations
in Mexico:

- Preponderance of U.S.-based multinationals
  and U.S. banking institutions.
- Substantial control by these multinationals
  of some of the most dynamic sectors of the
  Mexican economy.
- Subordination of operations in Mexico to
  external decision centers and foreign manage-
  ment.
- Displacement of native entrepreneurs.
- Decapitalization of the Mexican economy.

   The previous analysis of foreign investments in
Mexico leads into the political arena. The economic and
technological benefits implicit in direct foreign investments must be contrasted with the possible loss or reduction of national economic self-reliance. From this
perspective, the issue of the positive and negative
effects of foreign investments goes beyond the economic
dimension to a scenario where economic operations,
albeit important, are subordinated to a conjunction of
political factors. These factors are related both to
Mexican domestic politics, and to the maneuvering

capacity of the Mexican government in the international milieu.

The political implications of the effect of U.S. economic influence in Mexico must be viewed within the context of historical, political, economic, geopolitical, and strategic evidence. In short, the political impact of foreign investments in Mexico is directly related to the concept of "national interest," as a basis for analysis. But the "national interest" of Mexico must be weighed against the notion of the "national security" of the United States. According to Mario Ojeda,

> The perception of national security on the part of different agencies of the U.S. government, and the subsequent actions to enforce that perception, have often led to conflict in the relations between the United States and Mexico. As a general rule, the national security of the United States has determined the need for a continuous reinforcement of U.S. hegemony in the Caribbean and Central American area, which comprises the so called vital geographic perimeter for the defense of the United States, and of which, of course, Mexico is an indispensable component, That need has often clashed with Mexico's 'national interest,' because of what the Mexican government may or may not do. And, as a matter of fact, all political outcomes in Mexico, are evaluated in Washington, primarily in strategic terms.[66]

The national interest manifests itself in an acceptable degree of sovereignty. Sovereignty means internal supremacy and external independence; that is to say, a sovereign state must have complete legal and factual authority over all the subjects (individuals and groups) which compose it, and must be legally and factually independent from control by another state. It is the degree of relativity of Mexico's sovereignty vis a vis the United States that especially concerns us here.

The notion of sovereignty provides a useful parameter to assess the impact of U.S. business in Mexico. Through their massive investments, U.S.-based corporations control to a considerable extent some of the most dynamic areas of Mexico's economy, i.e. manufacturing and commerce, as well as the most strategic factor of development, i.e. technology. It would follow that U.S. economic influence potentially removes a large and vital part of the Mexican economy from national political control. It could be argued that, in many cases, economic decisions have responded to the needs of U.S. corporations rather than to the needs of Mexico. Therefore, the vulnerability of the Mexican government to actions taken by U.S. business corporations or by Washington is increased significantly. The most important result of this situation is the limitation to the scope and reach of political action by the Mexican government and, thus, to Mexico's national sovereignty.[67]

ATTEMPTS TO REGULATE FOREIGN INVESTMENTS

The real debate among Mexico's governing elites since the 1950s has not been whether or not to promote the entrance of new foreign investments. In this respect, up to now the issue is quite well decided in favor of foreign investments. Rather, the critical point has been how to have both foreign capital and domestic control. Parallel to the impressive growth of investments by multinational corporations in Mexico since the 1950s, two developments have underlined the continuous concern of the Mexican government about the activities of the multinationals.[68]

- The renewal of the process of nationalization of areas of the economy vital to national viability. In 1960, for example, the state acquired the last two foreign electrical companies through the state-owned Federal Commission of Electricity, an action which gave it the monopoly of electric energy. Likewise, by the mid-1960s, all foreign mining companies were forced to sell 50 percent of their constitutive capital to Mexican investors.
- As the model of "stabilizing development" gave way to the model of "shared development" during the early 1970s, foreign investments were seen by the Mexican government as unresponsive to the needs of integral development. Consequently, Echeverria's administration proceeded to attempt to control more effectively the multinational corporations.

The Mexican government decided to face what it saw as a challenge from the multinational corporations in a variety of ways: increasing the pressures of "Mexicanization" to new areas of the manufacturing sector; forcing the foreign-controlled industries to increase the use of domestically-produced parts; tying concessions of import permits to the levels of exports by the soliciting corporations; and new coordinated regulations to control the volume and activities of foreign investments.[69]
There have been laws controlling foreign investments in Mexico since 1944. However, because of the absence of a general law applicable to all foreign investments,

each presidential administration would take a different
approach. Also, the laws as they stood provided for
exceptions by administrative decree. By 1973, the need
for comprehensive legislation to control foreign investments had become apparent. In March of that year the
"Law to Promote Mexican Investments and Regulate Foreign
Investment" was enacted, and it went into effect two
months afterwards. Among the fundamental points of the
new legislation were: in no case would foreign investments be greater than 49 percent of the total in any
given enterprise; this same limit would apply to local
management of the companies; the creation of a "National
Commission of Foreign Investment," with the power to
change established percentages, and tending to greater
national participation when it would deem it necessary.[70]

While this law was being enacted in the Mexican
Congress, an incident occurred which helps to illustrate
the persistence of disagreement between the official
American and Mexican views in regards to foreign investments. The U.S. ambassador in Mexico at the time, Robert
H. McBride, in a speech given before the U.S.-Mexican
Managerial Committee in October 1972, strongly criticized
the imminent change by the Mexican government of the
"rules of the game" with respect to foreign investments,
praising their beneficial effects on Mexican development.
In response to McBride, and expressing the dissatisfaction of the Mexican government with his speech, the
Mexican Secretary of Commerce at the time, José Campillo
Sains, declared that, indeed, the rules of the game were
being changed," to adjust them to the needs and aspirations of our day."[71] Significantly, Ambassador McBride
was recalled and dismissed from his post within the same
year.

Another legal means of control of foreign investments is the "Law on the Registry of Technological Transfers and the Use and Exploitation of Patents and Brands,"
which went into effect in January 1973. This law
established the "National Registry of Technological
Transfers," whose main objectives are to avoid the importation of technology already available in Mexico, and to
regulate the payments that can be made by the multinationals for concept of royalties and technical assistance, which should not exceed 3 percent of net sales.[72]

In the context of these attempts to regulate the
activities of the multinational corporations, two related
facts should be mentioned: Mexico is one of the few
Latin American countries that have refused to sign with
the United States an agreement of guarantee to investments; and Mexico does not receive direct aid from the
United States. Another interesting related action took
place during the mid-1970s, in regard to the Mexican-
sponsored United Nations "Chart of Economic Rights and
Duties of the States." To this day, the United States

has not signed this international agreement, one of the few industrial powers still not to do so. Thus, while the United States lacks certain legal and economic means to pressure Mexico to be favorably disposed towards U.S. policies regarding foreign investments, it, too, has avoided entering into agreements that might hinder a U.S. response to actions against foreign investments by other countries.

These Mexican laws that regulate foreign investments and technological transfers are by no means flawless. It is doubtful whether the Mexican government has the administrative capacity to carry on the regulatory supervision of foreign enterprises. On the other hand, various devices to circumvent the laws are still extensively used in Mexico, such as the subterfuge known as the "name-lenders," which involves the registry of shares of ownership under the name of a Mexican citizen, concealing the real owner or beneficiary.[73] These facts add up to a situation where "the preponderance and control of foreign investments in the Mexican economy will continue to grow to the same extent that the system does not come to grips with the correction of these deficiencies."[74]

NOTES

1. Lorenzo Meyer, La resistencia al capital privado extranjero; el caso del petróleo, 1938-1950," in Bernardo Sepúlveda et al., Las Empresas Transnacionales en Mexico (Mexico: El Colegio de Mexico, 1974).
2. Bernardo Sepúlveda and Antonio Chumacero, La Inversión Extranjera en Mexico (Mexico: Fondo de Cultura Económica, 1973), Apendice Estadistico, Cuadro #1.
3. Sepúlveda et al., Las Empresas Transnacionales en Mexico, op. cit., p. 4.
4. For an example of this view on the situation of the Mexican economy at the time, see Raymond Vernon, The Dilemma of Mexico's Development (Cambridge: Harvard University Press, 1965).
5. Ibid., p. 193.
6. Olga Pellicer de Brody, "El llamado a las inversiones extranjeras, 1953-1958," in Sepúlveda et al., Las Empresas Transnacionales en Mexico, op. cit., pp. 75-77.
7. Ibid., pp. 78-82.
8. Ibid., p. 103.
9. Sepúlveda et al., Las Empresas Transnacionales op. cit., pp. 7-12.
10. Olga Pellicer de Brody and Esteban L. Mancilla, Historia de la Revolución Mexicana, Volumen 23, Período 1952-1960: El Entendimiento con los Estados Unidos y

la gestación del Desarrollo Estabilizador (Mexico: El Colegio de Mexico, 1978), pp. 55-56.

11. The stages in the government policy of resorting to external credit financing are analyzed by Rosario Green in El Endeudamiento Público Externo de Mexico: 1940-1973 (Mexico: El Colegio de Mexico, 1976).

12. Ibid., pp. 117-126.

13. Rosario Green, "La deuda pública externa de Mexico, 1965-1976," Comercio Exterior, Vol. 27, No. 11 (Mexico: November 1977), pp. 1281-1282.

14. Luis Angeles, Crisis y Coyuntura de la economía mexicana (Mexico: Editorial El Caballito, 1979), pp. 15-18.

15. Ibid., pp. 18-22.

16. Pellicer and Mancilla, op. cit., p..58.

17. Some examples of these works are: Howard F. Cline, Mexico: Revolution or Evolution: 1940-1960 (1962), which emphasized the validity of "desarrollismo;" James W. Wilkie, The Mexican Revolution: Federal Expenditure and Social Change (1967), which utilized quantitative indicators, i.e. public expenditures mainly, to underline what in the author's views were the successes of the Mexican Revolution, such as an improvement in social conditions; and Charles C. Cumberland, Mexico, The Struggle for Modernity (1968), which saw the revolution as the key element in the formation of the Mexican nationality and a necessary step in the road to modernity.

18. Clark W. Reynolds, document presented before the U.S. Congress, Joint Economic Committee, Subcommittee on Inter-American Economic Relations, Hearings on "Recent Developments in Mexico and their Economic Implications for the United States," Washington, D.C., January 17, 1977, p. 45.

19. For an analysis of the model of "shared development," see Gerardo Bueno, "Las estrategias del desarrollo estabilizador y del desarrollo compartido," in Bueno, Opciones de política económica en Mexico después de la devaluación (Mexico: Editorial Tecnos, 1977), pp. 21-51.

20. Mexico: La Política económica del nuevo gobierno (Mexico: Banco de Comercio Exterior, S.A., 1971), Chapter 1.

21. Carlos Bazdrech Parada, "El Dilema de la Política Económica," in La Vida Política en Mexico: 1970-1973 (Mexico: El Colegio de Mexico, 1974), p. 35.

22. Rafael Segovia, "La Reforma Política: el Ejecutivo Federal, el PRI y las elecciones de 1973," Ibid., p. 53

23. Carlos Arriola, "Los grupos empresariales frente al Estado (1973-1975)," in Las Fronteras del Control del Estado Mexicano (Mexico: El Colegio de Mexico, 1976), p. 69.

24. Directorio de organismos descentralizados y empresas de participación estatal (Mexico: Secretaría del Patrimonio Nacional, 1976).

25. For an analysis of the causes and effects of the 1976 peasant "seizures" of land in northwestern Mexico, see James W. Wilkie, Pulling, Hauling Mark Mexico's Land Reform" Los Angeles Times, December 26, 1976.

26. "Así se devaluó el peso: tiempo de la reconstrucción económica," Proceso, No. 2, November 13, 1976, Mexico, pp. 20-25.

27. Green, "La deuda pública externa de Mexico, 1965-1976," op. cit., p. 1285.

28. H.J. Robinson and T.G. Smith, The Impact of Foreign Private Investment on the Mexican Economy, SRI, Stanford, 1976, The American Chamber of Commerce of Mexico.

29. Reynolds, op. cit., p. 54.

30. C. Gribomont and M. Rimez, "La política económica del gobierno de Luis Echeverría (1971-1976); Un primer ensayo de interpretación," El Trimestre Económico, Vol. XLIV (4), No. 176, October-December, 1977, Mexico, p. 833.

31. "Mexico: The Road Back to Confidence," Time, February 21, 1977, pp. 16-22.

32. David H. Blake and Robert S. Walters, The Politics of Global Economic Relations (Englewood Cliffs, NJ: Prentice-Hall, Inc., 1976), pp. 80-81.

33. Raymond Vernon, Sovereignty at Bay (New York: Basic Books, Inc., 1971).

34. Richard J. Barnet and Ronald E. Muller, Global Reach: The Power of the Multinational Corporations (New York: Simon and Schuster, 1974), p. 26.

35. Ibid., p. 37.

36. Stefan H. Robock and Kenneth Simmons, International Business and Multinational Enterprises (Homewood, IL: Richard D. Irwin, Inc., 1973), pp. 37 & 44.

37. Ibid., p. 45.

38. J.N. Behrman, "Sharing International Production Through the Multinational Enterprise and Sectorial Integration," 4 Law and Policy in International Business 2, 1972.

39. Vernon, op. cit.

40. Fred G. Bergsten and Lawrence B. Krause (eds.), World Politics and International Economics (Washington: The Brookings Institution, 1975), p. 39.

41. Stephen Hymer, "Las Empresas multinacionales y la ley del desarrollo desigual," in Jagdish Bhagwati (ed.), La Economía y el orden mundial en el año 2000 (Mexico: Siglo XXI Editores, 1973), pp. 135-164.

42. Barnet and Muller, op. cit., p. 17.

43. Marcos Kaplan, "La concentración del poder político a escala mundial,"El Trimestre Económico, Vol.

XLI (1), No. 161, January-March, 1974, Mexico, pp. 102-103.

44. Barnet and Muller, op. cit., p. 17.

45. Charles S. Maier, "The Politics of Productivity: Foundations of American International Economic Policy after World War II," in Peter J. Katzenstein, Between Power and Plenty (Madison: The University of Wisconsin Press, 1978), pp. 23-49.

46. Ibid., p. 47.

47. Seymour J. Rubin, "Multinational Enterprise and National Sovereignty: A skeptic's analysis," 3 Law and Policy in International Business 2 (1971).

48. Reymond Vernon, "The Multinational Corporation," 5 Atlantic Community Quarterly 553 (1967-1968).

49. Detlev F. Vagts, "The Global Corporations and International Law," 6 The Journal of International Law and Economics 249 (1972).

50. Richard S. Newfarmer and Willard F. Muller, "Multinational Corporations in Brazil and Mexico: Structural Sources of Economic and Noneconomic power," Report to the Subcommittee on Multinational Corporations of the Committee on Foreign Relations, 94th Congress, 1st Session, Washington, 1975, pp. 55-56.

51. Ibid., pp. 53 54.

52. Ibid., p. 61.

53. Sepúlveda and Chumacero, op. cit., pp. 91-92.

54. Ibid., p. 87.

55. Ibid., p. 58.

56. Ibid., p. 59

57. Newfarmer and Muller, op. cit., pp. 73-80 and 125-131.

58. Mario Ojeda, "Mexico ante los Estados Unidos en la coyuntura actual," in Continuidad y Cambio en la Política Exterior de Mexico: 1977 (Mexico: El Colegio de Mexico, 1977), p. 59.

59. Manuel Aguilera Gómez, La Desnacionalización de la economia mexicana (Mexico: Fondo de Cultura Económica, Archivo del Fondo 47, 1975), p. 95

60. Sepúlveda and Chumacero, op. cit., p. 40.

61. Rosario Green "Deuda Externa y Política Exterior: la vuelta a la bilateralidad en las relaciones internacionales de Mexico," in Continuidad y cambio en la Política Exterior de Mexico: 1977, op. cit., pp. 76-79.

62. "Spread of U.S. Plants to Mexico Brings a Boom -and Complaints," U.S. News and World Report, March 27, 1972, pp. 57-59.

63. Vernon M. Briggs, Jr., "Mexican Workers in the U.S. Labour Market," International Labor Review, Vol. 112, No. 5, November, 1975, p. 364.

64. Sepúlveda and Chumacero, op. cit.

65. Ibid.

56

66.   Mario Ojeda, "The Perils of Proximity to a Powerful Country: The Viewpoint of a Mexican," type-written, p. 6

67.   Ibid.

68.   Miguel S. Wionczek, "La inversión extranjera privada: problemas y perspectivas," in Wionczek (ed.), La Sociedad Mexicana: Presente y Futuro (Mexico: Fondo de Cultura Economica, Lecturas 8, 1974), p. 136.

69.   Ibid., p. 152.

70.   "Ley para promover la inversión Mexicana y regular la inversión extranjera," in Fausto Zapata, Mexico: Notas sobre el Sistema Político y la Inversión Extranjera (Mexico: Publicidad y Offset, S.A., 1974), pp. 47-64.

71.   Speeches by the U.S. Ambassador to Mexico, Robert McBride, and the Mexican Secretary of Commerce, Jose Campillo Sainz, and the subsequent discussion during the meetings of the U.S.-Mexican Managerial Committee, in Acapulco, on October 12, 1977. Comercio Exterior, Vol. XXII, No. 10, October 1972, Mexico, pp. 937-944.

72.   "Different Fiscal Incentives and Comments to the Law of Foreign Investment and Registry of Technology," (Mexico: Mexican Institute for Foreign Trade, 1975), pp. 13-19.

73.   Aware of the gravity of the problem in December 1980, Mexican President José López Portillo sent an initiative for a new legislative measure to the Mexican Congress, through which reforms would be incorporated to the Fiscal Code, in order to establish stringent penalties to national and multinational enterprises that consent to the use of "name-lenders," as well as to the actual individual violators.   "Iniciativa de JLP: Hasta 6 Anos de Carcel a Prestanombres," Excelsior, November 30, 1980, p. 1.

74.   Samuel E. del Villar, "El Sistema Mexicano de regulación de la inversión extranjera; elementos y deficiencias generales," in Foro Internacional, Vol. XV, No. 3, January-March 1975, Mexico, p. 378.

4
Mexico's Energy Policy

MEASURE OF THE PETROLEUM BONANZA

Although most of the recent petroleum finds in Mexico have centered in the southeastern region of the country, there are other areas of substantial hydrocarbon accumulations. The main oil and gas producing areas are the following: the Northeastern Fields, located in the Piedras Negras-Monclova Province, which extends through the states of Coahuila and Nuevo Leon; the Tampico-Nautla area, which includes the Chicontepec Basin along the northern part of the state of Veracruz; the Reforma Fields in the southeastern states of Chiapas and Tabasco; and the Continental Shelf off the state of Campeche.[1] There are also other areas throughout Mexico that have been reported as promising sources for new petroleum provinces. In regards to medium-term objectives, exploratory work is under way in the states of Baja California and Chihuahua, as well as in the Continental Shelf of the Gulf of California and at sea off the state of Sinaloa. Longer-term objectives include exploration in the states of Michoacán, Guerrero, Nayarit, Oaxaca, and Jalisco. Additionally, preliminary exploration work suggests the existence of hydrocarbons in various places along the Central Plateau, Sonora, and the Chiapas mountain range.[2]

The Northeastern Fields are mainly producers of natural gas, although there are a few oil wells near the city of Reynosa. By 1978, close to 15 percent of Mexico's estimated natural gas reserves, which amounted to six trillion cubic feet of gas, were located in the Sabinas Basin, along the central part of the state of Coahuila and the northwest section of the state of Nuevo Leon.[3] The Sabinas fields, which extend over an area of 50,000 km^2, appear to be some of the most important in the Western Hemisphere, and superior to all the other natural gas deposits in Mexico put together.[4]

The Tampico-Nautla area, site of much of Mexico's oil boom of the early 1920s, includes the old fields

near Tuxpan and Poza Rica. Present efforts in this area
concentrate on the Chicontepec Basin, which covers more
than 3,000 km². These are generally shallower deposits,
found at an average depth of only 1,200 meters, and with
a low yield of between 50 and 100 barrels daily (b/d).
By comparison, the overall average production level of
Mexican wells at present, including of course the rich
southeastern area, is 500 b/d.[5]

According to PEMEX, the Chicontepec Basic holds
more than 100 billion barrels of oil, of which close to
18 billion are susceptible to exploitation. However,
this would require the drilling of more than 16,000
wells. By comparison, from 1938 to March 1979, the total
number of wells drilled in Mexico came to 15,895. Notwithstanding, PEMEX insists on the profitable exploitation of Chicontepec which, throughout the first thirteen
years of development, should yield 2,600 million barrels
of oil. As a start, by March 1979, there were 433 wells
in production in the area.[6] Initially, the news about
Chicontepec were received with awe in the United States,[7]
which has subsequently turned somewhat to skepticism
regarding the technical feasibility of fully developing
the area.[8]

Mexico's present oil bonanza centers in the southeastern states of Tabasco and Chiapas, and in the Continental Shelf off the state of Campeche. An analysis
of production figures for 1979 attests to this fact.
PEMEX divided its oil production figures for that year
in relation to three geographical zones, northern,
central, and southern, which correspond rougly to the
Northeastern Fields, the Tampico-Nautla area, and the
Reforma and Campeche Fields of the southeast, respectively. In 1979, out of a total production of 590.6 million barrels, that is, a daily average of 1.618 million
barrels, the northern zone produced 27,812,635 barrels
(5 percent), the central zone 53,403,515 barrels (9
percent), and the southern zone 509,354,215 barrels
(86 percent).[9] By 1980, the Reforma area was contributing 48.9 percent of the total production, and the fields
in the Continental Platform off Campeche accounted for
35.4 percent. For 1982 the relative importance of the
fields in the Continental Platform is expected to
increase to 63 percent of the total, while the Reforma
area diminishes its share to 26 percent.[10] In any case,
by mid-1981 it was possible to conclude that both oil
provinces were part of the same geological formation.[11]

The Reforma Fields in the states of Tabasco and
Chiapas have undergone a rapid development since 1972,
when the first discoveries took place. By 1975, five
oil fields were being exploited in the area, which
represented 310,000 b/d, at the time nearly half of the
total national production. The average yield per well
was over 4,200 b/d, in contrast with the then national

average of 110 b/d per well.[12] By April 1976, there were
80 wells in the Reforma area, which produced 442,000 b/d,
that is, an average of 5,524 b/d per well. The combined
production for both oil and associated gas was 950,000
b/d. By 1976, the fact that wellhead pressures had
remained basically unchanged through more than two years
of sustained production, confirmed the richness of the
Reforma Fields.[13]

By 1978, the picture that seemed to emerge from
PEMEX's data on the Reforma oil region, was that of a
huge deposit of approximately 7,000 km^2. The geological
structures in Reforma are extremely rich, and most drillings in the area have turned out to be commercially profitable. The first discovery of a "supergiant" petroleum
deposit during the 1970s took place in Reforma: the
"Antonio J. Bermúdez" field, with 6,500 million barrels
susceptible to exploitation, and an average production
of 8,000 b/d per well, as of 1978. Other "giant" fields
in the area, with more than 1,500 million barrels susceptible to exploitation, include the "Cactus," "Sitio
Grande," and "Iris-Giraldas" fields. By mid-1981 the
Reforma area was producing more than one million b/d.[14]
It has been estimated by PEMEX that, when fully
developed, the Reforma area could produce at least 3.5
million b/d. The total reserves of Reforma should
amount to over 25 billion barrels.[15]

Closely related to the mainland finds the most
spectacular and recent discoveries have taken place in
the Continental Platform off the state of Campeche. By
mid-1978, PEMEX had announced the existence of a "sea"
of oil offshore, comparable in size to the deposits of
Tabasco and Chiapas. In order to explore further, and
commence the exploitation of the area, PEMEX rented
several oil rigs and contracted the services of U.S.
engineers and geologists. The first drillings resulted
in an encouraging rate of success.[16] By August 1979,
PEMEX had accelerated the development of the Gulf of
Campeche deposits at the rate of one drilling platform
every two weeks.[17]

By March 1981, PEMEX had explored some 50,000 km^2
in the Continental Shelf, with detailed work being done
in 8,000 km^2. Actual development of oil deposits was
taking place within an area of 700 km^2, at a depth of
between 1,250 to 3,600 meters. There was a 64 percent
rate of successful drillings. With a production of
1,308,000 barrels per day, the Gulf of Campeche is at
present the most important oil province in the world.
The "Akal" field is the world's first in capacity of
production, with an output of 42,000 b/d per well.[18]

Many other areas in Mexico are susceptible of holding deposits of petroleum and natural gas. Mexico's
territorial extension is 1,967,183 km^2; including the
Continental Platform, the total increases to approximately 2.5 million km^2. According to PEMEX officials,

70 percent of this total area, i.e. 1.8 million km^2, corresponds to sedimentary basins, of which only 10 percent have been explored and exploited with relative intensity. The remainder, i.e. 1.6 million km^2, is likely to contain hydrocarbon deposits.[19]

In order to better understand the measure of Mexico's petroleum reserves, the basic scale of reference should be mentioned here. There are three categories used to estimate the magnitude of reserves: proven, probable, and potential. These terms express the degree of certainty of the deposits. Proven reserves are those whose location, size, and susceptibility to exploitation have been determined beyond any reasonable doubt. Probable reserves imply the likelihood of the existence of deposits. Potential reserves pertain to still preliminary estimates, reached according to the characteristics of geological strata usually associated with hydrocarbon deposits.

Since the early 1960s until the mid-1970s, estimates of Mexico's proven hydrocarbon reserves remained stable, at five to six billion barrels of crude oil and natural gas. Production steadily increased, albeit not rapidly enough to compensate for growing domestic demand, and by 1972 Mexico's annual petroleum output of close to 194 million barrels had reached the previous 1921 all-time high. By late 1976, the incorporation of the fields in southeastern Mexico had raised the level of production considerably, as well as the estimates of proven, probable, and potential reserves. On February 11, 1977, for the first time in its history, PEMEX produced more than a million b/d. By then, the new fields in the southeast already represented 60 percent of the entire output.[20]

During 1977, a year in which PEMEX expanded its exploration to cover twenty-five states across Mexico, petroleum deposits were being discovered at a rate of one each twenty days. By December of that year, PEMEX estimated its reserves, which always include natural gas as well as crude oil, to amount to sixteen billion barrels in proven reserves, thirty-one billion probable, and 120 billion potential.[21] In his second annual report, President Lopez Portillo in 1978 officially announced estimates of twenty billion barrels in proven reserves, thirty-seven billion probable, and 200 billion potential.[22] By August 1978, stepped-up explorations in the Bay of Campeche were beginning to raise speculations that Mexico's hydrocarbon wealth could place it eventually alongside Saudi Arabia as a producer.[23] Early 1979 estimates expressed that Mexico conservatively expected its offshore reserves and production to equal that of the entire North Sea by the mid-1980s, and that it had only begun to exploit its Gulf of Mexico potential.[24]

On the basis of these substantial increments in reserves, the production of hydrocarbons doubled in just four years. From 1977 to 1980, total output increased from 545.6 to 1,032.4 million barrels, i.e. an average of 23.7 percent per year. In 1976, the average daily production was 0.9 million barrels of crude oil and 2,115 million cubic feet of gas; by early 1980, these figures had increased to 2.1 million barrels of crude oil and 3,672 million cubic feet of gas. In spite of the growth of production, the ratio reserves/production improved from nineteen years in 1976 to 57 years in 1979.[25]

The program of production drawn up by PEMEX in 1976 had stated the goal of 2.25 million b/d for 1982. By July 1980, two and a half years ahead of schedule, this objective had been surpassed, with 2.276 million b/d. At that time, Mexico became the first producer of hydro-carbons in Latin America, ahead of Venezuela, and the fifth in the world, behind the Soviet Union, Saudi Arabia, the United States, and Irak.[26] In his fourth annual report of September 1980, President Lopez Portillo announced significant increases in estimates of reserves: 60.126 billion barrels in proven reserves, 38.042 billion probable, and 250 billion potential.[27]

Thus, in terms of both reserves and production, the growth of the Mexican petroleum industry has been spec-tacular. On March 18, 1981, the director of PEMEX was able to announce that available reserves had increased almost eleven times since 1976, to 67.830 billion bar-rels in proven reserves, 45 billion probable, and 250 billion potential.[28] At the time, the ratio reserves/ production was up to sixty years.[29]

There are two reservations that, to a certain degree, might qualify reserves estimates as well as production goals. In its figures for reserves, PEMEX includes natural gas as well as petroleum. Since the ratio is usually estimated at 35:65 respectively, petro-leum by itself would correspond to only two-thirds of total reserves. Additionally, partly as a result of the quick pace of development, in some cases drilling data have not been forthcoming parallel to announcements of increases in reserves. This point could raise some ques-tions in regards to reserve claims. However, in the light of achievements in both exploration and subsequent exploitation since the mid-1970s, these factors by no means appear to add up to a straitjacket for the Mexican petroleum industry.

In his fifth annual report of September 1981, President López Portillo announced that total produc-tion of hydrocarbons through 1981 had reached an average of 2.350 million b/d, an increase of 17.5 percent rela-tive to the same period in the previous year. Whereas in 1976 Mexico occupied the fifteenth place in the world with regard to production, at present it is the fourth

largest oil producer in the world, only after the Soviet
Union, Saudi Arabia, and the United States. Likewise,
Mexico's reserves are also the fourth largest in the
world, on the order of 72 billion barrels in proven
reserves, 58.650 billion probable, and 250 billion
potential.[30] By late 1981 it was a widely acknowledged
fact that Mexico had, indeed, sizable petroleum and
natural gas deposits, whose progressive exploitation was
bound to have a lasting impact in its domestic affairs,
as well as in its role in the international scenario.

ENERGY POLICY

Administration

       Until recently, the Mexican government had not
considered the need for a comprehensive energy policy.
Since the nationalization of the petroleum industry, each
energy field has been managed individually by state
enterprises. These state organizations could be clas-
sified in two groups: those involved in the production
process; and the institutions in charge of research and
development. The most important in the first group are:
Mexican Petroleum (PEMEX), created in 1938; the Federal
Electricity Commission, set up also in 1938; and Mexican
Uranium (URAMEX), established in 1979. The research
institutions that operate in accordance with these
organizations are: the Mexican Petroleum Institute,
established in 1965; the Electricity Research Institute,
created in 1937; and the National Nuclear Research Institute which, together with the National Atomic Energy
Commission, were established in 1979.[31]
       PEMEX is the most important Mexican company, second
in Latin America, and thirty-eighth in the world, with
sales for 7.290 billion dollars by December 1980.[32] This
figure would be substantially higher but for the fact
that domestic price levels are far below those prevalent
in the international market. To December 1979, PEMEX
employed 103,271 workers in its various areas of
activity. Whereas in 1976 production was 14.9 b/d per
employee, by 1980 this figure had risen to 26.1 b/d.
This represented a 75 percent increase in productivity.
By 1980, crude production was three times that of 1976,
while personnel had only increased at an average of
5.06 percent annually. From another angle, operating
expenses, which in 1976 accounted for 54 percent of total
sales income, represented only 31 percent of the total
in 1980. Of course, it could be argued that the extra-
ordinary wealth of the new wells, rather than specific
increases in productivity per worker, has been the key
to these improvements. Indeed, the number of barrels of
proven reserves for each PEMEX worker increased from
72,000 in 1976 to 560,000 by 1980.[33]

According to U.S. sources, "PEMEX can easily be
compared to a major American oil company." PEMEX itself
takes care of most of its own work: exploration, drilling, production, refining, basic petrochemicals, transportation and commercialization, technological development, and construction. For operations such as offshore
drilling and coring analysis, sometimes it contracts the
services of commercial specialized firms, just as major
American companies occasionally do.34

The Mexican Petroleum Institute includes five divisions: engineering, petrochemical and refining, training, exports, and exploration. The Institute is PEMEX's
primary consulting firm and architect/engineering con-
tractor. It appears to be an internationally competitive technical firm, holding more than 100 international
patents. The Institute is "an active, burgeoning petroleum technology firm" which, in addition, provides PEMEX
with onsite technical supervision at its major construction projects. Thus, the Institute not only develops,
but also implements and applies PEMEX's technical base.
This role as a fundamental technological support includes
training programs for most of PEMEX's personnel.35

Planning

The Secretariat of National Patrimony and Industrial Development (Secretaria de Patrimonio y Fomento
Industrial) is in charge of defining and implementing
national energy policy. Its jurisdiction includes the
Energetics Commission, established in 1973 and termed
by its officials as a "modest equivalent" to the U.S.
Department of Energy; its role is rather diminished by
the fact that it does not set any energy policy.36 However, the Energetics Commission formulates guidelines
about the administration and rational use of energy
sources. In other words, the commission is a state
instrument for developing strategies to meet energy
demands, according to available resources and the country's socioeconomic needs.37

With the creation of the Energetics Commission in
1973, the idea of a comprehensive approach to energy
policy began to take hold of Mexican government officials. At first, the main themes referred to self-
sufficiency, an extension of energy supplies to the
population, a diversification of energy sources, planning
mechanisms, financial stability, and the promotion of
research and technology. There were obvious internal
and external factors that blocked these measures, including: a lack of coordination among the various organizations in charge of the national supply of energy; a
discontinuity in the development plans of the sector,
due to the administration changes every sexenio (six-
year presidential term); after 1976, external pressures

regarding oil exports; domestic subsidies to the industrial sector; and a lack of reliable data concerning reserves. However, the fact that national development is contingent, to a significant degree, on energy strategies, reaffirmed the vital need for a comprehensive policy. It was a double-edged proposition. Energy policy must be geared towards production, mainly industrial growth, according to the basic tenets of Mexico's postwar process of development; and the industrial sector should cover, increasingly, the needs for capital goods in PEMEX and the Federal Electricity Commission.

There were two basic domestic considerations in the promotion of a comprehensive energy policy: the fact that Mexico's development and growing energy demands have relied predominantly on petroleum and natural gas; and the state policy of maintaining a low domestic price for these resources, in order to promote economic and industrial activities. Conversely, an energy plan would have to address the question of diminishing the overwhelming reliance on a single non-renewable resources, i.e. oil and natural gas, and of revising internal price policies.

By 1977, the main guidelines for a comprehensive energy policy during López Portillo's sexenio (1977-1982) already seemed clear: a) petroleum should not become an end in itself in the process of development; b) petroleum resources must be industrialized; c) for geographical as well as economic reasons, the United States would continue to be Mexico's most important oil client; d) petroleum resources must be given optimum utilization; e) hydrocarbons would constitute the axis of the energy policy; f) the process of development must make use of coal; g) nuclear energy should be used once reactors were available, but it would not be the base of Mexico's development; h) solar and geothermic energy must be incorporated to development, even before nuclear energy; i) hydraulic energy should also play a role.[38]

By the late 1970s, it appeared that the Mexican government was following a course of accelerated extraction of its petroleum resources, with the objective of achieving a sizable level of exports. In the past, Mexico had maintained a rather cautious energy policy, geared to production for the domestic market, and conservation of its oil resources. Now the new and sharply distinct goals revolved around three incentives for development: to achieve self-sufficiency for Mexico in refined products and basic petrochemicals; to increase the participation of finished products in contrast with primary products in the exports market; and to achieve a liberalization in the prices of petroleum products. This amounted to a recognition of the need to end with superfluous subsidies and excessive protectionism.[39] However, these objectives would be qualified, increasingly, by crude oil exports, a tendency which in

principle at least, would seem to undermine their
intended effectiveness.

In recent times, the Mexican government has shown an
affinity with planning, as a means to bring cohesiveness
and a common purpose to the process of development.
According with this trend, on April 15, 1980, President
López Portillo promulgated the "Global Plan for Development, 1980-1982," as a stage towards the creation of a
"National System of Planning." The Secretariat of Programming and Budget (Secretaría de Programación y Presupuesto) is in charge of the implementation of the
Global Plan, whose basic objectives are:

1. To reaffirm and strengthen Mexico's economic,
   political and cultural independence as a
   democratic, just and free nation;
2. To provide the population with employment and a
   minimum of welfare, giving priority to the
   needs with respect to food, education, health,
   and housing;
3. To promote a high, sustained, and efficient
   economic growth; and
4. To improve the distribution of income among
   the people, factors of production, and geographical regions.[40]

Energy policy is a crucial element of the Global
Plan for Development. In his presentation of the plan,
the Secretary of Programming and Budget, Miguel de la
Madrid Hurtado, emphasized that "oil is intimately tied
to the viability of the planning strategy." However,
"It is not a matter of implementing an oil growth policy,
but a policy of development that makes use of oil."
From this perspective, the exploitation and export of
oil would seem to be conditioned by the purposes of the
overall development strategy, and by the real absorption
capacity by the Mexican society, of oil resources and
income.[41] Indeed, this question encompasses the critical
dilemma that grows out of Mexico's petroleum wealth:
will Mexico's government and society be able to foster,
shape, and channel development in a positive way for the
nation as a whole, or will oil distort development in an
uncontrolled, and possibly unsatisfying fashion. In
other words, oil income is likely to further the third
basic objective of the Global Plan, i.e. economic growth;
but its impact on the achievement of the other three
objectives, i.e. Mexico's economic and political independence, social progress, and distribution of income,
still remains a dubious proposition.

Energy policy, introduced in Chapter XI of the
Global Plan, constitutes a basic support for the objectives of the general strategy of development. Chapter XI
enumerates the specific goals to be reached in this

field: to uphold the sole ownership by the nation of
all hydrocarbon resources in Mexico's territory, as well
as in the 200-mile "exclusive economic zone" in the Gulf
of Mexico and the Pacific Ocean; to generate sufficient
electric energy for the country's needs; to diversify and
take advantage of alternate energy sources; to promote
the manufacture of capital goods for the oil industry;
to diversify Mexico's foreign trade; to protect the
environment; and to propose to the international community the adoption of a "World Energy Plan," in order to
give an integral approach to the solution of the energy
crisis.[42] In the Global Plan, a maximum level is set
for production of petroleum, defined as 2.5 million barrels of crude oil daily, with a margin of flexibility of
10 percent, to guarantee domestic supply and exports.
This means that, according to the plan, the level of 2.7
million barrels of crude oil daily would be the maximum
expected production up until 1982.[43]

The Global Plan for Development gave an additional
boost to the promulgation of an energy program. During
September and October 1980, the Mexican Congress was
busy analyzing the basic points of such a program.[44]
Finally, on November 18, 1980, the Secretary of National
Patrimony and Industrial Development, José Andrés de
Oteyza, set in motion the National Energy Program. Among
other points, he emphasized the fact that not more than
50 percent of Mexican oil would be exported to any single
country, the need for appropriate technology, and the
urgency of rationalization in the use of oil. Specifically with respect to the 50 percent limit on exports,
Oteyza declared: "Of the one million and a half oil
barrels Mexico will export, the United States will
receive 730,000 or 750,000 barrels or crude daily."[45]

The Energy Program sets goals to 1990, and projections to the year 2000. It places energy in the overall
context of development, and delineates its role. In
other words, the main objective of the Energy Program is
to support national economic development, which implies:

> ...in the first place, to expand the production
> of hydrocarbons according to the needs of a
> balanced economic growth. Secondly, to obtain
> the resources derived from oil exploitation,
> in order to assign them to activities of the
> highest priority.[46]

Specifically, the objectives of the Energy Program
are as follows:

1. To satisfy the national needs for primary
    and secondary energy;
2. To rationalize the production and use of energy;

3. To diversify the sources of primary energy,
   paying particular attention to renewable
   resources;
4. To integrate the energy sector to the development of the rest of the economy;
5. To know with greater precision the energy
   resources in the country; and
6. To strengthen the scientific and technical
   infrastructure capable of developing Mexico's
   potential in this field and of benefiting
   from new techniques.[47]

The Energy Program stresses the fact that so far
Mexico has used its energy resources in an inefficient
way. This is underlined by the high intensity in energy
consumption per unit of GDP, an index comparable, and
even superior to those in highly industrialized countries. In other words, Mexico appears to have an energy-
intensive economy. Thus there is a need to modify consumption patterns and increase efficiency. In this
context, the diversification of energy sources is the
only way to diminish dependency on hydrocarbons.[48]
   The Energy Program establishes three levels of
priorities:

1. Energy and industrialization;
2. Energy and regional development; and
3. Energy and the external sector.[49]

In regards to energy and industrialization, the
program underlines the possibilities in refining, petrochemicals, and energy-intensive industries. The links
with regional development are related to the need for
spatial planning of urban and industrial growth, for a
strengthening and extension of infrastructure and services in the places where the oil industry has a greater
impact, and for a protection of the environment. The
relation between energy and the external sector basically deals with the limits of the economy to absorb
income from oil exports, and the role of these exports
in the diversification of Mexico's foreign trade.[50]
   There would seem to be a rather clear contradiction
between the promotion of energy-intensive industries,
and the already established high-intensity levels in
energy consumption in Mexico. It could be argued that
the solution lies in more efficient operations, but the
mode through which this increased efficiency can be
achieved is still undetermined. On the other hand, even
though apparently sufficient consideration is given to
the regional impact, the program goes on to emphasize
immediately afterwards that it is mainly at the national
level where gains from the expansion of the energy
sector will have an effect. Here, again, the seeming

inevitability of centralization would seem to override the preoccupation with regional imbalances. Finally, the capacity of the economy to absorb income from oil exports is not clearly defined.

However, the Energy Program does set a limit to petroleum exports, at a level of 1.5 million b/d, and of natural gas, at a level of 300 million cubic feet daily. Furthermore, to avoid an excessive dependency on a single product, it is underlined that hydrocarbons are expected not to account for more than 50 percent of current foreign income. Not more than 50 percent of Mexican oil exports should go to a single country. Parallel to this, Mexican oil exports should not account for more than 20 percent of the hydrocarbon imports of any country, with the exception of the Central American and Caribbean countries, whose needs up to 50 percent could be supplied by Mexico.51

The Energy Program emphasizes Mexico's unique international position, due to the magnitude of its petroleum and gas reserves, and to the comparatively low costs involved in their exploitation. Given the export projections of the program, and the expected increases in domestic demand, it is estimated that the production of crude oil and gas liquids will be around 3.5 million b/d by 1985, and around 4.1 million b/d by 1990. The production of natural gas will increase, respectively, to 4,300 million and 6,900 million cubic feet daily. A margin of 10 percent in additional production capacity should give the energy sector added flexibility. The rate of exploitation of actual proven reserves, as established by the program, would guarantee by 1990 a ratio reserves/ production of at least 23:1 for petroleum, and of at least 19:1 for natural gas, which are deemed to be adequate margins of security, to be enhanced as exploration proceeds.52 Independently of the exploitation policy that is followed, the Energy Program concludes that, because of technical reasons, which include safeguards against premature exhaustion of the fields, the maximum level of production of oil and gas in Mexico will not exceed during any period the equivalent of between 8 to 10 million b/d of crude oil.53

On February 5, 1981, the National Energy Program was published in Mexico's Official Diary, approved and signed by President López Portillo and nine secretaries, and thus it became a law. This, in effect, seemed to reassert the goal of the Mexican government in regards to the rationalization of activities of the energy sector.54

Infrastructure

According to the Global Plan for Development, "the industrialization of hydrocarbons is the fundamental part of energy infrastructure."[55] The priority given to infrastructure works is revealed by some of PEMEX's development objectives over a six-year period (1977-1982). As stated in 1978, these included: in refining, to double capacity to 1.7 million b/d; to accelerate the construction of gas processing plants, and of the gas pipeline system in Mexico, as well as of oil and gas distribution and transportation equipment in general, such as additional pipelines and tankers; in petrochemicals, to triple capacity to 18.6 million tons by 1982.[56]

Mexico's energy policy has given priority to the multiple uses and transformations of crude hydrocarbons into processed products. During the first three years of the López Portillo government, from 1977 to 1979, there was a significant increase in infrastructure geared to that end. In the area of industrial plants, there were the following works: twenty-eight refining industrial plants, eighteen plants for hydrocarbon treatment, twenty-four petrochemical industrial plants, and fifty auxiliary service installations. During these three years, the area of transportation, storage, and distribution expanded in the following way: 128 gas, oil, and petrochemical ducts, eighteen storage tanks, seventeen storage and distribution plants, and eleven port works. With respect to offshore structures in the Gulf of Campeche, again from 1977 to 1979, these included: ten drilling platforms, one likage platform, four platforms for temporary production, the setting of a thirty-six inch diameter oilduct 165 kilometers long, and sixty-five kilometers of recollection lines.[57] These works underscored the emphasis on infrastructure.

Domestic demand for refined products derived from petroleum has pushed PEMEX to sustain annual rates of increment of 9.3 percent on the average. By December 1979, refining of crude oil and liquids had reached the level of 1.1 million b/d, an increase of 42 percent from the December 1976 level. For the first time in its history, PEMEX surpassed the level of one million barrels of crude oil refined daily. The capacity of crude processing was raised by 31 percent from December 1976, to December 1979; during this same period, processing of gas liquids increased by 78 percent.[58] This was made possible by the incorporation to production of the new refineries of Cadereyta, with a projected capacity of 235,000 b/d, and Salina Cruz, with a projected capacity of 170,000 b/d. These refineries, together with the expansion in the capacity of older ones, have allowed Mexico to become self-suffient in processed products.[59]

Towards the end of 1980, Mexico had reached the eleventh place as a country in the refining of crude oil and gas liquids, by increasing the processing capacity of its ten refineries to 1,476,000 b/d, i.e. an average

annual growth rate of thirteen percent since 1977. As
a refining company, PEMEX now occupies the fifth place in
the world, surpassed only by four multinational corporations. Expansion is under way in the refineries at
Tula, Hidalgo, Salina Cruz, and Ciudad Madero, and there
are projects for new refineries.[60] The expected expansion of refining capacity during the 1980s will make it
necessary to build five plants equivalent in size to the
refinery at Minatitlan, the largest in the country.[61]
The increases in refining capacity underline the fortunate coincidence for Mexico of huge deposits of petroleum and gas, a rapidly expanding domestic consumption,
and a respectable level of industrial capacity.

In the primary petrochemical industry, during 1979
the production in PEMEX's seventy plants reached a
volume of 6.34 million metric tons of thirty-seven different products, such as ammonia, ethylene, polythylene,
methanol and ethanol. This represented an increment of
60 percent with respect to the 1976 level of production.
In spite of this increase, the supply of several important products still remained under the level of demand.[62]
This situation has been addressed since mid-1978, with
the construction of seventy-six additional petrochemical
plants, which would help PEMEX reach its goal of tripling
production to eighteen million metric tons per year.[63]
According to the rate of construction, by late 1981
Mexico was expected to be self-sufficient, and even an
incipient exporter, in most of the basic petrochemical
products.[64]

In 1980, the production of basic petrochemicals was
7.22 million tons, an increment of 83 percent over the
1976 level. The Cosoleacaque petrochemical complex is
at present the biggest ammonia-producing center in the
world, which guarantees Mexico sufficient nitrogen to
meet domestic demand for fertilizer, as well as a substantial surplus for exports.[65] On April 29, 1981, the
huge petrochemical complex at La Cangrejera started
operations. The twenty plants located in this complex
represent an initial incorporation of 3.5 million tons
per year to total petrochemical production, and will
make possible the fulfillment of the expansion objectives.[66]

One of the most important additions to PEMEX's
infrastructure has been the Central Duct of the National
Gas System, from Cactus to Monterrey. Originally initiated with the main purpose of selling natural gas to
the United States, at present it plays a crucial role in
meeting Mexico's domestic energy needs. The result of
the rupture in the negotiations for the sale of gas to
the United States in 1978 was a process of conversion
of Mexican industry to gas. By March of that year, the
Secretary of National Patrimony and Industrial Development, José Andrés de Oteyza, stated the intention of

supplying all the industrial zones in the country with
natural gas, and adding an extension to the gasduct from
Cactus to Reynosa-Monterrey all the way to Chihuahua and
Ciudad Juárez in the northwest. Gas was to become the
key to an ambitious project of industrial decentralization that would help to rationally distribute economic
growth through the establishment of development poles.[67]

On March 18, 1979, President López Portillo inaugurated the Central Duct. Its construction time was
seventeen months, the total length of the main line is
1,247 kilometers, and the cost was over 16,000 million
pesos. This was the most ambitious distribution project ever undertaken by PEMEX, and investments ran at
the rate of almost one billion pesos per month. The line
includes 1,102 km of forty-eight inch diameter duct, and
145 km of forty-two inch diameter duct.[68]

Towards the end of 1979, work was under way in
eighty-two additional ducts, in order to interconnect
the Central Duct with various locations in the country,
such as the polyduct Cadereyta-Monterrey-Torreón-
Jiménez, and also in other regions such as the polyducts
Rosarito-Mexicali and Topolobambo-Culiacan in the northwest.[69] In October 1980, the Secretariat of Health
and Welfare signed an agreement with PEMEX through which
the latter is to supply natural gas to the central valley
(where Mexico City is located), by means of a direct
gasduct from Cactus, Chiapas. The main objective of this
project would be to reduce the level of environmental
pollution in the capital through use of cleaner energy
sources such as gas.[70] By November 1980, the director
of PEMEX announced that the national duct network for
the distribution of hydrocarbons and gas would ultimately
extend 35,100 km, of which 15,800 km were already in
service. At the time, a new gasduct was underway between Salamanca and Leon, Guanajuato, alongside which
there will be an industrial corridor through the central
part of the country.[71] Early in 1981, construction of
a line was started in order to supply gas to the steel
works at Lázaro Cárdenas-Las Truchas, on the Pacific
Coast. Likewise, an additional forty-eight inch gas
line was being installed to double the volumes available
in the central valley.[72]

During 1980, for the first time, natural gas consumption exceeded that of gasoline, fuel oil and coal,
and its importance is expected to be still greater in the
coming years. In all, in that year 2,940 million cubic
feet of natural gas were processed, 97 percent more than
in 1976. In this operation, Mexico occupies the fifth
place in the world.[73]

The advances in infrastructure were dramatically
underscored by the director of PEMEX in his annual report
of March 18, 1981:

> During the period 1977-1980 we have installed
> an average of one high-capacity compressor
> every six days; we have laid 5,200 meters of
> pipelines per day; we have completed and put
> into operation one industrial plant every
> fourteen days; we have installed one offshore
> platform every nineteen days; we have built
> a storage tank every three days.[74]

In spite of PEMEX's impressive record of achievements, especially since 1977, a number of drawbacks still
persist. By September 1980, out of a total production
of 3,300 million cubic feet of natural gas per day, 300
million were being burned in the atmosphere.[75] However,
most flaring has been confined to offshore wells in the
Bay of Campeche. With the construction of gas delivery
systems to the shore, specifically a 336 km gasduct to
Ciudad PEMEX and a 165 km gasduct to Mérida, it is
expected that PEMEX will be able to use up to 97 percent
of the total production.[76] By March 1981, the director
of PEMEX acknowledged that 550 million cubic feet of gas
were still being glared at sea, but that the installation of compression platforms as well as the additional
gas pipelines, would soon eliminate the waste.[77]

There are indications that Mexico's industrial
sector is not keeping up with the capital goods needs of
PEMEX. In 1978, a year in which the petroleum industry
grew by 65 percent, PEMEX had to import 50 percent of the
machinery it needed. By 1979, PEMEX was forced to buy up
to 75 percent of its capital goods in foreign markets.[78]
In October 1980, the Mexican Petroleum Institute estimated that PEMEX would spend a total of thirty-three
billion pesos in foreign equipment during 1980. This
figure represented 30 percent of total imports by
Mexico's public sector.[79] The previous facts imply a
significant erosion of PEMEX's financial basis. Two
additional limiting factors to PEMEX's expansion are
its reduced tanker fleet and the lack of adequate port
facilities.[80]

PEMEX is pushing ahead to cope with these obstacles.
In March 1979, it was announced that a plant for the
production of machinery and capital equipment would be
built in the northern part of the country, with French
technology and financial support, which would eventually
supply the needs of PEMEX and the Federal Electricity
Commission. Additionally, by mid-1981, PEMEX owned
223 drilling rigs, thus becoming one of the main drilling
firms.[81] But in general terms, the scientific-techno-
logical panorama in PEMEX, as well as in Mexico as a
whole, is rather somber. There is an urgent need to
foster basic research for development, in order to
proceed from the stage of a user to that of a producer of
appropriate technologies.[82] Nonetheless, in what would

appear to be excessively optimistic projections, by
October 1980, PEMEX announced that by the end of 1981 it
would be using in its operations 90 percent of national
technology, and thus only 10 percent of imported technology.[83]

Action is being undertaken which shows a preoccupation with the need to develop human resources. As part
of the National Program for Science and Technology,
1978-1982, 2,924 scholarships have been granted through
the Mexican Petroleum Institute, for training in the
fields of petroleum and petrochemicals, as well as technical training in nuclear and solar energy. The Mexican
Petroleum Institute itself grew in size from 1966 to
1977, from 316 employees to almost 3,000, 75 percent of
whom were involved in research and development projects.
On the other hand, there have been increases in the
budget of the institute in the order of a 20 percent
level.[84]

With respect to tankers and port facilities, PEMEX
is also trying to build up its capacity. PEMEX's tanker
fleet is expected to increase its deadweight tonnage,
from 650,000 tons in 1977, to close to one million tons
in 1982. On the other hand, some shipyards are being
rehabilitated. Still, Mexican ports can only service
ships in the order of 25,000-30,000 tons of dead weight,
which excludes supertankers. This constitutes an obstacle to PEMEX's objective of exports diversification. A
temporary solution has been found in the Bay of
Campeche, through the use of a mooring buoy installed at
Cayo Arenas, with a captive tank tied to it, capable of
storing one million barrels. Crude oil is pumped from
the captive boat to the tanker ships that carry the loads
for export.[85]

At present, under the project "Ships, Pipelines and
Ports," a new pattern of transportation is taking shape,
based on sea and river routes, as well as the optional
use of pipeline systems, instead of the traditional
land roads. By the end of 1980, 793,000 tons of freight
had been transferred from land to sea and river transportation. These measures are aimed at complying with
the proposed goal of relieving congestion in overland
routes. Whereas formerly 78 percent of PEMEX freight
was transported by railroad and highway, and only 22
percent by water, by 1980 land movements had decreased
to 59 percent while sea transportation had increased to
41 percent.[86]

Finances

A key component of Mexico's energy policy is the
financial factor. The schemes for advancing rapidly and
in unison in the various stages of the petroleum production cycle obey a financial imperative. For example,

the development policies for the petrochemical and refining phases are expected to eliminate imports of chemical
products, which in 1976 still amounted to 700 million
dollars, and of fertilizers, which in that same year
totalled 350 million.[87]

Several fortunate circumstances would seem to
contribute to a bright financial outlook for PEMEX. Even
though the Reforma Fields are relatively deep and the
decline in the natural pressure of the wells demands
maintenance works, plus the additional expenses involved
in exploiting the offshore deposits in the Gulf of
Campeche, the total production costs for the average
barrel of Mexican oil are considerably lower than the
costs in other areas such as the North Sea fields.
Extraction costs for Mexican oil, which vary markedly,
are not expected to exceed an average of $2.50 per barrel,
and might be as low as $1.60. However, they are sub-
stantially higher than Saudi Arabia's $0.35 to $0.50 per
barrel.[88]

PEMEX's development program, introduced in 1977,
included a budget of 926 billion pesos for the entire
period 1977-1982. Investments were expected to reach a
total of 390 billion pesos. The magnitude of these
figures is easily perceived when compared to those of the
previous sexenio, during which budget and investment
totals amounted to 240,300 and 119,800 million, respectively.[89] Since 1977, moreover, expenditure levels and
investments have surpassed the original estimates by a
considerably margin. Just in 1979, PEMEX received financial resources that totalled 259,026 million pesos, an
increment of 57 percent over the 1978 level. PEMEX's own
income from its operations came to 184,372 million pesos,
71 percent of the total and 275 percent higher than in
1976. Credit financing represented 74,654 million, or
29 percent of the total. Of PEMEX's own income in 1979,
72,749 million corresponded to domestic sales, and
100,766 million to exports of crude oil, refined
products, and petrochemicals. Expenses amounted in 1979
to 258,884 million.[90]

During 1980, PEMEX's total income amounted to 362
billion pesos, a figure more than seven times higher than
that of 1976. Current disbursements came to 140,600
million pesos, more than five times those of 1976. Thus,
current savings totalled 221 billion pesos, i.e. twelve
times as much as the 1976 figure. The destiny of these
savings helps explain PEMEX's financial situation, as
well as its impact in the Mexican economy. In 1976, 38
percent of internal savings were assigned to the payment
of taxes, i.e., revenues for the public sector. By
contrast, in 1980 this proportion had increased to 73
percent of internal savings. In 1980 PEMEX paid 162
billion pesos in taxes, or twenty times more than the
1976 level. For 1981, taxes were estimated to have

increased to over 300 billion pesos. On the other hand,
the amount corresponding to investments during 1980 was
121,800 million pesos, or five times more than the figure
for 1976.[91]

As of December 31, 1980, total liabilities of PEMEX
amounted to 369 billion pesos, of which 193,400 million
corresponded to foreign debt on a short and long term
basis. That is, the debt increased five times from 1976
to 1980. PEMEX officials argue that the increment in
the debt does not have a detrimental impact on the financial stability of the company, when compared with the
substantial and growing value of the vast and ever
expanding petroleum reserves. In other words, the growth
in reserves has brought about the possibility of widening
PEMEX's credit capacity. And PEMEX has increased its
foreign debt as a function of its investment programs,
and as a result of its supportive role as a major source
of revenues for Mexico's public sector.[92]

On the other hand, PEMEX is a major recipient of
government expenditures. Mexico's national budget for
1981 allocated 418 billion pesos for the sectors that
were given priority in the Global Plan for development.
Among these, 36 percent, or 150,480 million pesos, were
destined to PEMEX's investments. As a whole, PEMEX
received 35.6 of the total budget for organizations and
companies within the public sector, i.e. 376,818 million
pesos. This is 10 percent higher than the 1980 figure.[93]
And there is the precedent of "additional" allocations:
during his fourth annual report, in September 1980,
President López Portillo announced an increase in that
year's budget by 206 billion pesos, most of which went
to PEMEX to "balance costs and operations related to the
new oil production level."[94] Thus, it is likely that,
given the industry's momentum, expenses in 1981 actually
exceeded estimates once again.

Alternate Energy Sources

There are three important variables that determine
energy demand: population growth, economic development,
and modes of utilization of energy sources. Energy
consumption in Mexico has also been influenced by government price policies. By keeping prices low, on occasion
even below production costs, the government has tried to
promote development. However, this artificial price
structure has also led to an irrational pattern of
consumption. This is one of the reasons that explain
the fact that many Mexican public companies operate at
a loss and, subsequently, increase the public debt. In
addition, there is the question of whether in recent
times petroleum resources have been exploited irrationally, i.e at an excessively rapid pace.[95] This general

situation has hindered the incorporation of alternate
energy sources other than petroleum.

By 1978, the general rate of growth in energy consumption in Mexico was 7.5 percent annually, and 7.7
percent for petroleum consumption. Between 1976 and
1979, per capita energy consumtion expanded at a rate of
5 percent per year.[96] In the world context, Mexico has
a relatively high level of energy consumption, and one of
the highest among developing nations. The consumption
of primary energy per unit of GDP in 1978, expressed in
thermic equivalent of crude oil, was of 0.8 in Mexico.
This figure can be compared with 1.1 for the United
States, 0.9 for Great Britain, 0.9 for Venezuela, and 0.6
for West Germany, during that same year.[97]

The indices of growth of energy consumption, and of
the GNP, have traditionally been intimately tied in
post World War II Mexico. According to official sources,
by 1979 the most important energy users were the following sectors: industry, 25 percent; transportation, 24
percent; energy, 34 percent; domestic consumption, 6
percent; and other uses, 11 percent.[98] A more detailed,
and somewhat different chart of energy users would show
the following percentages: industry, 26.38 percent;
transportation, 29.84 percent; residential, 8.09 percent;
agriculture, 0.69 percent, other uses, 1.00 percent;
nonenergy uses, 3.39 percent; PEMEX's own needs, 14.01
percent; and the electricity sector, 16.61 percent.[99]
In any case, it is clear that the industrial sector is
a dynamic energy user. The growth in energy use in the
field of transportation is a result, to a considerable
degree, of the rapid increase in the number of motor
vehicles, of 10.2 percent annually. The precarious level
of energy use by agriculture is a reflection of the
travails of this sector in recent years. And the rate
of growth in the domestic sector, well above the rate
of population increase, denotes an increment in per capita consumption, although not necessarily a more equitable spread among the various groups of the population.

Petroleum and natural gas are by far the predominant sources of energy in Mexico. In 1980, the production of primary energy came from the following sources:
petroleum, 64.40 percent; natural gas, 23.15 percent;
coal, 5.25 percent; hydroelectric works, 6.94 percent;
and geothermal, 0.26 percent.[100] Thus, out of its total
energy consumption, Mexico depends in a level of 87.55
percent on hydrocarbon energy. The Global Plan for
Development, in its section on energy, proposes a
strategy that would consistently widen the government's
information on Mexico's energy resources, as a basis
for diversifying actual sources. It seeks to promote a
greater use of hydraulic, geothermal, solar, and coal
sources, among others. This strategy acknowledges the
effect that domestic price structures have had on the

exploitation of new sources, and the need to use energy
more efficiently.[101] In his annual report of September
1981, President López Portillo emphasized that the electricity sector, in which demand grows at a rate of 11
percent annually, will be forced to double its electric
energy generating capacity of 17.1 MW every seven years.
Thus, efforts will have to be undertaken in order to
diversify its energy sources; specifically geothermal,
coal, and nuclear power, will progressively become
substitutes for hydrocarbons, which have other more productive uses.[102]

Mexico has sizeable sources of energy, other than
petroleum and natural gas.

Coal. Reserves, which were 172 million tons in
1976, had increased to 1,500 million tons by 1980.[103]
Traditionally, coal production in Mexico has been asso-
cited with the steel industry. However, at present
the Federal Electricity Commission is trying to foster
the development of other sources for electricity, such
as coal. Some Mexican sources foresee that by the end
of the century coal might supply 12 percent of the country's electricity needs. As a start, the first great
thermoelectic plant based on coal, "Río Escondido,"
Coahuila, is near completion. This plant will have a
capacity of 1.200 MW.[104]

Hydraulic energy. At present, this is the source of
almost 7 percent of the overall energy generated in
Mexico, and of close to 28 percent of electric energy.[105]
Even though Mexico is not relatively well-endowed with
great river systems close to its main population centers,
the government is pushing ahead with dam projects in the
southern section of the country, in order to supply an
increasing share of the national demand for electricity.
The great works at Chicoacen, Chiapas, constitute the
most recent example of this policy. In November 1980,
President López Portillo inaugurated the Chicoacen Hydroelectric Plant, which required an investment of twenty-
one billion pesos, and is expected to generate 8 percent
of Mexico's total electricity demand, i.e. 5,500 MW
per hour.[106]

Nuclear energy. This is another possibility that is
being given growing attention by the Mexican government.
During 1983 and 1984, the nuclear reactors at Laguna
Verde are expected to begin operations, with a capacity
of 1,308 MW. Together with another nuclear unit to be
built during the 1980s, by 1990 Mexico is expected to
have a nuclear-electric generating capacity of 2,500
MW. In this context, the objective of the Energy Program
is to build additional nuclear units throughout the

1990s, in order to have installed 20,000 MW of nuclear
capacity by the end of the century.[107]
     A drawback from the perspective of the goal of
energy independence, is the fact that Mexico must rely on
the United States for delivery of enriched uranium for
these nuclear plants. Nevertheless, URAMEX has increased
its exploratory activities, in order to guarantee the
production of 250 tons of uranium needed for the Laguna
Verde plant. By December 1980, the prospects appeared
to be good, with the discovery of sizeable uranium
deposits in the state of Oaxaca. With these finds, the
production of refined uranium might reach the level of
seventy tons in a two-year term. Apparently, Swedish,
French, and Canadian companies are actively trying to
obtain the contracts for the construction of the new
Mexican nuclear plants.[108]

     Geothermal energy. Mexico, a predominantly volcanic
country, is located in a privileged area for generating
geothermal energy. There are estimates of a minimum
geothermal potential of 20,000 MW. The importance of
this figure is well understood by comparing it with the
9,000 MW total electric capacity installed in Mexico at
present.[109] According to the goals of the Energy
Program, Mexico will have increased its geothermal
capacity from 150 MW in 1980 to 620 MW in 1990.[110]

     Solar Energy. Additionally, the Energy Program also
considers the "solar option," although only as a long-
term resource that will be the basis for decentralized
types of electricity systems.[111]
     The degree of success in promoting alternate energy
sources is bound to be a decisive factor, on a middle and
long range basis, in determining the flexibility of
development strategies and of foreign policy options.
Rising domestic demand for energy, if dependent solely
on hydrocarbons, could eventually lead to dwindling
reserves. And, to the extent that domestic needs require
a greater share of total output, the potential will
diminish for petroleum to be used by Mexico as a gener-
ator of foreign revenues, as well as a leverage for its
foreign policy. Thus, the stabilization of the domestic
energy market, in terms of a rationalization of consumption patterns and a diversification of energy sources,
would appear to be a must for Mexico's overall objectives of development.

NOTES

     1. See Joseph P. Riva, "The Geology of Mexico's Oil
and Gas Resources," (Appendix), in Mexico's Oil and Gas
Policy: An Analysis, Document prepared for the Committee

on Foreign relations, U.S. Senate, and the Joint
Economic Committee, Congress of the United States, by the
Congressional Research Service, Library of Congress,
95th Congress, 2nd Session (Washington: U.S. Government
Printing Office, 1979), pp. 59-67.

2. Informe anual del Sr. Director, Ing. Jorge Díaz
Serrano, en la ceremonia de aniversario de la Expro-
piación de la Industria Petrolera, Guadalajara, Jalisco,
March 18, 1980, in Nosotros los Petroleros, Pemex, Año
2, No. 8, March-April 1980, p. 15. Also, Report of the
Director General, Petroleos Mexicanos, Cuidad Madero,
Tamaulipas, March 18, 1981, p. 5.

3. Riva, op. cit., p. 60.

4. "Depositos de gas de 50,000 kms. cuadrados: lo
halló Pemex en el norte hace dos años y lo tuvo en
reserva," Excelsior, February 22, 1979, p. 1.

5. Informe anual del Director de Pemex, March 18,
1980, op. cit., p. 15.

6. Chicontepec: Un Desafío...una oportunidad
(Mexico: Pemex, March, 1979).

7. See, for example, "Petroleos Mexicanos finds oil
reservoir that might contain 100 billion barrels," Wall
Street Journal, November 14, 1978.

8. "Petróleo de México, 22,000 millones de barriles; Chicontepec, inaccesible: E.U. Gran discrepancia
con las cifras de Pemex," Excelsior, November 16, 1980,
p. 1.

9. Petróleos Mexicanos: Memoria de Labores, 1979
(Mexico: Pemex, 1980), pp. 8-9.

10. Jaime Corredor, "El Petróleo en Mexico," in
El Petróleo Hoy," Uno mas Uno, Mexico, March 18, 1981,
p. 8.

11. V. Informe de Gobierno del Presidente José López
Portillo, El Universal, Mexico, September 2, 1981, p. 24.

12. Alvaro Franco, "Recent Discoveries Vault Mexico
in New Position," The Oil and Gas Journal, October 21,
1974, p. 74.

13. Alvaro Franco, "New Reforma Finds Push Mexico
to New Oil Heights," The Oil and Gas Journal, May 17,
1976, p. 73.

14. Corredor, op. cit., p. 8.

15. Alvaro Franco, "Latin America's Petroleum Surge
Gathers Momentum," The Oil and Gas Journal, June 5, 1978,
pp. 68.70.

16. "Petróleo en 7,000 km.^{2} de la Bahia Campechana,"
Excelsior, date not available.

17. T.J. Stewart-Gordon, "Mexico: Offshore is in
the News," World Oil, Vol. 189, No. 3, August 15, 1979,
pp. 79-84.

18. Petróleos Mexicanos: Memoria de Labores, 1979,
op. cit., p. 9. Also, Report of the Director General,
1981, op. cit., pp. 7-9.

80

19. "Petróleo en 80% del país: Pemex," Excelsior, October 25, 1978, pp. 1 & 11. Also, Corredor, op. cit., p. 8.

20. "Petróleo: Reserva con las reservas," Proceso, No. 20, March 19, 1977, Mexico, pp. 6-8.

21. Informe anual del Director de Pemex, March 18, 1978 (Mexico: Pemex), p. 5.

22. "Segundo Informe de Gobierno de JLP," Excelsior, September 2, 1978, p. 32-A.

23. "Mexico's Oil Bonanza," Newsweek, August 14, 1978, p. 42.

24. Leonard LeBlanc, "The Rising of an Oil Power-house," Offshore, Vol. 39, No. 51, May 1979, p. 135-146.

25. Corredor, op. cit., p. 8.

26. "Nueva Marca de Pemex: 2.276 millones de bar-riles al dia. Se convierte en el quinto productor de hidrocarburos del mundo, y primero en A.L.," Excelsior, July 22, 1980, p. 4-A.

27. Cuarto Informe de Gobierno de JLP, Uno mas Uno, September 2, 1980, Special Supplement, p. 9-A.

28. Report of the Director General, 1981, op. cit., p. 6. Potential reserves include figures for both proven and probable reserves.

29. "Reservas seguras de petróleo y gas para 60 años: Díaz S.," Excelsior, March 19, 1981, p. 1.

30. V Informe de Gobierno, op. cit., p. 24.

31. Alejandro Carrillo C., Las Empresas Públicas en Mexico (Mexico: Instituto Nacional de Administración Pública, 1976), pp. 143-148.

32. "Pemex, Segunda Empresa de A. Latina," Excelsior, December 19, 1980, p. 4. In terms of volume of business transactions, the first place in Latin America corresponds to Petróleos de Venezuela (Venezuelan Petroleum).

33. Corredor, op. cit., p. 9. Also, Report of the Director General, 1981, op. cit., p. 18.

34. "Pemex" in U.S./Mexico Relations and Potentials Regarding Energy, Immigration, Scientific Cooperation and Technology Transfer, a Report prepared by the Subcom-mittee on Investigations and Oversight, and the Sub-committee on Science, Research, and Technology, of the Committee on Science and Technology, U.S. House of Repre-sentatives, 96th Congress, 1st Session (Washington: U.S. Government Printing Office, 1979), pp. 25-26.

35. "Mexican Petroleum Institute," in Ibid., pp. 27-28.

36. "Energetics Commission," in Ibid., p. 22.

37. Juan Eibenzhutz, "Panorama General de Energéticos en Mexico," Comercio Exterior, Vol. 26, No. 4, 1976, p. 29.

38. Boletín Informativo del Sector Energético, Comisión de Energéticos, Año. 1, No. 1, Mexico, 1977, p. 17.

39. Eduardo Turrent Díaz, "Petróleo y Economía: Costos y beneficios a corto plazo," Foro Internacional, El Colegio de Mexico, Vol. XVIII, No. 4, April-June 1978, p. 624.

40. Plan Global de Desarrollo, 1980-1982 (Mexico: Secretaría de Programación y Presupuesto, 1980), pp. 12-13.

41. Ibid., p. 25.

42. Ibid., pp. 266-272.

43. Ibid., p. 278.

44. "Divergentes opiniones en la Cámara de Diputados sobre el anunciado Plan Nacional de Energéticos," Uno mas Uno, September 11, 1980, p. 4; "El Plan de Energéticos aportará los criterios de explotación petrolera," Uno mas Uno, October 29, 1980, page not available.

45. "Uso Racional del Petróleo; no mas derroche: Oteyza. A ningún país, más del 50% de la exportación." Excelsior, November 19, 1980, pp. 1 & 23-A.

46. "Programa de Energía," Energéticos: Boletín Informativo del Sector Energético, Comisión de Energéticos, Secretaría de Patrimonio y Fomento Industrial, Año. 4, No. 11, November 1980, p. 6.

47. Ibid.

48. Ibid.

49. Ibid., pp. 6 & 9.

50. Ibid., pp. 9-10.

51. Ibid., p. 10.

52. Ibid., p. 22.

53. Ibid., p. 11.

54. "Publican en el Diario Oficial el Programa de Energía; es ley a partir de hoy," Excelsior, February 5, 1981, p. 4-A.

55. Plan Global de Desarrollo, op. cit., p. 277.

56. Gary J. Pagliano and David M. Lindahl, "Mexico's Oil and Gas Policy to 1888: An Evaluation," in Mexico's Oil and Gas Policy: An Analysis, op. cit., p. 19.

57. 3 Años de la Nueva Política Petrolera: 1977-1979 (Mexico: Pemex, 1979), pp. 33, 69 & 110.

58. Informe anual del Director de Pemex, March 18, 1980, op. cit., p. 18.

59. Petróleos Mexicanos: Memoria de Labores, 1979, op. cit., pp. 12-13.

60. "Pemex, quinto lugar mundial entre las empresas refinadoras," Uno mas Uno, November 10, 1980, pp. 1 & 16.

61. "Programa de Energía," op. cit., p. 23.

62. Informe anual del Director de Pemex, March 18, 1980, op. cit., p. 19.

63. Leonard Greenwood, "Construye Pemex 37 plantas petroquímicas; hará 39 mas," Los Angeles Times, June 12, 1978, cited in Excelsior, June 31, 1978, pp. 1, 8 & 9.

64. Informe anual del Director de Pemex, March 18, 1980, op. cit., p. 19.

65. Report of the Director General, 1981, op. cit., pp. 10-11.

66. Ibid. Also, "López Portillo puso en funciona-miento el complejo petroquímico en 'La Cangrejera'", Uno mas Uno, April 30, 1981, p. 17.

67. "Se creará un circuito de gas en el país," Uno mas Uno, March 3, 1978, pp. 1-2.

68. Ducto Troncal del Sistema Nacional de Gas (Mexico: Pemex, March 18, 1979).

69. Petróleos Mexicanos: Memoria de Labores, 1979, op. cit., p. 47.

70. "Gasoducto para las industrias metropolitanas," Uno mas Uno, October 29, 1980, p. 1.

71. "Construyen un gasoducto para formar un corredor industrial," Uno mas Uno, November 4, 1980, p. 1.

72. Report of the Director General, 1981, op. cit., p. 12.

73. Ibid., pp. 10 & 13.

74. Ibid., p. 16.

75. Alan Riding, "El auge petrolero desborda la capacidad técnica de Pemex," The New York Times, September 19, 1980, in Excelsior, September 20, 1980, p. 3.

76. Corredor, op. cit., p. 8.

77. Report of the Director General, 1981, op. cit., p. 7.

78. "Por el rezago fabril, Pemex importará 75% de su equipo," Excelsior, January 4, 1979, p. 1.

79. Petróleos Mexicanos gastará 33 mil millones este año en la compra de equipos extranjeros," Uno mas Uno, October 21, 1980, p. 13.

80. ""La Flota Petrolera, insuficiente," Uno mas Uno, May 30, 1978, p. 2.

81 "No mas importación: hará Mexico todo el equipo a Pemex," Excelsior, March 4, 1979, p. 1. Also, Report to the Director General, 1981, op. cit., p. 5.

82. In this context, see Leopoldo García-Colín Scherer, "La Ciencia y la Tecnologia del Petroleo: Situacion actual y perspectivas futuras en Mexico," Foro Internacional, El Colegio de Mexico, Vol. XVIII, No. 4, April-June 1978, pp. 678-690.

83. "90% de tecnología nacional utilizará Pemex en 1981," Excelsior, October 22, 1980, p. 5-A.

84. "Mexico's Program for Science and Technology, 1978-1982," in U.S./Mexico Relations and Potentials Regarding Energy, Immigration, Scientific Cooperation an Technology Transfer, op. cit., Appendix B, p. 47-48.

85. Report of the Director General, 1981, op. cit., p. 8.

86. Ibid., pp. 23-24.

87. "The Oil and Gas Development Plan," in Mexico's Oil and Gas Policy: An Analysis, op. cit., p. 20.

88. Richard B. Mancke, Mexican Oil and Natural Gas: Political, Strategic and Economic Implications (New York: Praeger Publishers, 1979), p. 71.

89. Turrent Díaz, op. cit., pp. 143-144.

90. Petróleos Mexicanos: Memoria de Labores, 1979, op. cit., pp. 50-53.

91. Report of the Director General, 1981, op. cit., pp. 16-17.

92. Ibid., pp. 17-18.

93. "Ley de Ingresos y Presupuesto de Egresos de la Federación para 1981" (Mexico: Secretaría de Hacienda y Crédito Público, 1980).

94. Cuarto Informe de Gobierno de JLP, op. cit., p. 3-A.

95. In regards to some of the obstacles to a rational exploitation of oil, see Jean Pierre Angelier, Producción y reservas de energía en Mexico, CIDE, Mexico, December 1976, p. 21.

96. Wolf Hafeler, "La Demanda de Energia," Boletín Informativo del Sector Energético, Comisión de Energéticos, Mexico, Año. 2, No. 7, 1978, p. 11. Also, Corredor, op. cit., p. 9.

97. "Programa de Energia," op. cit., p. 7.

98. Ibid., p. 8.

99. Raul Olmedo, "La crisis: la distribución de la energía," Excelsior, July 30, 1980, p. 26-A.

100. Rodolfo Torres, Perspectivas Energéticas de Mexico (Mexico: Asociación de Tecnología Apropiada, 1980).

101. Plan Global de Desarrollo, op. cit., pp. 271-272.

102. V Informe de Gobierno, op. cit., p. 24.

103. "Programa de Energía," op. cit., p. 25.

104. "Con carbón, 8 millones de Kv. este siglo," Excelsior, November 10, 1979, pp. 1 & 9-A. Also Corredor, op. cit., p. 9.

105. "Programa de Energía," op. cit., p. 29.

106. "21,000 millones de pesos, la inversión de la planta hidroeléctrica Chicoacen," Excelsior, November 29, 1980, p. 1.

107. "Programa de Energía," op. cit., p. 29.

108. Ronald Buchanan, "Enorme riqueza uranifera en la Sierra Madre," The Sunday Times, London; in Excelsior, December 11, 1980, p. 5-A.

109. Raul Olmedo, "El ejemplo de la energía geo-térmica," Excelsior, August 5, 1980, page not available.

110. "Programa de Energía," op. cit., p. 32.

111. Ibid., p. 33.

5
The Energy Situation
in the United States

It would be pertinent here to incorporate into the discussion the general context of the world energy situation, and U.S. responses to it, as the global scenario where Mexican petroleum must, by necessity, play its role. In order to better understand the meaning of the energy crisis, it is necessary to underline the peculiar characteristics of petroleum, as a raw material of not only economic, but also political and strategic importance. Petroleum is a critical factor in determining the possibilities of any nation, in terms of both domestic viability and international relevance. In this context, Mario Ojeda advances the following categorization:

1. those countries which have oil;
2. those which do not have oil, but control financial resources to acquire it; and
3. those which have neither oil nor sufficient financial resources to buy it from foreign producers.1

International politics and economics, to a significant degree, are contingent upon the changes in price, supply, and demand of petroleum. This is fact of present times.

Much of the economic growth in the post-World War II era was based on cheap energy. From 1967-1973, demand for hydrocarbons in the three main consuming regions, Western Europe, Japan, and the United States, increased by more than 500 million barrels annually, while production in these same areas expanded by less than a tenth of this amount. Thus, imports by these regions grew by 95 percent during this entire period, from 4.9 to 9.5 billion barrels per year. Practically all the increment in consumption was made possible through an increase in production by members of the Organization of Petroleum Exporting Countries (OPEC). More specifically, 80 percent of the increase came from Middle East countries.[2] This constitutes the background of the energy crisis of the 1970s, and of the growth in power of OPEC countries.

Petroleum prices were kept at a low and stable level through the worldwide control of the market by the fabled "Seven Sisters": Exxon, Shell, Mobil, Texaco, British Petroleum, Standard Oil of California, and Gulf. These companies, in effect, operated as a cartel from 1945 until 1973, concerting their transactions in the international oil trade, in order to maintain low prices. One of the results of this successful policy was that alternate sources of energy were gradually driven out of the market. During the 1960s, oil prices diminished progressively in real terms. This made possible the penetration of petroleum as the predominant energy source in Western Europe and Japan. In the United States, the effect of low oil prices was felt at various levels, all of which would contibute later on to increase U.S. dependence on foreign oil sources: the domestic market was protected by means of import quotas, which made U.S. oil prices rise well above those in the international market, and thus affected adversely U.S. industrial and trade competitiveness vis a vis Western European countries and Japan; coal production declined; starting in the 1970s, natural gas production also diminished; and the timetable for the construction of nuclear plants was significantly delayed.[3]

The main oil companies were able to maintain a low price structure by means of increases in production. In this way, even though the price per barrel of crude declined, oil producing countries registered an absolute increase in tax revenues: from 1,381 million dollars in 1960 to 4,886 million in 1970.[4] But the situation was to change soon, as the oil producing countries looked for ways to obtain more substantial profits.

The first initiative for the creation of OPEC belonged to Venezuela. This country, in 1949, offered its cooperation to Iran in the negotiations then underway between the latter and the Anglo-Iranian Oil Company. Afterwards, Venezuela's information on its tax agreements with the oil companies would be used by Iran, Saudi Arabia, and other oil exporting countries in their demands for additional revenues. In 1953, a formal agreement was signed between Iran and Saudi Arabia for the exchange of information regarding prices and oil policy. Finally, in Baghdag, in September 1960, as a reaction to the persistent trend towards lower oil prices (8 percent less in 1959; 6 percent less in 1960), representatives of Iran, Iraq, Kuwait, Saudi Arabia, and Venezuela, announced the creation of OPEC.[5]

There were three principal factors that contributed to the development of OPEC: the need, from the point of view of the petroleum producing countries, to check the capacity of the oil companies to lower prices at will; the awareness on the part of the already-established producers that the entrance in the market of new, lower-priced producers could affect their operations; and a new confidence by the oil exporting countries in their own technical achievements, enough so to compensate for any possible reaction by the oil companies.[6]

A few years later, in January 1968, the Arab countries members of OPEC signed an agreement that created the Organization of Arab Oil-Exporting Countries (OAPEC). Even though the OAPEC agreement stipulated that it would not affect the functions of OPEC, the fact that the Arab countries felt the need to underscore their common economic and political objectives was indeed significant.[7] Arab militancy, reinforced by political-military events in 1973, i.e. the "Yom Kippur" war, that galvanized Arab countries into action, came to the fore in unprecedented oil price increases: from 2.48 dollars per barrel in 1973 to 11.56 dollars in 1974, that is, an increment of 366 percent.[8] This action, in effect, signaled the end of the era of cheap energy.

The energy crisis, in plain terms, has meant a disruption in the production and commercialization processes of the main energy source in the contemporary world: from 40 percent to 50 percent of all the energy consumption comes from crude oil or derived products. But its causes and outcomes are not a matter easily agreed upon. According to various diverging perspectives, the roots of the energy crisis can be located in: the actual or imminent scarcity of world energy reserves, especially petroleum; the instability in the international oil supply, manifest through price variations and insecurity in the supplies; and the environmental and social degradation due to the growing dependence on oil and coal to meet energy demands.[9] Obviously, the relative weight of these factors, especially the first two, is directly related to the political context. Thus, it would be useful to analyze the energy crisis in terms of its impact on, and reaction from, five basic groups of actors: OPEC; the international oil companies; the Western industrialized countries; Third World countries; and the Soviet Bloc countries.

To a signficant extent, what the OPEC countries have done is to take over the petroleum market structure that had been created by the main oil companies, and to continue fixing prices also according to a political strategy, albeit a different one.[10] But diverging ideological perspectives within OPEC have threatened its very viability as an international cartel. Specifically, the "hard-liners," such as Lybia and Iraq, have frequently clashed with the "moderates", mainly Saudi Arabia, over matters related to price and supply levels.

After the abrupt increases of 1973-1974, oil prices began to fall in real terms, i.e. in relation to inflation. Specifically, from January 1974 to December 1978, official OPEC prices declined 25 percent in constant dollars, 40 percent in constant Marks, and 50 percent in constant Yens. Several factors contributed to this trend. First of all, the economic recession in the Western industrial nations during the mid-1970s, and the subsequent erosion in the value of the dollar, brought about a reduction in the demand of OPEC oil, and declining revenues for the cartel members.[11] On the other hand, during the second half of the 1970s, new sources of oil, such as Mexico, the North Sea, and Alaska, caused a temporary relative glut in the oil market.

Another factor that permeated the oil price structure during the 1970s was the continuing presence of the international oil companies as kingpins of commercialization. The size and diversity of the main oil companies, which limits their vulnerability, and their extensive control of refineries, pipelines, tankers and gas pumps, tend to explain their resilience. By 1978, the sales of the "Seven Sisters" had more than doubled the level of 1973. Most of the companies were successful in arranging deals with OPEC countries, through which they received a fee for pumping the oil, and bought a guaranteed share of the production for themselves, plus most of the remainder at a fixed price.[12]

According to a 1980 study for the National Office of Economic Research, written by the former head of economists of Allied Chemical Company, Avram Kisselgoff, the price increases by OPEC also brought about higher earnings for the main U.S. oil companies, in the three stages of operation: production, refining, and commercialization.[13] Even though the relative increases in their earnings tended to diminish through 1981, it is estimated that total earnings for 1980 were still 30 percent above the 1979 level: from 8.350 billion dollars in 1979 to 11 billion in 1980. Earnings for 1981 were expected to amount to 11.7 billion dollars, and for 1984 a total of 14.960 billion dollars.[14]

The role played by the oil companies is intimately tied to the actions by the Western European and U.S. governments in regards to the energy crisis. To begin with, the energy crisis is not by any means an isolated phenomenon, in its causes and consequences. At a macro-level, it is inscribed in the framework of a linear vision of history, central to contemporary Western civilization, and to much of the rest of the world by the effect of demonstration, which assumes unending progress and limitless expansion of the standard of living. Without entering here into a revision of the various estimates of availability of natural resources, i.e. of the possible exploitation of the physical environment, such a vision is ultimately a fallacy from either a material or a moral perspective. But this topic is well beyond the objectives of this volume, and a brief mention will suffice. At a micro-level, the energy crisis is related to the general economic situation in the countries members of the Organization for Economic Cooperation and Development (OECD), i.e. inflation, unemployment, and a negative balance of payments. In regards to energy policies since 1973-1974, there have been instances of sharp disagreement among OECD nations.

Diverging political responses by oil importing OECD nations to the sharp increases in oil prices were, from the beginning, divided in two currents. One, headed by the United States, tried to promote the formation of a common front to counteract OPEC. This initiative culminated in the International Energy Agency (IEA), established in Brussels in September 1974. The IEA has encouraged cooperation among its members,[15] in order to "...promote a secure petroleum supply, according to reasonable and equitable conditions."[16]

The opposing tendency, led by France, maintained that such a front would not be able to achieve the needed unity among its members, and thus would not have the negotiating power to check OPEC's maneuvers.[17] Indeed, to a certain degree Western European countries, and to a lesser extent Japan, have frequently favored bilateral negotiations and independent agreements. Such a course of action might appear to be contrary to the interests of the IEA, the United States, and the big oil companies. Parallel to this, since 1973, governmental control over the energy sector in Western Europe has increased signficantly.[18]

On the other hand, U.S. initiatives provoked an uncomfortable political situation for OECD countries that were potential oil exporters, such as Canada, Great Britain, and Norway. Some of these nations, as a matter of fact, concurred with OPEC measures. After all, it was the increase in prices itself that made the exploitation of oil profitable in areas such as the North Sea, that had previously been economically unfeasible. Nevertheless, by early 1981, the European Economic Community was considering a project to constitute a "petroleum bank," as a common reserve to act as a safety valve against supply deficits and price raises.[19]

From a general perspective, some authors see the energy crisis as a syndrome of a global crisis of the capitalist system, unable to maintain a rate of growth akin to raised expectations.[20] Within this context, there is the view that the energy crisis has been to a certain degree the result of price manipulation by the oil companies, with the objective of increasing profits. In this regard, one of the positive results for the United States would have been the partial reduction of

the comparative trade disadvantage of recent years vis
a vis Western Europe and, mainly, Japan.[21] However, this
point of view misses facts such as the growing deterioration of the U.S. balance of payments, and the erosion of
American global political leadership, both direct results
of the energy crisis. At any rate, even though there
might be reasons to think that the U.S. government tended
to stimulate actions by OPEC until 1973, as a means to
bring about a raise in prices in the international market
to levels closer to U.S. domestic prices, after that
year OPEC policies were by far too forceful, unpredictable, and disruptive of the international monetary
system, to serve American interests.[22]

If the increases in oil prices have pushed inflation
to perilous levels in Western developed nations, for
Third World oil importing countries in Latin America,
Asia, and Africa, the impact has been catastrophic. In
1978, Third World countries, with 71 percent of the
world population, were consuming 10.5 million b/d of oil;
by contrast, the United States, with approximately 6
percent of the world population, in that same year con-
sumed 18.3 million b/d.[23] In spite of the fact that
Third World countries consume only about 16 percent of
the total energy, their current payments deficit grew
from seven billion dollars in 1973 to more than seventy
billion in 1980. The standing debt of almost 100
developing countries increased six times over during the
1970s, to a total of 376 billion dollars by 1980.[24]
Developing countries must pay oil bills that amount to
fifty billion dollars per year and that, on the average,
absorb 26 percent of their export earnings; in some
cases, this last figure is considerably higher, for
example, in 1980, 60 percent for Turkey, 40 percent for
Brazil, and 30 percent for India. Oil expenditures are
expected to increase to 110 billion by 1990.[25]

In the United Nations, the danger of an economic
paralysis of the Third World has been given growing
attention, as proof of the urgent need for a "New
Economic Order" that would be based on monetary reform,
a transfer of financial resources, and an equitable
planning of energy production and consumption.[26] Even
though the possibilities of an OPEC "Special Fund" for
helping developing countries solve their financial problems have been widely considered, no effective and quick
solution is to be expected from these quarters. In
their price hikes, OPEC has given only marginal attention to their pledge of 1975, in Argel, to assist
developing countries.[27]

At the October 1981, summit of twenty-two leaders
from industrialized and developing nations, held at
Cancún, Mexico, near consensus was reported on the need
for the creation of an energy affiliate of the World
Bank. The proposed agency would manage a thirty billion

dollar fund to help finance exploration and development
of energy resources in Third World countries. In this
context, the active participation of the United States
would be essential. However, the Reagan administration
has opposed the idea, favoring instead the action of
private enterprise.[28]
     In the context of the energy crisis, those nations
which have oil and the political-military capacity to act
on a global scale, will try to assert their presence and
objectives. Specifically, the Soviet Union would appear
to gain from financial turmoil in western countries,
including inflation, recession, and social malaisse, and
from stagnation and increasing political upheaval in
Third World countries. Thus, the energy crisis must be
placed in a proper framework, political as well as
economic, strategic as well as commercial, and as a
danger signal that points to the fact that the means and
ends of development must be redefined, in order for the
western world to stand up to the challenge of an economically finite, and politically perilous environment.
     There have been contradictory signals, since 1973,
regarding the future energy supply scenario. According
to some observers, the relative oil glut since the
second half of the 1970s, a result of western economic
recession and growing oil production, means that scarcity
was just a passing phenomenon. The optimistic forecasts
in regards to petroleum supplies have been partly based
on the assumption that new technologies will make possible an increase in the recovery rate of deposits. But
the discovery of new sources, in itself, is supposed to
augment petroleum supplies. According to some 1975
estimates, by 1985 potential production of oil will be
twice as large as consumption: the exporting capacity
of oil-rich countries would amount to sixty-five million
b/d, while the import needs of industrialized nations
would be covered with thirty-two million barrels.[29] A
study of OECD published in 1977 expected supply by OPEC
countries to reach the level of forty-five million b/d
by 1980, well above the estimated world demand of 33.5
million b/d. By 1985, there would be an excess supply of
between 13 percent to 37 percent of OPEC's production
capacity.[30] By October 1981, new and hopefully more
accurate predictions underlined that there could be surpluses for the next five to ten years, as a result of
continued slow growth in world economies and further
energy conservation.[31]
     On the other hand, new sources such as Mexico and
the North Sea have considerably increased total output.
Additional possibilities are found in China which,
according to the China Business Review, published by the
National Council for U.S.-China trade, would be exporting fifty million tons of oil a year by 1990. Indeed,
by August 1980, China was producing 106.15 million b/d,

a level equivalent to that achieved by Great Britain in its North Sea wells.[32] All in all, some estimates put the amount of oil remaining to be discovered in the world at around one trillion barrels, with 30 percent to 40 percent of it expected to be found offshore, some in deep water areas that have yet to be explored.[33]

In the midst of the maze of estimates regarding oil supplies and prices, it is obvious that these depend on contingent situations of a triple nature: economic; political; and those related to time horizons. In order for the price of crude oil to decline significantly, there would have to be a sizeable drop in world demand (especially U.S. demand), a growing reliance on alternate energy sources, and a permanent expansion in the oil production of non-OPEC countries.[34] These conditions are not likely to coincide on a sustained basis.

Many recent indications tend to confirm the previous argument. A 1977 analysis of future oil supplies concluded that, regardless of the rate of economic growth and oil prices, up to a 50 percent increment above then prevalent levels, before the end of the century there would be a substantial gap between production and demand: demand would outstrip supplies by a margin of fifteen to twenty million b/d, that is, a 26 percent to 28 percent of total world demand.[35] According to a report by the Office of Technological Studies of the U.S. Congress, oil production in the western industrialized nations, under the most favorable circumstances, will remain stationary until the year 2000. In the United States, production is expected to decline to four million b/d. Additionally, by the early 1980s, the Soviet Union may be forced to interrupt its oil exports to Eastern Europe.[36]

A 1977 CIA projection estimated that the Soviet Union and the COMECON Bloc are likely to have a petroleum deficit of up to 4.5 million b/d by the mid-1980s, with its subsequent impact on the world market.[37] Indeed, in 1981 the Soviet Union, the biggest oil producer, increased its oil output by only 0.7 percent, the lowest rate of increment in recent times, in contrast with a 4 percent rate during the previous four years.[38] At present, the Soviet Union supplies only 75 percent of the petroleum demand of Eastern European countries, which means that a higher share of the latter's financial resources will have to be spent on oil from other sources.[39]

Developing countries constitute the most dynamic force in overall petroleum supply and price levels. Petroleum exporters, which number more than twenty countries and represent one-fifth of the population of the Third World, are industrializing at an accelerated pace, and increasing their energy use at a rate of 6.1 percent; oil-importing developing countries also share

the goal of industrialization. Together, these countries will play a crucial role in the 65 percent worldwide increase in energy consumption expected by the end
of the century. Energy use in less developed countries
is rising at a rate at least 30 percent higher than their
GDP. In all, the demand for crude oil in the Third
World, including the thirteen OPEC members, will grow
from eleven million b/d at present, to close to twenty-
four million b/d by the year 2000. Long-range import
needs of developing coutries may not be satisfied unless
there is a drastic reduction in sales to OECD nations,
or a substantial increase in overall production.[40]

If the previous situation appears to impede a sustained trend towards stability in petroleum supplies and
prices, the political milieu is even more unpredictable.
By 1978, sagging demand for petroleum was instrumental
in making Saudi Arabia lead and implement an OPEC
price freeze through the last two-thirds of that year.[41]
However, the Iranian upheaval and the Iraq-Iran War were
soon to show again the intimate relationship between
political and economic events. In particular, the war
between the two Persian Gulf oil exporting countries
has raised the possibility of a cut off in the transit
of oil tankers through the Strait of Ormuz, which would
economically strangle Western Europe and Japan. By
October 1980, most of the Iranian oil exports, and more
than two-thirds of Iraq's exports had been suspended.
This amounted to a loss of 3.15 to 3.35 million b/d
for exports markets.[42]

These factors contributed to a new round of price
hikes. By June 1980, OPEC members had agreed to raise
their base price from twenty-eight dollars to thirty-two
dollars per barrel of crude oil, with a maximum five
dollars premium.[43] By mid-November of that same year,
the price had gone up to fourty dollars per barrel for
cash transaction and up to fifty dollars for thirty day
sales, the highest levels in history.[44] The precipitate
price increases would call into question OPEC's unity,
and bring about an abrupt reversal of the upward price
spiral.

Even before the price increases of November 1980,
a drop in the demand of industrialized nations due to
recession, and to burgeoning existences that by the
beginning of that year had reached the level of five to
5.5 billion barrels, were already eroding the basis for
OPEC's price structures.[45] Saudi Arabia, in order to
prevent excessive raises in prices, by October 1980 had
increased its production from 9.5 to 10.5 million b/d.[46]
For their part, the twenty-one nations members of IEA
responded to the price increases by announcing in
December 1980, that they would reduce their oil imports
and start to use their reserves instead.[47] These
factors, in addition to the bitter pricing battle that

ensued through 1981, had by mid-year effectively undermined the unity among OPEC members and forced a downward
revision of prices. Skyrocketing prices and diminishing
demand had, in effect, resulted in a mini-glut.

The key to a price compromise has been the high
level of production of Saudi Arabia's less expensive
crude oil, which by October 1981, represented nearly half
of OPEC's total production of 21.5 million b/d. Apparently, Saudi Arabia's policy has been to maintain the
price of oil at a level low enough to prevent conservation measures and alternate sources of energy from substantially eroding the demand for petroleum. At the same
time, the Saudi's benchmark price for their oil during
1981, at thirty-two dollars a barrel, effectively under-
cut competition from other oil producing countries,
pressuring them into reaching a price agreement.48

On October 29, 1981, at Geneva, OPEC again established a common price structure. Saudi Arabia agreed
to increase its price two dollars per barrel, in return
for a two dollar reduction by other members of their
thirty-six dollar base price. Thus, a new common benchmark price of thirty-four dollars per barrel was reached,
to be frozen at that level until the end of 1982. OPEC
members were allowed to attach surcharges to this base
price, in order to account for transportation and crude
quality differences, but at a maximum level of a four
dollar premium per barrel. This meant, apparently that
under no circumstances would the price per barrel of oil
be above thirty-eight dollars.49

Nevertheless, these measures taken by OPEC were not
sufficient to avoid the effects of a worldwide oversupply on oil prices, combined with a continuing decline
in demand, which in non-Communist nations was expected
to fall to 44.9 million b/d during 1982, down from 52.2
million b/d in 1979, this in spite of the fact that
total OPEC production had, by October 1981, fallen to
20.5 million b/d from a high of 31 million b/d in
1979. By early March 1982, the IEA reported that
petroleum use during the two previous months was five
to seven percent below the levels of a year before. At
the same time, an outside producer, Great Britain, put
into effect a four dollar cut that reduced the basic
price for its high-quality North Sea oil to thirty-one
dollars per barrel. Some OPEC officials attributed the
problems with falling prices to a concerted action by
outside producers to maintain full ouput and thus undermine OPEC's sales, while in unison consumers were drawing
millions of barrels a day from inventories. By February
1982, oil exporting countries had already become net borrowers of funds from major western banks, for the first
time since the end of 1978. The general situation
engendered considerable bitterness within OPEC, directed
mainly towards Saudi Arabia, which refused to cut its

production without an agreement among all members. Faced
with a crisis, OPEC decided to hold an emergency consul-
tation in March 1982.50

On March 18, 1982, OPEC oil ministers met in Vienna
to try to prevent a general reduction in prices. The
only feasible alternative appeared to be a commitment to
holding production to a level sufficiently low to reverse
the price slide. In this regard, Saudi Arabia was the
key to an effective curtailment in output levels, as a
measure to ensure more bargaining power for OPEC.51
Towards the end of March 1982, OPEC had decided to reduce
production and cut some surcharge quotes. OPEC members
agreed to limit their total crude output to 17.5 million
b/d starting in April, down from an estimate of 18.2
million b/d. Specifically, Saudi Arabia would reduce
its production to a level of seven million b/d, while
Nigeria, Algeria, and Libya cut prices for their oil
by $1.50 to two dollars a barrel, to an average of
thirty-five dollars a barrel, and other members also
reduced their surcharge quotes. OPEC retained the
thirty-four dollars a barrel price for its benchmark
grade, Saudi Arabia's light oil.52

Predictions for the impact of OPEC's decision to
trim production and lower some prices were mixed, but
outside observers tended to agree that it would take
from three to six months to ascertain whether the
strategy succeeds. In any case, the likely result will
be a period of fluctuating prices, until the market
stabilizes. More important than the actual cuts in production is OPEC's credibility, that is, whether its
members will actually uphold their respective production
quotas and price levels. OPEC has pledged to take
further action if necessary. On the other hand, OPEC
members are pressured by previous domestic budget com-
mitments, which were established during a period of
substantially higher revenues.53 Thus, the matter
could turn into a running confrontation between short-
term domestic social expectations and economic expansion,
and the long-term viability of OPEC as a cartel.

In any case, the ultimate effect of OPEC's attempt
to regain control of the petroleum market is contingent
upon factors outside its reach. Production and price
policies by non-members play a significant role. Future
oil price levels will also shift according to the
economic situation in consuming nations. If lower oil
prices result in a relative transfer of wealth away from
oil-producing countries and oil companies to various
national economies, this might bring about a respite in
terms of the inflation rate and as an incentive for
economic growth. An end to OPEC's pricing feud, i.e.
to the dual pricing structure that plagued the organization during most of the 1981 and early 1982, could mean
a reassessment of the energy picture in western

industrialized nations. There is the possibility of a
repetition of another round of "energy profligacy,"
which originally set the stage for OPEC's ascent.54 New,
stable OPEC prices might also result in decreasing
efforts to develop alternate energy sources. Moveover,
political disruption, such as renewed hostilities in the
Middle East, could very rapidly dispel the apparently
reassuring petroleum supply scenario. A relatively
minor alteration of any of the previous factors could
mean, on a short-term basis, a return to a new period
of tight petroleum supplies.

Conversely, under conditions of relative stability
in the petroleum market, OPEC policy conceivably could
seek formulas that would link prices to the rate of
inflation in the main oil-importing nations, and to the
value in real terms of certain key world currencies.
Such an arrangement, by far not a distasteful one considering other more ominous scenarios, would strengthen
a long-term tendency towards moderate, progressive raises
in petroleum prices.

In regard to time horizons for changes in oil price
and supply levels, the picture is not settled. On a
short-range basis, it is widely acknowledged that fuel
supply difficulties will be present as an almost universal phenomenon during most of the 1980s, though
taking various forms in different parts of the world.55
According to extended estimates, a 1980 CIA study states
that world oil supplies are likely to last only between
sixty to ninety years. There is a "precipitate decline"
of "supergiant" oil fields (those of at least five billion barrels), and of "giant" fields (500 million barrels or more), which are being found only at a fraction
of the rate of previous years. These huge fields are at
present the source of more than 75 percent of the
recoverable oil.56 According to another global projection of the energy sector to the year 2030, the period
of "confusion" up to the year 2000, during which the
world will face a progressive scarcity of "clean" fuels,
must be overcome by a period of "transition", immediately
afterwards, during which energy needs will have to be
increasingly supplied by alternate sources.57

The energy crisis, with its economic and political
variables, contributes to shape an international scenario
according to the degrees of vulnerability of the actors.
In this respect, Helio Jaguaribe has noted several overlapping categories: countries or regions without
resources to face the crisis; those that are being forced
to revise their economic and social policies to adapt
to the new conditions; democratic nations whose consensus
mechanisms are being sorely tested by the economic
impasse; and those countries whose legitimacy is based
on an apparently all-encompassing ideology, albeit under
diverging methods of political control.58

In an unstable international milieu, qualified by these groups of actors, disorientation as to the mutually acknowledged and accepted boundaries of political inter-play could lead, according to Jaguaribe, to three pos-sible outcomes:

1. a Third World War;
2. the consolidation of a "world regime" under "shared direction" by the superpowers; or
3. the emergence of a new international system, based on widely agreed-upon economic trans-actions.[59]

The definition of, and agreement on the meaning, causes, and effects of the energy crisis, will be a crucial factor in determining which path will be fol-lowed in the end.

IMPACT OF THE ENERGY CRISIS IN THE UNITED STATES

It is necessary to analyze the energy crisis in the United States in relation to general patterns of con-sumption, for if the goal of development is limitless expansion of demand, ours being a finite world, there is no possible way of avoiding a turning point sooner or later. In this context, is it a crisis indeed, or rather a shortcoming of a particular mode of civilization, i.e. industrialism, based on an excessive rate of energy con-sumption? Of course, it could be argued that the United States also produces a disproportionate share of the world's industrial and agricultural goods. But this fact by no means would dispose of the innate faults of a life style and a system of production based on the irra-tional exploitation of non-renewable resources.

After World War II, exploitation of petroleum in the United States accelerated sharply. The United States, in fact, was a net oil exporter, mainly to Western Europe, until 1947. As early as during the 1950s, some U.S. geologists were disputing the excessively optimistic estimates of hydrocarbon reserves, among them L.G. Weeks and M.K. Hubert. By 1956, based on a revision of avail-able data, Hubert predicted that U.S. petroleum produc-tion would reach a peak from ten to fifteen years after-wards. A few years later, in reply to greater supply expectations raised by the main oil companies, Hubert reaffirmed that new discoveries had already reached a maximum level in 1957, and that proved reserves were at their highest in 1962. Hubert was saying, in effect, that during the 1960s, U.S. oil production would enter a phase of decreasing yields.[60]

Grim reality would confirm Hubert's assertions. What the 1973-1974 oil price hikes did was to question

the up-until-then assumed abundance of cheap energy. But
the signs of an impending crisis were at hand well before
that time. After 1961, proved oil reserves in the United
States entered into a steady decline. The U.S. petroleum
industry could not keep up with the staggering increases
in demand of the 1960s and early 1970s. Nevertheless,
some of the most important markets and industries in the
United States, such as the automobile industry, the
transportation system, and the home-heating market, were
developed on the premises of cheap, abundant energy.[61]

Between 1955 and 1976, U.S. petroleum demand almost
doubled, from 8.5 million b/d to 17.4 million b/d.
Production of oil and natural gas increased at a slower
pace. In 1970, petroleum production reached its peak,
9.64 million b/d. By 1965, the United States had
ceased to be self-sufficient in petroleum and, after
1970, imports grew at a rapid pace. By 1976, the United
States was importing 7.3 million b/d, that is, 42 percent
of national demand.[62] Whereas in 1973 the United States
imported 35 percent of its oil, by 1977 the figure had
risen to 48 percent.[63]

The sources of oil imports on which the United
States relied became increasingly less secure and more
politically explosive. During 1976, Canada reduced its
oil exports to the United States. Parallel to this,
Saudi Arabia replaced Venezuela in the position the
latter had occupied since World War II, as the main U.S.
external source of crude oil and derived products.
Imports from OPEC countries grew from 47 percent of the
total before 1973 to close to 67 percent in 1976. This
included a tripling of purchases from Arab OPEC nations,
a disturbing strategic prospect. The cost of oil imports
increased rapidly, from four billion dollars in 1971 to
eight billion in 1973, forty-five billion in 1977, and
forty-two billion in 1978. By 1979, the petroleum bill
had exceeded the fifty billion mark.[64] In his "Energy
Address" to the nation of April 5, 1979, President Carter
presented a gloomy picture:

> Just ten years ago, we imported hardly any oil.
> Today, we buy about half the oil we use from
> foreign countries. We are by far the largest
> customer for OPEC oil, buying one-fourth of
> that foreign cartel's total production. This
> year, we will pay out fifty billion dollars
> for imported oil -- about 650 dollars for
> every household in the United States.[65]

Domestic oil production has failed to meet increasing demand. In 1978, oil imports diminished somewhat
as oil from Alaska's North Slope added 1.2 million b/d to
domestic supply. However, at the time this proved to
be only a temporary respite, since it was not reinforced

by stringent restraint measures, and it was partly erased
shortly afterwards by the effects of the Iranian upheaval
on world oil supply and prices.66

As a result of government measures, but mostly
because of economic reasons, during the first two-thirds
of 1980 crude oil imports by the United States dropped
from 8.3 million to 5 million b/d. This represented a
contraction of 19.3 percent.67 However, price increases
nullified any possible gains from this decline in demand.
In April 1980, government officials were announcing that:

> With the doubling of oil prices in the last
> twelve months, we are spending ninety billion
> dollars per year for imported oil -- and the
> price is rising at the time. Our 1980 oil
> import bill is equal to the net assets of
> General Motors, Ford, IBM, and General Electric
> combined. If we continue to spend for imported
> oil at this rate, in twelve years we will have
> exported cash equal to the trading value of all
> stocks listed on the New York Exchange -- well
> over a trillion dollars.68

There is no way to overestimate the impact of the
energy crisis on the American economy. Since the first
oil price increase round of 1973-1974, the U.S. economy
has been painfully vulnerable to trade imbalances and
inflation. The unhappy combination of inflation and
recession so prevalent in the mid and late 1970s was
directly related to OPEC's price increases.

Specifically, foreign oil price hikes have meant
that substantial income has been shifted to OPEC which
otherwise would have been spent on goods and services
within the U.S. market. The fact that energy demand is
relatively fixed in the short run, i.e. it cannot be
reduced significantly by conserving fuel or by using
substitutes for oil, made it unavoidable for consumers to
pay higher energy bills. Indirectly, higher energy
prices have had repercussions on everything that uses
oil or substitutes, even for several years after the
initial impact. Internally, this has implied additional
inflation; externally, growing trade deficits. The
depreciation of the dollar in foreign markets during
the late 1970s completed the vicious circle, by further
raising oil imports and inflation. In short, the net
effect of the energy crisis has been a decline, or at
least a stagnation, of the American standard of living,
this in spite of the 12 percent reduction of oil prices
in real terms from mid-1974 to 1978.69

A comparison of the average economic growth rates
in the main western industrialized nations during the
period 1950-1973, and 1973-1978, clearly presents a
picture of a fall in the rates of growth and

productivity. In the United States specifically, the growth rate fell from an average of 2.6 percent during the first period to 0.4 percent during the second. One of the main reasons for the decline was the sudden increase in energy prices. 70

By April 1979, one of the primary immediate impacts of the curtailment of foreign oil supplies on the U.S. economy, in spite of constantly higher prices, was the reduction of industry stocks to dangerously low levels. This augured a crucial need to dispense partially with gasoline production in order to rebuild distillate fuel oil stocks for industry.71 But the energy problems referred to a much wider framework than the simple reduction of oil consumption:

> The task ahead is clear. We have to bring the highly inflationary price of energy under control, stop the outflow of dollars, and wean ourselves away from the excessive dependence on Middle East oil, which has grown to the point where it threatens our national security.72

The energy crisis represents a danger to the United States from two sources: domestic malaise and foreign strategic dependence. Internally, unless policy measures to prevent them are effective, progressive increases in the cost of fuel and rationing, a breakdown of the transportation system, unemployment, and inflation, could wreak havoc with America's social structure and even its political system.73 Externally, the security threat from vulnerable sources of supply, which are concentrated in the politically volatile area of the Middle East, underline the need to find appropriate solutions.74

UNITED STATES ENERGY POLICY

If the voice of alarm had been given since the 1950s by some scientists worried about the growing gap between U.S. energy production and reserves, on the one hand, and demand on the other, it was not until the early 1970s that political circles began to show their concern about the situation. During 1971, President Nixon expressed his awareness of a possible energy scarcity, and the need to promote research and development of new sources. By April 1973, these programs had not given the expected results, and Nixon proceeded to eliminate government restrictions on petroleum imports. When the crisis of late 1973 arose, the response of the Nixon administration centered on production: oil companies were given incentives, such as the authorization to raise prices, as a means to increase the domestic supply of petroleum. Other signs of government action were the adoption of a

general 55 mph speed limit all over the nation. Nixon's
"Project Independence", geared as its name implied to
achieve energy self-sufficiency and sever external links
of dependence, fell short of its goal. Some of the
reasons for its failure were an excessive optimism
regarding the production and price levels of alternate
sources of energy, and environmental considerations.[75]
     The failure to increase domestic supplies led to
conservation measures. A 1974 policy project by the Ford
Foundation stressed the need to cut in half the annual
rate of increment in energy demand through conservation.
This reduction, according to the project, would not
affect the growth of the economy, but it would effectively contribute to reduce petroleum needs through the
end of the century. The project was the first integral
policy approach designed to face energy shortcomings.
However, because of strong opposition from the private
sector, it was never implemented.[76]
     During the 1976 elections, the energy question was
not a central theme of the Ford-Carter campaign debates.
Both men coincided in the triple need to cut petroleum
imports, to free the prices of natural gas, and to support a strategic petroleum reserve. While Ford emphasized strong federal budgetary support for creating a 90-
day reserve, Carter went further and proposed an energy
plan that would deal with the various dimensions of the
problem.[77]
     After his election, Carter placed James R. Schlesin-
ger in charge of the energy sector. The bitter winter
of 1976 reinforced the objective of a comprehensive
energy plan, but political problems related to Carter's
inability to deal with Congress were to plague its enactment. The energy plan that finally emerged in November
1978, after protracted negotiations in Congress, was a
modified version of the original. Nevertheless, it was
a recognition to a new awareness in the government
regarding energy problems. Energy questions had gained
a position of priority. An indication of this fact was
the creation in 1977 of the Department of Energy at the
level of a Secretary, headed by Schlesinger.
     Carter's energy plan, i.e. the National Energy Act,
was in reality a package of energy-related measures,
centered on two basic objectives: conservation and
utilization of alternate energy sources. In regards to
conservation, the National Energy Conservation Act of
1978 required governors to submit plans to the Secretary
of Energy on the procedure through which oil and gas
dealers would advise customers about conservation measures in each state. Furthermore, it encouraged conservation by putting into effect a series of grants,
loans, and federal programs to assist public and federal
facilities in installing energy-saving devices and
switching to solar heating and cooling.[78]

The Energy Tax Act of 1978 reinforced these measures by granting tax credit to homeowners who installed energy-saving equipment, and by imposing a tax starting with 1980 automobile models, on those which did not meet a minimum standard of economy. The Public Utilities Regulatory Policy Act was based on the principle that electricity rates should encourage the conservation of energy and the efficient use of resources. In regard to the promotion of alternate energy sources, the Power Plant and Industrial Fuel Use Act of 1978 tried to reduce the nation's dependence on imported oil by expanding domestic coal production; this would be achieved by limiting the use of oil or natural gas in certain facilities, which would then turn to coal for their energy needs.[79]

Another section of the energy package, the Natural Gas Policy Act of 1978, created for the first time a single national market for natural gas. Through this act, all states now gained access to 40 percent of the natural gas production, which had previously been out of the interstate market, due in part to the higher prices available in the producing states. Since this situation had caused gluts inside the producing states, it was expected that the nation as a whole would benefit from more abundant supplies. Initial price increases would be smaller for homes, schools, and hospitals than for large industries. In regards to new natural gas, price controls would end by 1985. The Natural Gas Policy Act purported to help reduce dependence on imported oil by stimulating home production through increased prices and accelerating the switch from gas to more abundant energy sources.[80]

The National Energy Act acknowledged that growth in world oil production could not keep pace indefinitely with demand. While new oil findings might postpone the day when oil production started its inexorable downward trend, the Act underlined the fact that new finds were not replenishing existing reserves. Thus, there was a crucial need for conservation and use of alternate energy sources.[81]

During 1979, energy questions remained one of the priority policy areas in the Carter administration. The central preoccupation was now to set forth a phased decontrol of oil prices, to begin on June 1 of that year throughout twenty-eight months, until September 1981, when federal government controls on oil were to cease anyway. The objective of phased decontrol would be to encourage production of oil and gas. Thus, it appeared that conservation and alternate sources of energy by themselves were not enough to face the energy crisis. However, since decontrol could further augment what the Carter administration deemed to be already large profits by the oil companies, there would also be a "windfall

profits tax" on the oil companies, in order to retain
part of the extra earnings and channel them into an
"Energy Security Fund." This fund would be geared to
"protect low income families from energy increases, to
build a more efficient mass transportation system, and
to put American genius to work solving our long-range
energy problems."[82] Congress would later approve these
measures.

In addition to the previous announcements, Carter
proposed other steps to encourage production. One of
these would be the resumption of previously stalled talks
with Mexican officials, in order to reach an agreement
on sales of Mexican natural gas to the United States,
"at a price that is fair for both countries."[83] These
talks would eventually clear the way for an agreement.

The details of Carter's new offensive on the energy
field were spelled out in what was called a "Response
Plan", that included conservation as well as production
measures, such as: crude oil price decontrol mechanisms;
increased production from sources such as the Naval
Petroleum Reserve at Elk Hills; state, local, and private
initiatives to reduce petroleum use; natural gas projects; electric energy transfers; a lead phasedown for
gasoline; emergency building temperature restrictions;
immediate reductions in federal energy consumptions;
emergency weekend sales restrictions; and allocation and
price control rules in case of emergencies.[84]

To present a comprehensive view of the new initiatives or, as President Carter put it, "to build on the
foundation of the National Energy Act", by May 1979,
the Department of Energy designed the Second National
Energy Plan. This plan addressed three fundamental
themes: U.S. dependence on potentially unstable supply
sources, which implies a vulnerability to interruptions
and sudden price increases; the possibility that supply
and demand forces might cause world and domestic oil
prices to rise well above the rate of inflation, depress-
ing the long-term economic growth index; and the need to
develop an energy strategy that holds down economic and
political costs to the United States.[85]

The National Energy Plan II introduced a near term
(1979-1985), a mid-term (1985-2000), and a long-term
(2000 and beyond) strategies. The challenge of the near
term would be to insure appropriate energy producing and
consuming equipment in degree and kind, so as to start
reducing dependence on foreign oil. During the mid-term,
the United States would continue to hold down energy
consumption and oil imports, and to develop the capa-
bility to shift from reliance on oil and gas to new and
higher-cost forms of energy technologies. Finally, the
challenge for the long term would be to go beyond the
"transitional" energy supplies of the mid-term, such as
some renewable technologies, enhanced oil recovery, oil

shale, and coal-derived products, towards a set of
"ultimate" technologies, such as renewable and advanced
nuclear technologies. "The nation's long-term objective
is to have renewable and essentially inexhaustible
sources of energy to sustain a healthy economy."[86]

The agenda for action of the National Energy Plan II
included a number of federal policies and programs.
Grants and tax incentives would continue to be instrumental in increasing energy efficiency, thus enhancing
conservation. Financial incentives and the reduction of
institutional barriers would be major tools to raise
domestic oil and gas production. The use of coal, as
the nation's most abundant fossil energy resource, would
be encouraged in place of oil and gas wherever economically and environmentally feasible. Nuclear reactors
were expected to continue to meet a growing share of the
electrical energy needs. And, finally, an effort was to
be made to enhance the capacity to use renewable
resources such as solar and geothermal energy.[87]

By mid-1979, the Carter administration again underlined its commitment to deal with the energy crisis. The
1977 oil import level was set as the maximum allowed,
leaving conservation and domestic production as the only
avenues for higher energy consumption. To insure these
targets, import quotas were set. A commitment of funds
and resources was made to develop alternative sources of
fuels. Carter asked Congress to require by law that
utility companies cut their massive use of oil by 50
percent within the following decade, and switch to other
fuels, especially coal. He also urged Congress to create
an Energy Mobilization Board, in charge of completing
key energy projects. Finally, Carter reemphasized a
conservation program, at the state, county, and city
levels.[88]

Carter's energy proposals faced numerous obstacles
from pressure groups, within Congress itself, and from
lobbies, which favored above everything else the liberalization of prices as incentives to production.
Carter's proposals, which originally had underlined the
need for conservation and the use of alternate sources
of energy, progressively incorporated measures such as
phased decontrol, whether by own conviction, or perhaps
in order to lessen the opposition to his programs. Some
observers have also pointed out that the energy proposals
were designed in too much of a hurry and secrecy, which
harmed Carter's already-strained relations with Congress.
On the other hand, the barrage of legislative initiatives
received by Congress may have weakened their passage.[89]

There has been a continuing debate since 1973 over
the role of the American oil companies in the energy
crisis. Obviously, there is a wide, and hard to discern,
margin of negotiation between the U.S. government and
the oil companies. There are both coincidences and

divergencies between the perspectives of the two in
regard to national security, the standard of living,
economic stability, and the proper rate of profits.[90]
There are questions regarding the degree of compatibility
between the interests of the U.S. government and those
of the oil companies. The issue remains undefined and
open to debate. During 1979 the Carter administration
became worried over the role of the oil companies in
the gasoline supplies shortages of 1978-1979. However,
in a mid-1979 report by the Department of Energy, it was
stated that no evidence had been found of hoarding of
oil by refiners, and that the refiners had kept their
stocks within normal levels.[91]

PERSPECTIVES

What are the perspectives of U.S. energy policy? In
regard to exploitation and production, intensive efforts
were being carried on by 1979, and world instability in
the petroleum market was spurring domestic drilling.[92]
By late 1980, oil companies were drilling at deeper
levels than ever, 15,000 feet or more. During 1980, a
record 60,000 new oil and natural gas wells were estimated to have been drilled in the United States; by
comparison, only 27,602 wells were dug in 1973. At the
same time, an attempt was being made to develop new
techniques to recover some of the 75 percent of oil that
remains in the subsoil after using conventional pumping
methods.[93] According to official sources, these efforts
were expected to succeed in keeping oil production in
the United States near 1980 levels of approximately
nine million b/d, through the year 2000. In addition,
petroleum consumption was expected to be at significantly
lower levels by 1985: up to an 8 percent reduction that
would allow a savings of as much as 1.5 million b/d.[94]

In 1980, the Department of Energy projected conservation measures that by the year 2000 could bring about
savings on the order of approximately 20 percent in
energy use.[95] Among alternate sources, coal constitutes
by far the brightest hope. Under the authority of the
Fuel Use Act, by 1980 the Department of Energy was ordering industry and utilities to convert from oil to coal,
with the goal of displacement of the equivalent of a
million b/d of oil by 1990. However, many environmental
problems related to the burning of coal remain to be
solved.[96] In August 1980, it was announced that the
biggest commercial plant for the production of oil from
coal would be built in West Virginia, at a cost of 1,400
million dollars; the investment would be partly guaranteed by West Germany and Japan, which would benefit from
the technology.[97]

Crucial to the achievement of the previous objectives is the rational distribution of energy throughout the United States. This would involve the construction of much additional infrastructure, including pipeline systems. For example, the size and development of additional Alaskan reserves and California production would determine the size and desirability of a west to east pipeline.[98] By late 1980 the U.S. pipeline network had continued to grow steadily, despite inflationary costs for construction.[99]

A key part of U.S. energy policy, in regard to lessening the political vulnerability of the United States vis a vis foreign oil sources, is the strategic petroleum reserve. In 1977, President Carter proposed the creation of such a reserve, in the order of 500 to 1,000 million barrels of oil.[100] By March 1978, 150 million barrels were already in reserve, and the one billion objective was expected to be reached by 1983.[101] However, by 1979, the State Department opposed the strategic reserve, arguing that it would destabilize the world market; leaders of the oil industry, as well as Saudi Arabia, supported this view.[102] By September 1980, ninety-two million barrels were in reserve, sufficient for only eighty-six days of normal consumption. At that time, the Department of Energy suggested that the initial objectives fell short of actual strategic needs, and should be increased four times over.[103]

These discrepancies in official energy policy objectives seemed to subside with the election of President Reagan. Since early in 1981, the Reagan administration announced that the United States would buy crude oil for the strategic reserve, at an accelerated pace and directly in the international market.[104] By mid-1981 the new Energy Secretary, James B. Edwards, declared that the United States was taking advantage of more flexible market conditions, to increase its strategic petroleum reserves at a rate of 200,000 b/d. The ultimate objective had been expanded to 120 days of supply.[105] In this context, a significant development was the incorporation of Mexico as a direct supplier to the strategic reserve, by September 1981.

If a lesson must be learned from a decade of various approaches to face the energy crisis, it is the extreme difficulty of putting into effect an efficient program of energy conservation in a society and an economic system such as those of the United States. According to some observers, factors such as the American political process itself, and the coexistence of multiple pressure groups, do not bode well for the prospects of success.[106]

It would appear that energy policies should be flexible and multi-faceted: the goals of conservation and production must be carefully balanced. However, the Reagan administration has directed its efforts mainly

towards production and away from conservation. This is
likely to imply a number of things, such as: a lessening
of environmental standards; the opening up of more
federal lands for oil and gas exploration; and the
encouragement of the nuclear industry.

Early in 1981, the Reagan administration moved to
eliminate the last oil price controls, well ahead of
schedule, in order to spur domestic exploration and production.[107] Likewise, federal subsidies in the industry
were abolished, an action which has resulted in serious
economic difficulties for small exploring and refining
companies. On the other hand, decontrol was bringing
about the closure of various retail gas sales operations,
which had been maintained in light of government regulations.[108]

The Reagan administration has remained committed
to the objective of eliminating governmental interference in the field of energy. This determination was
sharply underscored in March 1982, when President Reagan
vetoed a bill that would have given him the power to
allocate petroleum supplies and control prices in future
emergencies, asserting that the free market would work
more effectively in a crisis without the hindrance of
any federal schemes.[109] However, pressure from various
Congressional leaders and consumer groups have given rise
to a number of compromises in several energy-related
areas. On March 1, 1982, President Reagan announced that
he would not send Congress legislation to speed up the
decontrol of natural gas. Nevertheless, the administration still sees natural gas decontrol as an essential
component of its energy policy, and is likely to pursue
the issue through intermittent action by the Federal
Energy Regulatory Commission.[110]

During his presidential campaign, Reagan had pledged
to dismantle the Department of Energy, as an additional
step to limit federal involvement in energy markets.
Accordingly, in December 1981, the Reagan administration
introduced a plan which would in fact abolish the department, and transfer most of its functions to the Commerce
Department, and the rest to the Departments of Interior,
Justice, and Agriculture. However, under strong Congressional resistance, legislative approval of such a
measure seemed unlikely, at least during 1982. Some
legislators interpreted the move as mostly a political
maneuver, which would have virtually no effect in
reducing the budget and, additionally, might give a
wrong impression to OPEC and allies alike, in regard to
American resolve in energy policy matters.[111] Furthermore, by April 1982, a coalition of members of Congress,
individuals, and interest groups, called into question
Reagan's scuttling of conservation measures, by suing the
administration in order to force the release of 21.8

million dollars to finance the Solar Energy and Energy
Conservation Bank.[112]

By mid-1982, the worldwide surplus of petroleum
represented a respite for American consumers and a curb
on inflation. Continuing a trend that began in 1979, oil
imports declined from 6.75 million b/d in February 1981,
to 4.85 million b/d a year later, a drop of 28.2 percent.
By March 1982, total imports were at the level of early
1972. For 1982 the United States was expected to spend
approximately sixty billion dollars to pay for imported
oil, in comparison with about seventy billion dollars in
1981.[113] However, lower prices have also meant a number
of detrimental side effects, as well as a challenge to
government policies.

Falling petroleum prices have hurt the oil industry
in terms of diminishing profits, stock prices, and capital investment programs. Oil companies plan to increase
exploration outlays during 1982 only by 14 percent, to
95.3 billion dollars, in contrast with a 39 percent
increase in 1981. As a result of price decreases, independent wildcatters have slowed down their drilling
activities, and this may bring about a reversion to a
long-term declining trend in domestic oil production.
Likewise, because of a cost squeeze, a growing number of
oil refiners have either closed down or reduced operations. Some of the top companies have also discarded
plans for extracting oil from coal, tar sands, and shale
rock. Lower prices seemed to be undermining the incentives for conservation.[114]

For the Reagan administration, caught in the midst
of burgeoning budgetary deficits, the petroleum glut has
resulted in declining "windfall profits" tax revenues
from oil companies. According to some estimates, the tax
reduction could mean an increase in the federal deficit
by ten to twenty billion dollars.[115] That prospect has
motivated both the White House and Congress to consider
the possibility of an energy tax, which could assume the
form of either a boost to the federal excise tax or
retail gasoline sales (at four cent per gallon in mid-
1982), or an import surcharge on foreign oil. The second
option would raise billions of dollars in tax revenues,
undermine OPEC through an "immunization" against ulterior
price increases when the oversupply ends, prop up conservation efforts, and encourage the exploitation of domestic energy sources. It has been estimated that a five-
dollars-a-barrel levy would increase revenues by almost
ten billion dollars, although partly offset by the subsequent inflationary impact.[116] Furthermore, the possibility has been advanced of a tax on all oil, which
would not antagonize friendly exporters as much as an
import fee.[117] Either option was considered to be
unlikely in an election year such as 1982.[118]

In spite of the reassuring supply outlook by mid-1982, a number of indicators underscored the cyclical nature of the world petroleum scenario. American crude oil imports have declined substantially, but still account for 25 percent of all U.S. needs. This means that the dependence on foreign sources has not been broken, with the corresponding vulnerability to new price increases or interruptions in supply. The end of the global recession might very well result in another "up" cycle, even under conditions of an unlikely absence of major political turmoil. Within the United States itself, diminishing incentives for conservation and exploitation of alternate fuels could be the prelude to another round of price hikes.[119]

Early in 1982, the Department of Energy projected rising imports as oil companies stop drawing on their stocks. Indeed, the factors that have caused the oil glut could be just temporary. Specifically, the lack of preparedness of the Reagan administration to manage a new disruption of the oil market might prove to be disastrous. In the end, the search for a balanced policy-making approach to the unnecessary dichotomy between energy-producing and energy-saving schemes, remains very much in effect.[120]

EFFECTS OF MEXICAN OIL EXPORTS
ON U.S. DOMESTIC MARKET

In the light of special geopolitical circumstances, i.e. geographic proximity, trade, strategic considerations, Mexico's oil exporting potential is bound to have a growing impact on the U.S. energy situation. This importance is manifest as a crucial source of petroleum in case of an external threat to U.S. national survival. Mexico's basic political stability and continuity, in contrast with the political unpredictability of Persian Gulf and African sources, enhances its prospects as a reliable supplier. In short, according to Edward J. Williams:

> The United States certainly sees more Mexican oil as desirable under any circumstances, and it is not too difficult to project a scenario in which petroleum exports from Mexico would be absolutely crucial.[121]

The point of view of Mexican analysts tends to reaffirm the previous assessment, albeit qualifying it with a dose of skepticism regarding Mexico's prospective gains from the exchange. It is feared that the United States might incorporate Mexican hydrocarbons to its global energy plan, as a means to maintain American

hegemony. In this context, the main objectives behind
U.S. purchases of Mexican oil would be: to increment its
crude oil reserves; to insure the external supply of
petroleum and natural gas necessary to cover domestic
deficits; to sustain a "loyal exporter" as a precaution
against future conflicts with Arab countries or adverse
OPEC policies; and to solve the need for secure energy
sources, while U.S. energy policy and consumption patterns undergo necessary adjustments and new alternate
energy sources become available.[122]

Richard B. Mancke has summarized, from the U.S.
perspective, the role of Mexico as a U.S. petroleum
supplier:

> Expanded imports of Mexican petroleum will help
> the United States to achieve three important
> domestic goals...: reducing U.S. vulnerability
> to sudden interruptions in oil supplies, assuring
> that the United States satisfies its basic energy
> needs efficiently, and reducing environmental
> damage.[123]

In terms of U.S. national security, the view is
widely shared by American analysts that it is in the
interest of the United States that Mexico develops its
hydrocarbon resources "as rapidly and completely as
possible."[124] The reason for this derives from the
divergence in political, economic, and ideological perspectives between the United States and the group of
countries that control a large share of the world's oil
exports, and from the growth in military and naval
strength by the Soviet Union. Obviously, the full inser-
tion of Mexico in the present framework of U.S. petroleum
suppliers would support the U.S. position in regards to
actual and potential threats to its energy, and thus to
its national security. Indirectly, in reference to
Mexican exports to countries other than the United
States, the existence of alternate oil sources would also
alleviate pressures on world supply and prices.[125]

In a context of economic efficiency, Mancke sees
three main areas of economic benefits for the United
States, arising from growing imports of Mexican oil:

1. a sizeable reduction in total spending for
   energy, because increased imports of more
   secure Mexican oil should reduce the need
   to commence large-scale, commercial production of higher-cost domestic alternatives
   (such as synthetic gas or oil made from
   coal, oil shale, nuclear power, and solar
   energy) in order to ensure an adequate
   level of energy security;

> 2. a sharp reduction in capital demands and, as a corollary, less rigid capital stock require-
> ments; and
> 3. strengthened exports, which will improve the U.S. balance of trade.[126]

Mancke is suggesting, in fact, that Mexico's oil exports to the United States might add a third option, at least in terms of time margin, to the two basic alternatives faced by U.S. energy policy, i.e. conservation, or increased domestic production. In short, Mexican oil exports might solve, albeit temporarily, the dilemma of spending billions in alternate energy sources, or continuing to rely on high levels of imports from unstable foreign sources.[127]

However, there are some basic weaknesses to these arguments. To begin with, the postponement of the critical U.S. energy dilemma, i.e. conservation vs. increased domestic production, is by no means a solution to the problem, and might even retard such a solution by giving rise to a new spurt in domestic consumption, on the basis that new, secure supplies have been assured. On the other hand, Mexico's socioeconomic situation would not necessarily improve according to growing oil exports.

The purchase of large amounts of Mexican oil might reduce the need for capital demands in the United States, but at the price of postponing a definite solution to the energy problems. And, in any discussion in regards to the development of domestic oil and alternate energy sources, U.S. pressure groups and domestic politics must be taken into account. Mexican exports are bound to have a large impact on U.S. domestic production. It has been argued that Mexican oil could displace petroleum from Alaska's North Slope (ANS) producers. Thus, there is a need to reconcile imports of Mexican oil with present policies that encourage sales of ANS crude in the Gulf Coast refining market. As a matter of fact, Mexican exports might undermine ANS sales both in the Gulf Coast and in the west coast refineries. By August 1978, Mexico was discounting[128] its oil to the extent required to gain a share in the U.S. market. As a result, Arabian light crude oil was being displaced, as Mexican oil became available. Furthermore, at that time "Mexican oil (was) also displacing ANS crude oil, causing ANS to be discounted on the Gulf Coast as well."[129]

This phenomenon might be beneficial to U.S. consumers, since ANS producers "would be forced to discount Alaskan oil to the extent necessary to undersell Mexican oil and to maintain their market shares. Slightly lower crude oil costs for domestic U.S. refiners could be the result."[130] However, if Mexican exports were to increase substantially, at reduced price levels, the situation might deter production and exploration in Alaska's North Slope. The competitive position of the producers of ANS could improve by the construction of the PACTEX Pipeline,[131] because of the savings in transportation costs over the present transit costs of the Panama Canal route. If this were to materialize, Standard Oil of Ohio (SOHIO), the largest ANS producer, which also has a sizable investment in PACTEX, would likely discount its oil to the extent needed to outsell Mexican oil in the Gulf Coast refining market. Since it has alternative markets, in the end "Mexico will probably price its oil just low enough to back out Arabian light but not low enough to displace ANS crude on a large scale."[132]

However, there are contrasting views regarding the extent of the impact of Mexico's oil exports on U.S. Gulf Coast refineries and Alaskan North Slope crude oil. According to U.S. official sources, the importation of sizable amounts of Mexican crude oil to Gulf Coast refineries "could render ANS crude oil unmarketable anywhere in the United States except the west coast, even with the PACTEX Pipeline, unless ANS prices are heavily discounted." And, needless to say, there are critical discounting margins beyond which ANS production and exploration might be discouraged.[133]

The effect of oil imports from Mexico on the U.S. domestic market could be further underlined by reference to two additional indicators: the "marker" standard in oil transaction, and transportation cost. There are two important factors that help to establish the price of crude oil and determine the "marker": refining values and transportation costs. Towards the end of 1979:

> ...Arabian light crude oil (was) the 'marker' crude oil against which other crude oil is measured. Due to significant differences between transportation costs for Arabian light crude oil and Mexican-Reforma crude oil to U.S. Gulf Coast refineries, however, the potential exists for significant discounting of Mexican-Reforma crude oil, and this discounting could lead to the Mexican-Reforma crude replacing the Arabian light crude oil as the 'marker'.[134]

Specially in regards to transportation costs, these are determined by factors such as the size of tankers, distances, and prevalent world scale rates. Due to the fact that freight rates are expected to increase through the 1980s, "the transportation differential between Mexican and Arabian light crudes will probably widen over the next decade." As the transportation differential increases, "this discounting in conjunction with surpluses could create downward pressure on the price of ANS crude.[135]

In short, the import of significant quantities of
Mexican crude oil would: bring about pressures to discount U.S. Gulf Coast price for ANS oil, which would
reduce the netback to the wellhead; in the absence of
a west coast pipeline (PACTAX), hinder ANS production
and exploration; progressively push both Arabian and ANS
oil out of U.S. Gulf Coast refineries. These possibilities raise potential federal policy issues in regards
to the need for incentives and compensations to Alaskan
North Slope producers in order to sustain exploration
and development of oil fields there. Other areas of
concern would be the potential levels of discounting by
the various actors, estimates on quantities and geographic penetration in the United States of Mexican oil,
and availability of oil for the Strategic Reserve Program.[136]

On the other hand, in all likelihood the U.S. balance of trade would benefit from the growing imports of
Mexican petroleum. Factors such as geography, population density, and economic growth objectives, underline
the fact that Mexico will purchase larger amounts of
U.S. goods. According to Mancke:

> ...since compared with any eastern hemispheric
> OPEC member, Mexico will spend a far higher
> fraction of any rise in its foreign exchange
> earnings for U.S. goods and services, a policy
> that encourages a rise in Mexico's share of the
> total world oil trade will lead to a net increase
> in the demand for U.S. exports. Therefore, the
> net effect...would be to reduce the U.S. balance
> of trade deficit.[137]

However, it would be an altogether different proposition for the United States to openly encourage or
pressure Mexico to raise its level of petroleum production and exports, even though it might benefit the U.S.
balance of trade, without due consideration to the domestic socioeconomic impact in Mexico. Any significant
increases in Mexico's hydrocarbon exports must be carefully weighed against the overall effect in Mexico's
internal milieu. And, obviously, domestic conditions
in Mexico are of utmost importance for the United States.
Mancke seems to assume that the more oil Mexico produces
and exports, the better off it will be, in terms of
stability and "rapidly rising living standards."[138] But
this is not necessarily so. As a matter of fact, unrestricted development of Mexico's oil industry, with a
corresponding increase in exports and earnings, might
well have the opposite effect, in social, economic,
political, and ecological terms.

By 1979, Mexico had already displaced, in order of
importance, two traditional U.S. petroleum suppliers,

Venezuela and Canada.[139]   It is by now clear that
Mexican hydrocarbon exports can indeed contribute to
alleviate the energy problems in the United States.
However, as it has been seen, their impact is complex
and intimately tied to U.S. domestic energy policy.
Regardless of the extent of Mexico's petroleum export
potential, its ultimate significance is contingent upon
future patterns of U.S. energy consumption and production. In a context of expanding oil consumption, in time
all of Mexico's exports might turn out to be just a
transient palliative. On the basis of a 1978 conjecture
of 100 billion barrels in proven reserves, it was estimated that Mexico would not be able to supply the equivalent of more than three or four years of petroleum consumption by the noncommunists world, in terms of expected
1990 levels of petroleum needs.[140]
        Mexico as an oil exporter represents for the United
States, on the one hand, valuable time to reach an
adequate equilibrium between conservation and production,
and on the other, a unique opportunity to lay the foundation for a better mutual understanding. In effect, this
is a two-sided proposition that goes beyond a mere commercial exchange, to encompass the complex social,
economic, and political amalgam of relations between the
two nations.

NOTES

1. Mario Ojeda, El poder negociador del petróleo:
el caso de Mexico," Foro Internacional, El Colegio de
Mexico, Vol. XXI, No. 1, July-September 1980, pp. 44-47.
        2. Nazli Choucri, "Dudas en torno a la OPEP,"
Technology Review, appeared in Contextos, Secretaría de
Programación y Presupuesto, Año 1, No. 21, 11-17 December
1980, Mexico, p. 34.
        3. Jorge Sábato, "Apocalipsis Petrolero?," South,
appeared in Contextos, No. 21, ibid., p. 43.
        4. Manuel Mejido, Los Aventureros del Petróleo
(Mexico: Editorial Grijalbo, 1980), p. 41.
        5. Choucri, op. cit., pp. 33-35. "Estatutos de
la Organización de Países Exportadores de Petróleo
(OPEP)," and "Resoluciones de la Organización de Países
Exportadores de Petróleo," in Luis Arauz (ed.), Legisla-
ción Petrolera Internacional (Mexico: Siglo XXI
Editores, 1978), pp. 23-37 and 38-163.
        6. Choucri, ibid., p. 33.
        7. "Convenio por el que se establece la Organiza-
ción de países arabes exportadores de petróleo," in
Arauz, op. cit., pp. 165-176.
        8. Luis Pazos, Mitos y Realidades del Petróleo
(Mexico: Editorial Diana, 1979), p. 105.

114

9. América Latina y los Problemas Actuales de la Energía, Comisión Económica para América Latina (Mexico: Fondo de Cultura Económica, 1975), Chapter 1.

10. Sábato, op. cit., p. 47.

11. "La baja demanda de crudo y la erosión del dólar provocan pérdidas a la OPEP," Uno mas Uno, Mexico, May 3, 1978, p. 24.

12. "The Seven Sisters Still Rule," Time, September 11, 1978, pp. 42-49.

13. Leonard Silk, The New York Times, June 23, 1980, title and page not available.

14. "Cede la ganancia de petroleras: E.U.," Excelsior, July 22, 1980, pp. 26 & 29. Also, Thomas C. Hayes, "Exxon Net Off 20.6% in Quarter," New York Times, 1981, date and page not available.

15. Originally: Belgium, Canada, Denmark, West Germany, Ireland, Italy, Japan, Luxemburg, the Netherlands, Norway, Great Britain, and the United States. At present, there are twenty-one members in the IEA.

16. "Texto completo del Pacto Petrolero de las Naciones Consumidoras. Convenio referente a un programa energético internacional," in Arauz, op. cit., pp. 351-379.

17. Helio Jaguaribe, "La Crisis del Petróleo y sus alternativas internacionales," El Trimestre Económico, Fondo de Cultura Económica, Vol. XLIV (3), No. 175, July-September 1977, Mexico, p. 654.

18. Oystein Noreng, Oil Politics in the 1980's (New York: McGraw Hill, 1978), p. 24.

19. "Proyecta la CEE la Creacion de un Banco Mundial del Petróleo," Excelsior, February 5, 1981, p. 4.

20. Francisco Mieres, Crisis capitalista y crisis energética (Mexico: Editorial Nuestro Tiempo, 1979).

21. Ibid., p. 26.

22. Oystein Noreng, "La Relación entre la OPEP y los exportadores que no la integran," Comercio Exterior, Vol. 29, No. 8, August 1979, Mexico, p. 868.

23. Juan Maria Alporte, "El Petróleo y los espacios periféricos," Uno mas Uno, November 18, 1980, page not available.

24. Melvyn Westlake and Nicholas Hirst, "Necesidad de un nuevo acuerdo petrolero," The Times, appeared in Contextos, Año 1, No. 20, 4-10 December 1980, p. 6.

25. "Energía y Países en Desarrollo," The Economist, appeared in ibid., p. 17. Also, Douglas Martin, "Poor Lands' Need for Oil Swelling," The New York Times, October 21, 1981, p. 34.

26. "Riesgo de Paralisis en el Tercer Mundo al faltar energía, aseguaran en la ONU," Excelsior, December 7, 1980, p. 4-A. "Declaración sobre el establecimiento de un Nuevo Orden Económico Internacional," in Arauz, op. cit., pp. 264-304.

27. "Desdeño la OPEP al III Mundo al elevar sus precios," Excelsior, April 1, 1979, p. 1.

28. See Clyde H. Farnsworth, "Reagan Bids Third World Adopt Free Enterprise to Battle Poverty," The New York Times, October 16, 1981, pp. 1 & 4. Also, Charles J. Hanley, "Here are Some of the Issues Facing the Summit," St. Louis Globe-Democrat, October 22, 1981, p. 17-A.

29. Joseph A. Yager and Elear B. Steinberg, Energy and U.S. Foreign Policy: A Report to the Energy Policy Project of the Ford Foundation (Cambridge, MA: Ballinger Publishing Co., 1975), pp. 251-255.

30. World Energy Outlook, OECD, New York, 1977.

31. "Continued Oil Surplus Forecast," St. Louis Globe-Democrat, October 7, 1981, p. 15-A.

32. Erik Fhalstad, "China, Potencia Petrolera en 1990," Excelsior, July 22, 1980, pp. 1 & 27-A. Also Ian Mackenzie, "China descubrió un nuevo yacimiento petro-lífero," Excelsior, August 8, 1980, pp. 1 & 27-A.

33. Rich McNall, "Oil and Gas Prospects of Deep Offshore," Petroleum Engineer International, Vol. 52, No. 10, August 1980, pp. 10-12 & 14-16.

34. Lawrence Whitehead, "Petróleo y Bienestar," in Las Perspectivas del Petróleo Mexicano (Mexico: El Colegio de Mexico, CEI, 1979), pp. 265-266.

35. Carroll L. Wilson, Workshop on Alternative Energy Strategies (WAES), Energy: Global Prospects 1985-2000 (New York: McGraw Hill, 1977).

36. A partir del año 2000 la producción de petróleo bajará en los países productores industrializados: Oficina de Estudios Tecnológicos del Congreso de E.U.," Uno mas Uno, October 20, 1980, p. 14.

37. The International Energy Situation: Outlook to 1985. Central Intelligence Agency, April 1977.

38. "Aumentará la URSS su producción de crudo 0.7% en 1981; el menor incremento de los ultimos años," Uno mas Uno, October 20, 1980, p. 14.

39. Juris Kaza, AP-Dow Jones, "Escasez de Crudo golpea al Comecon," Excelsior, July 16, 1980, pp. 26 & 28.

40. "Poor Lands' Need for Oil Swelling," op. cit. "La demanda de crudo en el III Mundo subirá a 23 millones 500 mil barriles diarios en el año 2000, informe de la OPEP," Uno mas Uno, November 17, 1980, p. 15. "El Consumo Mundial de Energía se elevará 65% en veinte años, Excelsior, February 5, 1981, p. 4. And "La demanda petrolera de los países del Tercer Mundo aumentará sustancialmente en el año 1990," Uno mas Uno, February 2, 1981, p. 14.

41. "Arabia Saudita propuso no aumentar los crudos por un período de cuatro años," and "Conferencia de la OPEP: Los precios del petróleo congelados hasta fin de año," Uno mas Uno, May 8, 1978, p. 15.

42. "Las Exportaciones Petroleras de Iran e Irak," The Oil and Gas Journal, appeared in Contextos, 23-29 October 1980, p. 12.

43. "Acuerda la OPEP subir a 32 dólares el barril de crudo," Excelsior, June 11, 1980, p. 1.

44. "Guerra de nervios para ajustar los precios del petróleo," Excelsior, December 9, 1980, p. 1.

45. "Prevé Venezuela una baja en la demanda mundial de crudo," Uno mas Uno, August 25, 1980, p. 15.

46. "Mexico no elevó los precios de su petróleo debido al aumento de la producción saudita," Uno mas Uno, December 10, 1980, p. 18.

47. "Reducirán sus importaciones de crudo y empezarán a utilizar sus reservas 21 paises desarrollados," Uno mas Uno, December 10, 1980, p. 18.

48. "Price Rift in OPEC May Close," The New York Times, October 16, 1981, pp. 27 & 36. Also, "Early OPEC Price Accord Predicted," The New York Times, October 29, 1981, pp. 29 & 36.

49. "OPEC Members Unite to Freeze Oil Price at $34,' The New York Times, October 30, 1981, pp. 1 & 31.

50. "Price Rift in OPEC May Close," op. cit. Also, "Petroworries," Time, November 2, 1981, and Steven Rattner, "OPEC Sets Review of Oil Market," The New York Times, March 4, 1982, p. 31.

51. Steven Rattner, "Key Talks Start Today at OPEC," The New York Times, March 19, 1982, p. 29.

52. Youssif M. Ibrahim, "OPEC Members Agree to Pare Output Levels," The Wall Street Journal, March 3, 1982, P. 3.

53. Ibid. Also, Douglas Martin, "OPEC: Trying to Be a Cartel," The New York Times, March 16, 1982, p. 36.

54. Martin, ibid.

55. B.A. Rahmer, "Peculiarities of a Regional Crisis," Petroleum Economist, Vol. XLVII, No. 3, March 1980, pp. 101-103.

56. Roberta Horning, The Washington Star, September 28, 1980, "Entre 60 y 90 años durará al mundo el petróleo, indica un estudio de la CIA," in Excelsior, September 29, 1980. For a detailed study on location, size and potential of oil fields throughout the world, see Richard Nehring, Giant Oil Fields and World Oil Resources, Rand Corporation (R-2284-CIA), June 1978.

57. B.I. Spinrad and W. Sassin, Sustainable Energy Supplies for Our World, International Institute for Applied Systems Analysis, appeared in Energéticos, Comisión de Energéticos, SEPAFIN, Año 3, No. 11, Mexico, November 1979.

58. Jaguaribe, op. cit., pp. 657-658.

59. Ibid., p. 658.
60. M.K. Hubert, U.S. Energy Resources, A Review as of 1972, Document #93-40 (Washington, DC: U.S. Government Printing Office, 1974).
61. National Energy Plan II, a Report to the Congress Required by Title VIII of the Department of Energy Organization Act (Public Law 95-91), U.S. Department of Energy, May 1979, pp. 16-17.
62. Data from the Independent Petroleum Association of American (1955-1971, and the Monthly Energy Review (1972-1976), cited in Marcela Serrato, "Las Vicisitudes del Plan Energético de Carter," in Las Perspectivas del Petróleo Mexicano, op. cit., pp. 280-281. For an analysis of the factors leading to a halt in hydrocarbon production in the United States, see Richard B. Mancke, The Failure of U.S. Energy Policy (New York: Columbia University Press, 1974).
63. National Energy Plan II, op. cit., p. 18.
64. Ibid.
65. Text of the President's Energy Address to the Nation, The White House, Office of the White House Press Secretary, April 5, 1979, p. 2.
66. National Energy Plan II, op. cit., p. 18.
67. Juan Maria Alporte, "Petróleo: Estados Unidos ante su crisis," Uno Mas Uno, September 30, 1980, p. 15.
68. "Coal: The Dynamo of Energy Independence," an address by John C. Sawhill, Deputy Secretary of the U.S. Department of Energy, Johnstown, Pennsylvania, April 14, 1980, p. 1.
69. National Energy Plan II, op. cit., pp. 19-20.
70. Edward F. Denison, Accounting for Slower Economic Growth: The United States in the 1970's (Brookings Institution, 1979).
71 Response Plan: Reducing U.S. Impact on the World Oil Market, U.S. Department of Energy (DOE/IR-0048), April 1979, pp. 13-14.
72. "Coal: The Dynamo of Energy Independence," op. cit., p. 1.
73. For an early analysis of possible domestic effects of a growing energy crisis, see Lawrence Rocks and Richard P. Runyon, The Energy Crisis (Crown: 1973).
74. National Energy Plan II, op. cit., pp. 21-22.
75. Serrato, op. cit., pp. 284-285.
76. A Time to Choose: America's Energy Future. Final Report by the Energy Policy Project of the Ford Foundation (Cambridge, MA: Ballinger Publishing Co., 1974), cited in Serrato, ibid., pp. 285-286.
77. Serrato, ibid., p. 286.
78. A New Start: The National Energy Act, U.S. Department of Energy, Office of Public Affairs (Washington: U.S. Government Printing Office, 1979).
79. Ibid.

118

80.   Natural Gas Policy Act of 1978 (Public Law 95-621 (92 Stat. 3350), 95th Congress, November 9, 1978.
81.   A New Start..., op. cit., p. 8.
82.   Text of the President's Energy Address to the Nation, op. cit., pp. 1-3.
83.   Ibid., p. 4.
84.   Response Plan..., op. cit.
85.   National Energy Plan II, op. cit., p. 31.
86.   Ibid., pp. 1-7.
87.   Ibid., pp. 7-12.
88.   Remarks of the President in his address to the Nation, The Oval Office, the White House, Office of The White House Press Secretary, July 15, 1979, pp. 1-8.
89.   Serrato, op. cit., p. 310-311.
90.   Eugenio Anguiano Roch, Segundo Comentario a Serrato, ibid., p. 318.
91.   Report to the President on the activities of Oil Companies Affecting Gasoline Supplies, U.S. Department of Energy, July 24, 1979.
92.   Rich McNally, "World Instability Spurs Home Drilling," Petroleum Engineer International, Vol. 51, No. 7, June 1979, pp. 21-25.
93.   "The Seven Lean Years," Time, December 22, 1980, p. 43.
94.   Secretary's Annual Report to Congress (DOC/S-0010-80), U.S. Department of Energy (Washington: U.S. Government Printing Office, January 1980).
95.   Ibid., pp. 2.1 to 2.17.
96.   "Coal: The Dynamo of Energy Independence," op. cit., pp. 2-6.
97.   Robert D. Hershey Jr., "Construirán en Virginia la mayor planta de petróleo a base de carbón," The New York Times, July 31, 1980, in Excelsior, August 1, 1980, p. 3-A.
98.   For an analysis of alternative transportation systems, see Petroleum Supply Alternatives for the Northern Tier and Inland States Through the Year 2000 (DOE/RA/0042-1&2), U.S. Department of Energy, Assistant Secretary for Resource Applications, Energy Supply Transportation Division, Washington, October 31, 1979.
99.   Carl Seaton, "U.S. Pipeline System Continues to Grow," The Oil and Gas Journal, Vol. 78, No. 32, August 11, 1980, pp. 59-66.
100.   Serrato, op. cit., p. 287.
101.   Juan Roldán, EFE, "E.U. sigue almacenando petróleo, indiferente al derrumbe monetario," Uno mas Uno, March 9, 1978, p. 15.
102.   Tad Szulc, "E.U., vulnerable a una grave escasez de crudo," The New York Times, November 28, 1980, in Excelsior, November 29, 1980, pp. 1, 8, & 31.
103.   John J. Fialka, "E.U. sería vulnerable en extremo ante otro embargo petrolero. Urge reforzar la reserva estrategica," The Washington Star Service, July

11, 1980, in Excelsior, July 12, 1980, p. 26-A. Also, "Estados Unidos cuenta con reservas de hidrocarburos para solo 86 dias, Uno mas Uno, September 26, 1980, p. 14.

104. "Compra directa de petróleo hara E.U. para incrementar su reserva," Excelsior, January 19, 1981, p. 3-A.

105. "Acumula E.U. enormes reservas petroleras," Excelsior, July 6, 1981, p. 1.

106. Richard R. Fagen, "El Petróleo Mexicano y la Seguridad Nacional de los Estados Unidos," in Las Perspectivas del Petróleo Mexicano, op. cit., p. 331.

107. "Libera Reagan los precios del petróleo y sus derivados," Excelsior, January 29, 1981, p. 1

108. "Big Oil's Surprising Problems," Time, April 27, 1981, p. 44.

109. "President is Upheld On Oil Veto," The New York Times, March 25, 1982, p. 31.

110. "Reagan Drops Gas Bill Plan," The New York Times, March 2, 1982, p. 35. "U.S. Energy Unit Slows Drive to Lift Natural Gas Prices," The New York Times, March 24, 1982, p. 29.

111. "Energy Unit's End Detailed," The New York Times, December 18, 1981, p. 33. "President Appears Ready to Drop Proposal to Abolish Energy Department," The New York Times, December 16, 1981, p. 13. "Department of Energy Stays Alive," The New York Times, February 15, 1982, p. 21.

112. "Suit Seeks U.S. Release of Fund for Energy Aid," The New York Times, April 7, 1982, p. 23.

113. "Oil Imports Down 28.2%," The New York Times, March 19, 1982, p. 34.

114. "Cost Squeeze on Oil Refiners," The New York Times, March 18, 1982, p. 43. "U.S. Oil Rush Begins to Slow," The New York Times, March 30, 1982, p. 35. "A Brave New Energy World," Time, April 19, 1982, pp. 60-61.

115. "Decline in Oil Prices Benefits U.S. Economy But Has Drawbacks," The Wall Street Journal, March 24, 1982, pp. 1 & 15.

116. "Talk of an Oil Import Fee," The New York Times, April 8, 1982.

117. "Tax All Oil, and Natural Gas Too," The New York Times, April 14, 1982, p. 26.

118. Clyde H. Farnsworth, "Washington Watch. Oil-Import Fee: Little Chance," The New York Times, March 15, 1982, p. 20.

119. "U.S. Oil Rush Begins to Slow," ibid., "A Brave New Energy Workd," ibid.

120. "Energy Department Predicts Gasoline Prices Will Jump 6 Cents a Gallon in '82," The News, Mexico, January 6, 1982, p. 20. Ernst R. Habicht Jr., "Prepare for the Next Oil Shock," The New York Times, March 2, 1982.

121. Edward J. Williams, The Rebirth of the Mexican Petroleum Industry (Lexington, MA: C.D. Heath and Co., 1979), p. 61.

122. Roberto Peña Guerrero, "Crisis: reajuste, hegemonía y dependencia," Relaciones Internacionales, CRI, Facultad de Ciencias Políticas y Soc., UNAM, Vol. VI, No. 21, April-June 1978, Mexico, p. 58.

123. Richard B. Mancke, Mexican Oil and Natural Gas: Political, Strategic, and Economic Implications (New York: Praeger Publishers, 1979), p. 124.

124. Fagen, op. cit., p. 334.

125. Mancke, op. cit., pp. 124-131.

126. Ibid., p. 131.

127. Ibid., pp. 131-133.

128. A discount is defined as "the difference between the current price differential and the refinery value differential." "Impact of Mexican Crude Oil Exportation on U.S. Gulf Coast Refineries and Alaskan North Slope Crude Oil," in Petroleum Supply Alternatives... Vol. 2, op. cit., p. 517.

129. David M. Lindahl and Gary J. Pagliano, "Impact of Mexican Oil and Gas on U.S. Energy Policy," in Mexico's Oil and Gas Policy: An Analysis, a report prepared for the Committee on Foreign Relations, U.S. Senate and the Joint Economic Committee, Congress of the U.S., December 1978 (Washington: U.S. Government Printing Office, 1979), pp. 45-46.

130. Mexico's Oil and Gas Policy: An Analysis, ibid., p. 4.

131. "...a large-diameter line that would move 500,000 b/d of mostly North Slope crude oil from Long Beach, California, to Midland, Texas," Lindahl and Pagliano, op. cit., p. 46.

132. Ibid., pp. 46-47.

133. "Impact of Mexican Crude Oil Exportation on U.S. Gulf Coast Refineries and Alaskan North Slope Crude Oil," op. cit., p. 499.

134. Ibid., p. 508.

135. Ibid., pp. 512 & 514.

136. Ibid., pp. 520-523.

137. Mancke, op. cit., p. 136.

138. Ibid., p. 123.

139. In that year, Mexico exported to the United States 162.74 million barrels, Venezuela 136.63 million, and Canada 104.67 million. The main four suppliers to the U.S. in 1979 were: Saudi Arabia (503 million barrels), Nigeria (414 million), Lybia (288 million), and Algeria (218 million). Survey of Current Business, U.S. Department of Commerce, March 1980.

140. "Western Energy Policy After Carter," Lloyd's Bank Review, London, January 1978, p. 37.

6
Mexico:
The Domestic Cauldron

SOCIOECONOMIC ENVIRONMENT: 1976 TO PRESENT

A Diagnosis

The goals of Mexico's process of socioeconomic development could be measured in terms of the following criteria:

1. A more equitable distribution in income, through greater efficacy and honesty in the fiscal mechanisms and a structure of progressive taxation.
2. An increase in productivity levels in all the sectors of the economy. This goal is parallel to the first one since, as the possibilities of consumption of the population become greater, there must be an increment in the availability of goods. Productivity is also a key factor in slowing the inflationary spiral.
3. A rate of employment creation above that of the increment of the economically active population. This is a vital objective in promoting the self-satisfaction of basic needs by an increasing percentage of the population, thus freeing state resources for other critical areas of development.
4. An improvement of educational levels, congruent with the modalities of development.
5. An improvement and extension of social programs, tending towards an ever increasing coverage of the population, indispensable for their full incorporation to the productive and creative activities of national development.
6. An improvement in basic infrastructure, in order to achieve an effective national integration.
7. An extension of birth control programs, in order to bring demographic growth down to an acceptable level.

8. The promotion of political-administrative
decentralization, and the establishment of
fiscal incentives for industry in the interior
of the country (outside the cities of Mexico,
Guadalajara, and Monterrey). The objective of
these measures would be to slow down the excessive increase of population in a few, over-
crowded, and unbalanced urban centers, with
their subsequent negative impact in terms of
maladministration of public resources.

These previous objectives implicit in Mexico's
process of development must be inscribed within a framework of complex social and economic problems, intimately
related to each other.

Official Policy: 1976 to the Present

According to Mario Ojeda, during the postwar era, a
series of factors effectively contributed to strengthen
Mexico's process of development, among them:

- Domestic political stability.
- A sustained rate of economic growth.
- Alternate sources of foreign currency (besides
  exports and international financial organiza-
  tions), i.e. tourism.
- Self-sufficiency in basic foodstuffs and petro-
  leum.
- A low rate of inflation.
- Solvency in the world's financial markets.
- An "escape valve" for unemployment and underem-
  ployment, through migration to the United States.[1]

However, by the late 1960s these factors had ceased
to have, to various degrees, their former positive
influence. From 1970 to 1976, matters took a turn for
the worse. Domestic political stability was threatened
by a flagging economic performance, and by the acrid
conflicts between public officials and the private
sector. Income from tourism was increasingly canceled
out by the growing expenditures of Mexican tourists in
other countries, especially the United States. In this
way, Mexico lost an important compensating element for
its chronic trade deficit. Agricultural production continued its long and steady decline, both for domestic
consumption and exports. During a brief period Mexico
lost its self-sufficiency in petroleum. The rate of
inflation soared. As a result of the previous situation,
Mexico's position in the international financial markets
was progressively eroded. Finally, a precarious economic
situation in the United States made Washington redouble,

to be sure more in intent than in effectiveness, its efforts to stop illegal Mexican migration.[2]

When the López Portillo administration took over in 1976, the stage was set for decisive political action in order to overcome the crisis, and embark upon new schemes of development. In his first annual report, in September, 1977, the Mexican president defined the prevalent situation at the time:

> Mexico...is living a severe crisis. The development of the country was sustained for a long time by political stability, moderation in price increases...and a fixed monetary parity with the dollar....Of these three supports we lost several years ago the proportionality of prices, which unleashed inflation...Later, our currency was devalued, unemployment increased, we fell into a recession, the financial system proved to be inadequate, and the situation was complicated by a lack of confidence.[3]

According to López Portillo, inflation, massive movements of capital, and radical changes in the relative values of currencies and raw materials, had created an essentially different scenario. Thus, there could not be a return to previously acceptable rules for socio-economic development. The old pattern of growth, according to the president, was finished, and new approaches would be needed.[4]

A key element characteristic of López Portillo's regime has been the reliance on planning mechanisms, as a means to consolidate the guiding function of the state in the process of development. During his campaign for the presidency, López Portillo had coined the slogan "Alliance for Production," i.e. between the public and private sectors, as a response to the economic crisis. In his acceptance speech of December 1, 1976, he defined the context of operation of the Alliance, in effect a new framework of organization in order to produce, distribute, and consume according to Mexico's own intrinsic needs. The Alliance for Production would offer "to everyone viable alternatives geared to reconcile the national objectives of development and social justice, with the specific demands of the various factors in the economy."[5]

The Alliance for Production set the pattern for a series of programs, such as: the Plan for Urban Development, the Plan for Industrial Development, the Plan for Agricultural and Cattle Development, the Mexican Food System, and various political, economic, and administrative reforms. By early 1980, all of these plans had been integrated into the Global Plan for Development, 1980-1982.

The Global Plan for Development has defined the model Mexico is to follow as a nation, based on:

A productive system capable of offering the national goods necessary for the consolidation of development and national autonomy, and the social goods to cover the normal needs of food, health, education, social security, and housing...6

Within the framework of the National System of Economic and Social Planning, the strategy of the Mexican government would be geared to fulfill four basic objectives of development policy:

- To reafirm and strengthen Mexico's independence as a democratic, just, and free nation, in the economic, political, and cultural spheres....
- To provide the population with employment and a minimum of welfare, giving priority to food, education, health, and housing needs....
- To promote high, sustained and efficient economic growth....
- To improve the distribution of income among persons, factors of production, and geographic regions.7

At present, two elements determine the priority of Mexico's development efforts: petroleum, and food production. By March, 1980, with the creation of the Mexican Food System (known by its Spanish acronym of SAM), the setting of limits to oil exports, and the postponement of Mexico's entrance to GATT, the model of development promoted by the Mexican government appeared to emphasize the goal of national autonomy.

The Mexican Food System has tried to overcome the lack of response by private enterprise in regards to the agricultural sector, namely in the area of basic foodstuffs for domestic consumption. The official encouragement of and preoccupation with food production as an element essential to national sovereignty would be summarized by López Portillo in frank terms:

...The objective is national self-sufficiency...
It would be painful for us that, having solved the energy problem, we were to fall into the trap of losing (the battle) through the mouth. We will not tolerate this!8

An additional indication of the importance the Mexican government places on food production is the Law for Agricultural and Livestock Production. Enacted in early 1981, this law constitutes a further attempt to encourage productivity in this sector, and stresses the public interest in self-sufficiency over private interests.[9]

But the petroleum industry is the key factor that has brought renewed confidence and high expectations in regards to socioeconomic development. The petroleum bonanza means for Mexico the possibility of a new model of development, able to compensate for domestic disequilibriums. Official Mexican government assessments of the significance of the oil wealth have shown clear optimism. By March 1978, President López Portillo could already declare confidently that "petroleum will erase the ancestral misery of the Mexicans."[10] In his second annual report, on September 1, 1978, the Mexican president underlined the recovery of the nation's economy and predicted accelerated economic growth for the next few years.[11] By early 1979, in the words of López Portillo, petroleum had become the "axis of progress."[12] In other words, the exploitation of oil would seem to open the possibility for Mexico to "liberate itself economically and socially."[13] As the Mexican president posed the issue:

> That a country without petroleum fails, cancels its possibilities of development, is lamentable but explainable, but that in these moments, in this last third of the XX Century, a country with oil should become disorganized, to the extreme of not solving its economic and social problems, would be grave. Such a country would definitely cancel its historical project, would not deserve a worthy place in history.[14]

The expectations arising from Mexico's petroleum wealth were underlined in a mid-1978 study by Mexico's National Bank. Petroleum could become, according to this analysis, the key to national development. It would generate funds for various industries, provide the necessary energy for an increase in the production of goods and services, create demand and employment through PEMEX's purchases, strengthen Mexico's financial stability in foreign markets, and promote the industrial capacity to achieve new projects.[15] Indeed, according to a prestigious international analysis firm based in Mexico, 1981 was expected to be the first of two years of accelerated growth, with a goal of upwards of an 8 percent increase in the GNP. A "powerful petroleum sector" would be the basis for a year in which "the Mexican economy will be one of the most dynamic in the world."[16]

Mexican government officials have frequently expressed their assurances that development will not come to rely excessively on oil. Since mid-1977, President López Portillo has often reiterated that Mexico's diversified economy will allow it to place the exploitation of

petroleum within a rational context.[17] By early 1979,
former Secretary of the Treasury, David Ibarra Muñoz, and
the former General Director of the Bank of Mexico,
Gustavo Romero Kolbeck, had announced a new strategy to
generate foreign funds, in which petroleum would pass to
occupy a second place in importance, while the exports of
manufactured and semi-elaborated products would become
the pivot of economic development.[18] In August 1981,
former PEMEX Director, Jorge Díaz Serrano, emphasized
that Mexico's economy was not becoming "petroleum-bound,"
but that, on the other hand, financial inputs from hydrocarbon resources constituted a fundamental element to
attain social justice. Mexico, said Díaz Serrano, "is
not an oil country, but a country with oil---hydrocarbons
are not an end in themselves, nor the final objective of
the efforts underway."[19]

     The self-assurance and ebullience of Mexico's public
officials since 1977 was positively reflected in U.S. and
international government and financial circles. Late in
that year, France's Le Figaro was predicting that "Mexico
was destined to become a new Saudi Arabia," a favorable
assessment of the situation, apparently.[20] By April
1979, the Petroleum Economist considered Mexico's rapid
ascent as an important oil producing and exporting country as "the most stimulating event since the 1973 oil
embargo." According to that London based publication,
the revision of Mexico's financial and monetary policies
by the López Portillo administration had placed the
country again on a sound economic basis, and attracted a
new wave of foreign investments.[21] By mid-1978, the U.S.
press was giving increasing attention to Mexico's oil
wealth, emphasizing the promising perspectives for sustained economic growth under new pragmatic policies.[22]

An Assessment

     How does the socioeconomic situation in Mexico stand
in the context of governmental policies, rhetoric,
and forecasts? To begin with, there must be a distinction between two often interchangeably used terms.
Economic growth is not the equivalent of development.
The latter involves a conjunction of economic and social
progress. The relationship between these two factors is
critical. A balanced process of development would tend
to spread among the various sectors of the population the
gains achieved through economic growth. Social progress,
for its part, enhances the possibilities of economic
growth by expanding the domestic market.

     Following this appreciation, it could be argued that
Mexico's postwar "stabilizing development," while stimulating industrialization and economic growth, resulted in
a deterioration of the distribution of income and
unemployment rates, and the stagnation of the agricultural sector. Likewise, "shared development" failed

in its objective of improving income distribution, because it lacked a comprehensive fiscal reform and resorted instead to external financing.

Redvers Opie has underlined six main problems related to Mexico's development: inflation; demographic growth; lagging agricultural productivity; low levels of industrial efficiency and international competitiveness; the problem of the "mix" between public and private enterprise; and the need for direct foreign investment capital.[23] The traditional avenues of solution to these various problems involve controversial views concerning the direction Mexican development should follow. According to Opie, an improvement in agricultural productivity would be the means to both expand the domestic market and create a surplus for exports. Increased industrial efficiency would go hand in hand with a shift in the structure of manufacturing into capital accumulation and the exports market. Mexico's "mixed system" would orient itself towards greater participation by private enterprise. And foreign direct investment capital, mainly through the action of multinational corporations, would contribute to job creation and general economic development.[24]

Mexican sociologist Rodolfo Stavenhagen challenges the previous perspective of the situation, through a number of "myths" which should not be confused with reality. One of these myths is that growing exports are a solution to Mexico's problems. If exports consist mainly of raw materials and semi-manufactured products, this would underline the lack of autonomous internal development. On the other hand, exports can indeed contribute to improve the balance of trade, but only if imports diminish, too. A deterioration in the terms of exchange can also spur inflation.[25]

According to Stavenhagen, another myth would be that an increase in production contributes automatically to the general welfare of the population. Deficits in the production of basic articles such as foodstuffs are often related not to a low level of output but to an unbalanced structure of production and an unequal system of distribution. A third myth would be that measures such as a devaluation and/or a liberalization of prices can improve economic health without substantial structural changes. Finally, there would be the myth that only large entrepreneurs can increase production in the agricultural sector. This production is usually geared to exports, which is detrimental for the domestic market, and takes away financial and technical resources from the poorest regions and groups of the population.[26]

It is fashionable in Mexico these days to proclaim that the postwar model of development is no longer valid. It would be pertinent to analyze some of the shortcomings of the process of development during the 1950s and

1960s, which tended to worsen domestic economic disequilibriums and social inequalities,[27] and to explore its persistent effects, now under the aegis of petroleum.

In many academic as well as financial circles, Mexico's economic performance following World War II was widely described as a "miracle." Specifically, high indices of economic growth, related mainly to the development of the industrial sector, an impressive infrastructure, improvements in the social services, and political stability, were some of the signs of the miracle. Some critics of this "miracle" during the early 1970s, Fernando Carmona et. al., questioned these assumptions by referring to certain fallacies such as: the official manipulation of statistical data; the lack of equilibrium in the economy, in sectorial as well as social terms; the "bureaucratic-political labyrinth," that enhanced nepotism and favoritism; the failure to improve significantly the nutritional, health, and educational standards among great sectors of the population; and the monopoly of political power.[28]

However, the authors of the Mexican Miracle failed to suggest alternatives to the situation they explored. Furthermore, whatever social and economic progress Mexico has experienced during the last few decades should not be dismissed lightly, especially when the enormous increase in population, and therefore in demands, is taken into consideration. Faced with internal diversity and external limitations, the job for Mexico's political leadership has not been easy, and its achievements would seem to be substantial.

Nevertheless, there are some clearly identifiable drawbacks. Writing in 1979, Enrique Padilla Aragon argued that Mexican development tends to be dependent, fluctuating, unbalanced, and unequal.[29] To a great extent Mexico relies on foreign investments and loans. But the determining factor is its strong dependence on a single market, i.e. the United States. Says Padilla: "...our economic development accelerates or is set back according to the economic policy of the United States in relation to the world and to us."[30] Mexican development also fluctuates, i.e. it is a cyclic type of development.[31] It suffers from various types of disequilibriums, i.e. between occupation and income, productivity in agriculture and industry, regional imbalances, and a breach between exports and imports.[32] Finally, the main problem, according to Padilla, is "redistribution of income and the internal market." In the early 1970s 50 percent of Mexico's population perceived only 15 percent of the total income.[33] To a varying degree, since 1976 these four characteristics have continued to plague Mexico's process of development.

Until the early 1970s, Mexican development had enjoyed both growth and stability. This was possible, according to Roger D. Hansen, because financing schemes followed the "monetarist" admonition of avoiding governmental deficits, as well as the structuralist dictum that investments in infrastructure must be kept at a proper level. Foreign credit financing was available at moderate interest rates.[34] However, something has obviously gone wrong since then. By early 1981, official Mexican estimates put the rate of inflation at close to 28 percent, and the IMF expected inflation to reach the figure of 32.5 percent by the end of that year. U.S. sources stated that, in spite of an average 8 percent rate of increase of the GNP in 1979 and 1980, inflation was limiting Mexico's progress.[35] In mid-1980, President López Portillo referred to inflation as the "cost of the consolidation of progress," i.e. industrialization and modernization.[36]

Nevertheless, inflation remains a serious threat to the Mexican economy, and by the early 1980s persisted at a level of around 30 percent. Part of it is undoubtedly related to the external sector, i.e. a result of turmoil in international financial markets, and the high costs of imported capital goods for the petroleum industry. According to U.S. analysis, there are also significant domestic components, three of which could be identified: a growing domestic demand which exceeds the supply of goods and results in bottlenecks in the economy; the fact that imports which might satisfy domestic demand and lower prices are constrained by trade barriers; and wage compensations demanded by Mexican organized labor to offset inflation, which have often resulted in actual wage increases, and a subsequent increase in demand for limited products.[37] However, any actions by the Mexican government to counter this situation would run contrary to social and nationalistic policy objectives and, thus, would be politically unfeasible.

Inflation has also been spurred by the critical situation in the agricultural sector. Starting in the 1940s, Mexico's economic growth was based on the primary sector. The government invested heavily in irrigation, and agricultural production began to increase by 4.4 percent a year. According to Richard D. Hansen, the agricultural sector had to provide: increasing amounts of foodstuffs to the rapidly expanding urban population; raw materials; export earnings to finance the import of capital goods; labor for the secondary and tertiary sectors; savings for industrial and infrastructure investments; a market for the goods from the industrial sector. Mexico became virtually self-sufficient in food production, and its output of raw materials for the industrial sector increased rapidly. Agricultural exports since 1940 grew at a rate of 6 percent annually, and represented from 25 percent to 50 percent of total

exports income. A sizeable proportion of the rural
population became available for urban occupations.
Savings from agriculture were transferred to other economic sectors. And, finally, rural Mexico seemed to
represent a growing domestic market for Mexican industry.[38]

But agriculture, the hen that laid the golden eggs
for Mexico's process of development, increasingly
faltered. From 1965 to 1976, output grew only by an
annual average of 1.6 percent. In the words of Redvers
Opie:

> At some point in the process of industrializing
> the country, the contribution of Mexican agriculture
> to GDP would be expected to decline. But total
> agricultural production would seem to have declined
> too early and too rapidly.[39]

The participation of agriculture in the total goods
and services produced in Mexico, which was 20.2 percent
in 1950, diminished to 9.4 percent in 1965, 5.6 percent
in 1975, and 5.2 percent in 1979.[40] From 1970 to 1979,
the agricultural sector's contribution to Mexico's
foreign trade declined by 23 percent.[41]

The reasons for the crisis in the agricultural
sector are varied. At the beginning of 1980, the surface under cultivation and the grain tonnage obtained
were basically the same as fifteen years earlier.[42] During the 1970s, agriculture suffered from a scarcity of
investments.[43] Cultivation of basic grains for domestic
consumption, such as wheat, corn, and beans, dropped,
while crops for export or cattle feeding, such as sesame
and sorghum, increased their volumes.[44] This was
propitiated by speculation in the basic foodstuffs
market by Mexican as well as multinational corporations.
The situation of scarcity in basic agricultural products
contrasts with the expansion of the cattle industry,
geared towards beef exports.[45]

Due to a combination of drought and frost, between
1979 and 1980 Mexico's grain harvest collapsed cata-
strophically. Through the entire decade of 1970s, grain
imports by Mexico had amounted to 16.637 million tons.
By contrast, during 1980 alone the figure would reach a
total of 12 million tons, the largest quantity of grains
ever purchased.[46]

The huge purchases brought havoc to Mexico's railroad system, in charge of transporting grain imports
from the U.S. border, and apparently unable to cope with
the task.[47] The traditional surplus in the agricultural
trading balance had, by mid-1980, turned into a deficit
of 180 million dollars, due to low production and
massive imports.[48] At the time, continued sizeable
purchases were predicted for 1981, in the order of ten
million tons of grain.[49]

The "easy" solution to the agricultural problem, i.e. to import foodstuffs with funds from petroleum exports, would seem to hinder the implementation of structural changes in the countryside, needed in order to achieve a more rational and effective production, and to run counter to nationalistic objectives. The Mexican government appeared to be aware of these problems. Since late in 1978, President López Portillo had emphasized that "oil (was) not enough; without foodstuffs, there can be only a half-way development."[50] The Mexican president, by late 1980, was counting on the Mexican Food System (SAM) to achieve a sufficient minimum level of food consumption for all Mexicans.[51] In December 1980, the Secretary of Patrimony and Industrial Development, José Andrés de Oteyza, was underlining that the best utilization of earnings from petroleum would be in the agricultural sector, to encourage food production.[52]

In his fifth annual report of September 1981, the Mexican president announced the recovery of the agricultural sector. During 1980-1981, harvests were the highest in history, i.e. 23.489 million tons of basic foodstuffs, an 11 percent increment over the previous record figure of 1978, and 29.5 percent in excess of the 1976 level. The production of fertilizers more than doubled during 1980, from 2.2 to 5 million tons. The Mexican government seems to have made the decision to reach self-sufficiency in food as a means to neutralize dependence on the United States. By 1982, trends pointed to self-sufficiency in corn and beans.[53]

The López Portillo administration has taken strong measures which involve extensive subsidies to producers and consumers of agricultural products. Besides the rise in production itself, the surface under cultivation is expanding rapidly, a 17.9 percent increase in 1980 in relation to 1979 levels, to a total of 12.7 million hectares. The strategy is proving to be very costly. During 1980, credits to the agricultural sector increased by 61 percent, and for 1981 it was estimated they would amount to 290 billion pesos. Basic price guarantees to producers increased by 40 percent during 1980, and in 1981 would represent an apportionment of 38 billion pesos. Still, Mexican officials point to the fact that oil income is being spent at home.[54]

According to a Mexican critic, Raul Olmedo, even if self-sufficiency in basic foodstuffs were to be reached, it would mean nothing if income and employment levels in the rural sector are not raised.[55] Olmedo thinks that insufficient food production is a result of a low level of demand, which springs from the weak consumption possibilities of great sectors of the population. Whereas potential demand is enormous, as precarious indices of nourishment attest, real demand, based on earnings, has not grown accordingly.[56]

Some Mexican officials are apparently well aware of the social implications from this agrarian dilemma. By late 1980, former Mexican Secretary of Agrarian Reform, Javier Garcia Paniagua, declared that the social inequalities in the countryside were "brutal."[57] Income distribution problems are deep-seated, and they are likely to plague Mexico through the remainder of the century. The level and intensity of these inequalities, and the success or failure of the government to improve them, might well determine social peace in Mexico. By mid-1980, a group of Mexican analysts were warning that the Global Plan for Development would not reach its goals, since it was addressed to problems pertaining to a certain economic juncture, i.e. the so-called exhaustion of the model of import substitutions, and not to deep structural problems, such as the maldistribution of income.[58]

Income distribution continues to be extremely unbalanced, and certain small groups receive a disproportionate share of the total income. According to Victor L. Urquidi, by the early 1980s 40 percent of the national income corresponded to barely 10 percent of the population, while the lower 40 percent of the population earned only 10 percent of the national income. This unequal concentration of economic wealth means that the living conditions of the majority of the population are well below what they could be, were there a more equitable distribution of the national income. By September 1981, the Mexican President was addressing the issue of income distribution. According to López Portillo, the impressive economic growth rates of 9.2 percent in 1979, and 8.3 percent in 1980, are having a clear impact on the increment of family income, of 4.7 percent between 1977 and 1980. From another perspective, the various social security institutions cover 48 million people, i.e. more than 65 percent of the population, 20 million of whom have been incorporated since 1977.[59] But conclusive proof of improvements in the distribution of income remains elusive, and the quality of benefits under social programs varies sharply.

Socioeconomic pressures are directly related to demographic growth. Mexico practically doubled its population between 1960 and 1980, from 36,881,000 to 69,752,000 people. During this period, life expectancy increased from 59.2 to 64.4 years. As a result of population policies adopted in 1973-1974, together with comprehensive family planning programs, Mexico's birth rate seems to have dropped from 3.6 percent in 1973 to 2.6 percent by 1980. For 1990 the goal is an annual growth rate of one percent.[60] Still, Mexico's population of 72 million by 1982 will be well over 100 million around the turn of the century, and further reductions in the fertility rate will require a continued effort. One of the most formidable problems derived from present population levels is the age structure of the population: more than 45 percent of the people are 15 years old or under. There are simply not enough resources to achieve an adequate level of nutrition, health, education, and housing for such an overwhelming proportion of minors.

This phenomenon of rapid demographic growth in Mexico could be better understood in the following terms:

1. The estimated demographic growth for relatively short time spans, of 20 to 30 years, leads to levels of population density similar to those of developed, industrialized nations, without a nearly comparable urban, industrial, or agricultural infrastructure.

2. Mexico's economic policies, and efforts at developmental planning, cannot by any means underestimate the impact of the demographic factor, not only in terms of total population increases, but also of its structure, i.e. the fact that the economically active portion of the population continues to decrease relative to the dependent sectors.

3. Demographic growth, and population structure, generate an ever greater need of investments on equipment and social services than is the case in countries with smaller demographic increases and a more balanced age structure.

Closely related to demographic growth, the high rate of urbanization causes multiple and sharp problems, among them the incapability to create urban industrial jobs in sufficient numbers, and to supply adequate social services, equal to the prevailing needs. Almost two-thirds of the Mexican population live in urban centers, and peasants continue to migrate to the cities, most of them to join the ranks of the poor, marginal population of the urban slums. Accelerated urbanization frustrates the efforts to provide adequate public services to an increasing population, and depletes resources that, otherwise, would be channeled towards the agrarian sector. Industrial and bureaucratic centralization in a few, larger cities emphasize the negative effects of urbanization.

Unemployment and underemployment represent one of the fundamental obstacles to achieving a better distribution of income. Although data is not altogether reliable, it is estimated that both of these phenomena affect close to 50 percent of Mexico's population. The main causes of unemployment are demographic growth and the situation in the agricultural sector.[61] The age structure of the population determines that the country has an adult labor force of only 18 million. This means that

28 percent of the population support the remainder.
Still, less than half the workers have permanent jobs.
The task of bringing down the level of unemployment is
staggering: The Mexican economy would have to create
more than a million jobs per year.[62] In other words, the
indices of employment creation, 2.5 percent a year between 1950 and 1970, and 2 percent from 1970 to 1979,
must be brought up to a goal of 4.2 percent, in order to
safely surpass the annual increment of job demand, of
3.4 percent.[63] President López Portillo is placing the
hopes for employment creation on vast industrial investments.[64] By September, 1981, the Mexican president was
reporting that during the period 1977-1980, industrial
production registered a growth of 8.1 percent per year.
This contributed to the creation of 3,250,000 new jobs.[65]
But, in the past, because of tendencies towards capital-
intensive industrialization, this scheme has been only
partly successful.

Here, again, hopes are also placed on the oil
industry to create jobs.[66] But the petroleum industry is
basically a capital-intensive industry, employing relatively few workers per plant. Thus, the success of a
liaison between the oil industry and the employment
market would depend, rather, on the ability to transfer
funds from the first into a wide arrangement of productive activities.

In this respect, there are a number of critics who
maintain that, far from representing a contribution to
Mexico's economic standing, petroleum exploitation has
increased its economic vulnerability. In other words,
PEMEX has borrowed and spent more than it has received
from its exports.[67] Indeed, a number of official estimates would seem to confirm this assertion. By the
beginning of 1981, the Secretary of Patrimony and Industrial Development announced that, in 1980, income from
petroleum exports amounted to 10.4 billion dollars (more
than twice the level of 1979), but the commercial and
payments deficit grew because imports totalled 18 billion, 7 billion more than expected.[68] On the other hand,
during the second three-month period in 1980, Mexico
paid 2.88 billion dollars in foreign debt services,
while petroleum exports income only reached the amount
of 2.565 billion.[69]

In the midst of economic turmoil in 1976, the
Mexican government had approached the International
Monetary Fund (IMF) for a loan, which was granted under
certain conditions, i.e. an austerity program that would
have set limits to deficits by the public sector as a
percentage of the Gross Domestic Product. Petroleum
changed this situation, and relieved Mexican economic
policy from IMF pressures. Since the late 1970s, international financial institutions and banking consortia
have undertaken sizable loans to Mexico. With climbing

credit needs derived from an expansionist economic policy
headed by PEMEX, and which surpassed the level of oil
exports revenues, Mexico has incurred a steadily growing
foreign debt.

In 1981, the public foreign debt grew by 14.9 billion dollars to 48.7 billion. If the private sector's
foreign debt of 15 billion dollars is added, the total
rises to more than 63 billion dollars. This figure makes
Mexico one of the most indebted nations in the world.
During 1981, the debt service grew by 36 percent, and out
of Mexico's national budget of 3320.6 billion pesos for
1982, these debt payments represented a substantial
share, 722.1 billion pesos.[70] It was estimated that
Mexico would have to raise 12 billion dollars in new borrowing during 1982, at high interest rates given the constraints of the international credit market.[71]

During his annual message of 1981, President López
Portillo pointed out that Mexico's total international
reserves were at a record high of 10.397 billion dollars,
66 percent over the 1980 level and the highest in history.[72] However, in this respect it should be noticed
that the central bank reserves, as a percentage of the
bank's total assets, had fallen from between 30 to 50
during the 1950s and 1960s, down to about 14 percent by July 1981. The worldwide oil glut which began by
mid-1981 hurt economic confidence and provoked a flight
of about 4 billion dollars. Additionally, Mexico's
anticipated exports earnings fell short by six billion
dollars. The current account deficit almost doubled to a
record 10.8 billion dollars. Even though the government
announced measures to reduce public outlays by 4 percent,
actual spending was about 12 percent over budget, and in
1981 the federal deficit grew to 14.2 percent of the
Gross National Product.[73]

These factors, together with a steady rise in consumer prices which just between 1977 and 1980 reached a
level of 106 percent, pointed to the possibility of a
sharp devaluation of the Mexican currency. The peso had
been allowed to "float" since the 1976 devaluation, and
it had slipped from a parity of 22.74 pesos to the dollar
in late 1977, to close to 26 pesos by late 1981. But,
as a matter of fact, the central bank supported the peso
in financial markets.[74] The Mexican government tried to
avoid a devaluation. In December 1981, it raised domestic oil prices by 120 percent, at the risk of slowing the
rate of economic growth, in order to lower consumption
and reduce PEMEX's borrowing needs. However, faced with
a growing flight of capital spurred by high U.S. interest
rates, speculation against the currency, and the exhaustion of its reserves, by mid-February 1982, the Mexican
government opted for a devaluation.[75]

In retrospect, the devaluation would seem to have
been inevitable. On February 18, 1982, after the announcement by the government that it would no longer

support the currency in exchange markets, the peso's
value fell abruptly by more than 30 percent. By May
1982, the peso was hovering at a parity of about 46 to
the dollar. The move had been expected for some time,
and thus it did not bring about the panic of the 1976
devaluation. While reaction was muted, the impact of
the currency drop was bound to be deep and persistent.76

On the positive side, the government was counting
on the devaluation to stimulate Mexico's exports other
than oil. Recently, the liquidity of Mexico's financial
system has suffered from a heavy imbalance in its foreign
commercial transactions. This is not a new situation:
Mexico's balance of trade, with the exception of the
year 1949, has been unfavorable for the last 49 years.
But the present characteristics and volume of the deficit
are indeed different. Specifically, two key factors that
determine the performance of the external sector since
1978 are the steady growth in imports, and the decline
in manufactured exports. Imports have increased partly
as a result of growing domestic demand, derived substantially from the expansion of the petroleum industry.
And the balance of trade in the manufacturing sector
has worsened, in spite of continuing domestic energy
subsidies. The total commercial deficit for 1980 was
$3.265 billion.77 By 1981, the Mexican government was
trying to reduce imports by the public sector, with
midly encouraging results, but non-petroleum exports
continued to be sluggish. This situation was expected
to change somewhat with the devaluation.

Likewise, tourism, which had been declining as a
source of revenues due to rising domestic prices, should
benefit from the devaluation. Mexicans will be discouraged from traveling and spending abroad, while local
resorts are bound to be more attractive to foreigners.
The first beneficiaries of the devaluation were Mexican
businesses along the border with the United States,
swarmed with American consumers cashing in on sudden
bargains that included much cheaper gasoline.78

On the other hand, the devaluation has also meant
detrimental socioeconomic effects. Real economic growth
for 1982 was expected to reach a rate of 4.5 to 5 percent, that is, a 3 to 3.5 percent decrease from the
rates of the years 1979 to 1981.79 A halting economy
might underscore the social problems of unequal income
distribution. Mexico's middle and lower classes have
felt the brunt of reduced purchasing ability and, in
spite of government imposed controls on a wide variety of
goods, inflation was likely to continue at a high rate.
Likewise, Mexican private companies with obligations in
dollars and other foreign currencies must somehow cope
with a higher debt level.80

In political terms, the devaluation brought about
the resignation of the Secretary of the Treasury, David
Ibarra Muñoz, and the General Director of the Bank of

Mexico, Gustavo Romero Kolbeck. Indirectly, there is
also a problem of loss of credibility in official measures. Government officials announced that, unlike
after the 1976 devaluation, there would not be a fixed
exchange rate, but the peso would be allowed to decline
gradually in value.[81] Additionally, the government put
into effect a number of financial and budgetary austerity
measures, including a cutback in public spending.[82]

The devaluation has brought into relief Mexico's
substantial deficit in its commerce with the United
States. According to the Mexican government's Foreign
Trade Cabinet, from 1975 to 1978 oil exports brought
about a reduction of this deficit, from 26.390 billion
pesos in 1974 to 12.387 billion in 1978. However, the
dynamism of the Mexican economy resulted in renewed sharp
increases in imports, which soon neutralized income from
oil. By 1979, the commercial deficit with the United
States surged to 38.712 billion pesos, and in 1980 a
deficit of 64.512 billion pesos was reached. In 1978,
oil accounted for 39.5 percent of sales to the U.S. and
this figure had risen to 61.2 percent by 1980. In general terms, there would seem to be a correspondence between the sharp increases in Mexico's trade deficits, and
the consolidation of petroleum as its main export to the
United States.[83]

During 1980, foreign investments in Mexico increased
by 1.66 billion dollars, and were expected to go up by
3 billion in 1981. Investments by subsidiaries of U.S.
corporations registered an increase of 347 million dollars in 1978, and 1.3 billion in 1980, channeled mostly
to the manufacturing sector of the Mexican economy.
Parallel to this, between 1979 and 1980 the current
account deficit of Mexico in its balance of payments with
the United States grew by 230 percent: from outflows of
797 billion dollars in "hard" currency for 1979, to
2.631 billion by 1980.[84]

Economic growth in Mexico is still related to a few
basic detonating factors: petroleum exports, purchases
of capital goods for Mexican industry (especially those
related to the oil industry), and the entrance of new
flows of investments. Mexico continues to depend on the
U.S. market for these key components of its trading
relationships.

THE POLITICAL PIVOT

An Overview: The State and the Private Sector

According to Bo Anderson and James Cockcroft, the
Mexican government is primarily concerned with promoting
four national goals: political stability, economic
growth, public welfare, and Mexicanization. Political

stability involves the perception of basic political
institutions, decision-makers, and modes of transferring
power as legitimate by most of the people. Economic
growth relates, as usual, to increases in categories such
as industrial productivity and per capita income. Public
welfare implies the improvement of living standards for
the bulk of the population. And Mexicanization refers
to the policy of achieving national control, public or
private, of the process of development.[85]

In Mexico, these goals are closely linked with the
mystique of the Mexican Revolution, and the concepts of
"mixed economy" and "state capitalism," i.e. the state
viewed as leading the country to higher levels of economic growth, social progress, and national consciousness. State action takes place within a political space
in which the main actors are, in order of importance,
the Mexican President, the "official" Institutional
Revolutionary Party (PRI), and pressure groups of various
political persuasions.

The Global Plan for Development, 1980-1982, reaf-
firms the "predominance of the state and the public
sector" in Mexico's economy.[86] In his annual report of
September 1981, President López Portillo underscored
that "planning for development supposes the leading
function of the state in its various processes."[87] This
preponderant role of the state does not spring from
direct control of most of the Mexican economy. The
private sector still contributes about half of the country's total investment, to 45 percent for the public
sector and 5 percent for foreign capital. Rather, the
state controls some key factors in the process of development. Raymond Vernon has pointed out the overwhelming
role of the Mexican state in regulating the supply of
credits, imports, and public facilities.[88]

The public sector comprises a complex of powerful
economic institutions. Three of these, the Banco de
Mexico (Central Bank), the National Banking and Insurance Commission, and the Secretariat of Finance and
Public Credit, regulate the financial operations of the
private sector. Traditionally, the government has
maintained a degree of control over prices in the private sector, usually to protect domestic industry.
Several public financial institutions such as Nacional
Financiera, are active in the promotion of agricultural
and industrial activities. State enterprises and decentralized organizations, of which PEMEX is by far the
most important, have in recent years accounted for
10 percent to 15 percent of Mexico's GNP.[89]

Since 1977, the growth index of state decentralized
enterprises has been more than double that of the total
for the entire manufacturing sector. Even excluding
PEMEX, this accounts for 11 percent of GNP. According

to official estimates, the 350 state decentralized
enterprises employ 470,000 persons and contribute with
more than 75 percent of total exports, although most of
this latter figure is made up by foreign oil and gas
sales.[90]

At first sight, Mexico's petroleum bonanza would
seem not only to restore to the state the influence it
had lost during the crisis ridden mid-1970s, but to
reinforce its role as the controlling force of the economy. In the words of E.V.K. Fitzgerald,

> The onset of oil and gas exports on a massive
> scale in the nineteen eighties means that the
> Mexican state will have, for the first time,
> resources of its own to allocate to economic
> and social infrastructure; this should permit
> the public sector to complete the task of
> restructuring the economy through direct
> investment.[91]

In other words, the growing financial capacity of
the state is likely to have a substantial impact on
Mexico's "mixed economy." Indeed, by mid-1980 the
Mexican Institute of Foreign Trade reported that the
public sector had attained a surplus in its commercial
balance during the first five months of that year,
amounting to 2.032 billion, which compensated in 79.4
percent the commercial deficit of the private sector,
of $2.559 billion. Hydrocarbon exports were the
decisive factor in the 199 percent increment in exports
income during this period, relative to a similar period
during 1979. However, the public sector had deficits
in both agricultural and manufactured products
transactions.[92]

Thus, petroleum income would seem to alter the
previous political equilibrium between the public and
private sectors. The increase in petrodollars for the
government could diminish the leverage of the private
sector to advance its goals. Capital flight constitutes
the main element of pressure available to the private
sector to impinge upon the orientation of national
economic policy. This possibility would tend to weaken
as the state increases its disposable funds through oil
exports.[93] This seems to be the general situation in
oil-exporting countries. According to Marcos Kaplan,

> The multiple impact of petroleum in producing-
> exporting countries is manifest and focuses on
> the strengthening of the state and its functions,
> of its powers, and of its relative autonomy, to
> retransmit itself to all the aspects and levels
> of national society.[94]

However, the plain fact of the increase in the
financial weight of the public sector, does not necessarily mean that there should be a conscious attempt to
swamp the sphere of action of the private sector. From
1940 to 1970, the role of the state in Mexico was to support domestic private enterprise through means such as
tax exemptions in order to achieve an accelerated and
sustained process of industrialization.[95] And there is
at present no real indication that the Mexican government
intends to do otherwise. The Mexican refusal to enter
into GATT seems to confirm this assessment. Some Mexican
analysts see schemes such as the Alliance for Production,
as basic incentives to foster the activities of the
private sector. In this context, the larger enterprises
would be the ones with the most to gain out of price
liberalization policies at a domestic level, and government measures to support industrial recovery.[96]

Indeed, President López Portillo has emphasized the
need to protect domestic industry against foreign competition, and from the limitations implicit in Mexico's
present stage of development.[97] Specifically, in October
1981, the government's Public Works Bank (BANOBRAS),
extended a credit for $680 million to the Alfa Industrial
Group, Mexico's largest and fastest growing private conglomerate, which was suffering a financial squeeze due
to overextension of operations and the rise in worldwide
interest rates.[98]

Pressure Groups and Political Parties

Mexican critic Roger Bartra has stressed the manifestations of Mexico's "heavy centralism and authoritarian presidentialism." According to Bartra, the
Mexican federal system is merely a legal formulism. As
the traditional power of the regional "caciques" has
eroded, the sway of the central government over the provinces has increased. Most of the governors are imposed
by the executive, says Bartra. With the exception of
four state governments that constitute a "crystallization
of regional power," i.e. the states of Mexico, Nuevo
Leon, Jalisco, and Veracruz, all the rest would be either
in a situation of extreme dependence vis-a-vis the central power, or as mere administrators for it.[99]

On the other hand, the PRI has been able to maintain
an overall control over political processes through its
three sectors: the National Confederation of Popular
Organizations (CNOP), which represents the interests of
Mexico's middle class; the Confederation of Mexican
Workers (CTM); and the National Peasants' Confederation
(CNC).

A number of elements explain PRI control over Mexico's middle sectors, such as the heterogeneity of CNOP's component groups, which make it difficult for them to act in unison, and the expansion of the national bureaucracy, whose members depend on the government for their jobs. Government employees constitute a sizable part of the sector and are, thus, a powerful force contributing to close identification with the official PRI line. Centralized control of Mexico's organized labor through the CTM and its durable leader, Fidel Velázquez, gives the PRI the capacity to mobilize workers in the urban sectors. The hold of the CNC throughout the countryside, based on its possibilities for patronage of peasants, remains practically unchallenged.

But political power in Mexico is by no means monolithic. There are new patterns of authority, as well as new political actors.100 One of the key elements that must be incorporated into an analysis of Mexico's changing political environment is the growing role of pressure groups.

Taken as a whole, the private sector is perhaps the most formidable source of pressure on the central government. As Richard B. Mancke asserts:

> Ironically, it has been the 'nonrevolutionary' private sector that, historically, has had the most influence on the PRI. Though officially excluded from the PRI's formal structure, there are at least three structural reasons why industry interacts closely with government. First, railways, communications, utilities, and several key industries, such as petroleum, are all in the public sector. Second, government pricing, credit, tariff, and investment policies have a direct impact on private business. Third, and probably most important, the PRI is able to control labor and thereby wins the gratitude of the private sector.101

On the other hand, the activities of private business help to mobilize employment and capital, vitally important elements in Mexico's process of development.102 In this respect, some conservative Mexican critics have argued in favor of a full return to private capital of its traditional activities in the Mexican economy, expecially in the manufacturing sector.103

At the other end of the political spectrum, the leftist leaning Mexican magazine _Proceso_ has given particular attention to what it sees as a political environment, under President López Portillo, extremely receptive to the activities of the private sector. The initial action by the government in this direction would

have been the formation, in December 1976, of the
"Alliance for Production," an agreement reached between
the government and leaders of industry and organized
labor, with the objectives of promoting investments and
economic growth. According to Proceso, since 1977 there
has been an expansion of the fusion between private
industrial and banking capital which is bound to tighten
its hold on the Mexican economy.[104]

Some Mexican critics go even further in their analysis and see the appearance of a bureaucratic entrepre-
neurial complex as part of a project of privatization of
political power. This would amount, in effect, to an
alliance between the government and private enterprise,
in order to maintain the present model of development,
based on capital accumulation, rapid economic growth,
and renewed industrialization.[105] However, present
political processes in Mexico cannot be viewed from such
a narrow perspective, as the strengthening of any
particular group, no matter how relevant it may be.

Nevertheless, the resources available to Mexico's
private sector are formidable. In a mid-1980 list of the
500 most important enterprises in the world, published
by the magazine Fortune, there were 16 Latin American
state and private firms, of which 3 were Mexican. The
most important Mexican company was PEMEX, third in Latin
America and 39th in the world, with sales for $7.290
billion. The other two were private firms. The Alfa
Group, with headquarters in the city of Monterrey, ranked
8th in Latin America and 299th in the world. Alfa is the
most important private enterprise in Latin America, with
sales for $2 billion and total assets at a level close
to $5 billion. Alfa has diversified its activities
beyond its initial nucleus as a steel company, into
petrochemicals, tourism, electric appliances, food processing, and capital goods. The VISA Group (Industrial
Securities, S.A.), also located in Monterrey, ranked
15th in Latin America and 453rd in the world, with sales
for 781 million dollars.[106]

The political demands by Mexico's private sector
have traditionally been channeled through a representation of their interests in Mexico's bureaucratic-political apparatus. For example, the Secretariat of Industry and Trade has generally tended to represent
Mexico's manufacturing interests. Likewise, the Secretariat of the Treasury has over time worked towards the
maintenance of a "good investment climate," and sound
financial management.[107] Thus, the private sector
appears to have direct institutional means to present
its views in governmental circles.

The private sector has a direct stake in the
expansion of petroleum exploitation, and present laws
mandate the extensive use of Mexican subcontractors in
the development of the industry. By the same token, oil

income would seem to strengthen the Mexican economy and pave the way for larger investments and operations by private companies.[108] However, an overheated economy has also brought about rising interest rates, a sign of strain in the capacity of the Mexican banking system to finance purchases on credit. In any case, in spite of the willingness of the private sector to expand its activities in the petroleum industry, the state is unlikely to relinquish to any degree its direct control of the industry.[109]

The harmony of interests between Mexican and American business groups derives from their multifaceted association. Mexican private firms in Monterrey and Mexico City, as well as banking groups such as Bancomer and Banamex, share joint ventures with U.S., Western European, and Japanese multinational corporations. Likewise, the Mexican private sector relies on credit financing from U.S. conglomerates such as the Bank of America and the Chase Manhattan Bank.[110]

After the January 1981, meeting between President López Portillo, and then President-elect Reagan, the leaders of three of Mexico's most powerful private sector organizations, Ernesto Rubio del Cueto, President of CONCAMIN (Confederation of Industrial Chambers), Jose Porrero, President of CANACINTRA (National Chamber of the Transformation Industry), and Jorge Chapa, President of CONCANACO (Confederation of National Chambers of Commerce), stated their hopes for a better commercial relationship and a relaxation of bilateral tensions. High on their agenda was the need for lesser trading barriers in the United States to Mexican manufactured exports.[111]

It would be safe to assert that the American Chamber of Commerce in Mexico represents the views of U.S. investors quite closely, since in its membership of approximately 2,200 corporate members "is represented the major part of U.S. direct private investment in Mexico.[112] Al R. Wichtrich, former President of that association, has stated that its "main objective (is) to promote trade between the host country and the United States....There is no question in my mind that U.S. private foreign investment is one of the best ways to stimulate the economic development of Mexico."[113]

Wichtrich praised the measures put into effect by President López Portillo early in his administration, which gave "reassurance of a more understanding and conciliatory attitude toward the private sector."[114] Apparently, a good working relationship has developed in the last few years between Mexican officials and the leaders of the American Chamber of Commerce in Mexico. The latter, according to Wichtrich

...dialogue with the Mexican Government, we do
talk to them, we do try to place before them our
position, certainly we are not going to tell them
what they should do or not do...They have their
problems. As I mentioned before, it is a sovereign
country. We try to show them where perhaps they
are making a mistake and try to prove...how they
should adopt certain attitudes, perhaps, foreign
investment would be more welcome.[115]

One of the objectives of the American Chamber of
Commerce in Mexico is to underline "this mutuality of
interests between the U.S. transnationals and the Mexican
government."[116] Jorge Domínguez has noted in the behavior
of this pressure group an attempt to widen and influence
the information available to the Mexican government and
to mold a more favorable political climate for foreign
investments. At the same time, "specific foreign firms
have also lobbied to defend their particular interests
against adverse governmental policies," such as in the
case of automobile and pharmaceutical firms in the 1960s
and 1970s.[117]

John Pluntket, President of the American Chamber of
Commerce in Mexico at present, views the relationship
between Presidents López Portillo and Reagan as instrumental in strengthening friendly relations between the
"leading Latin American country" and the United States.
Pluntket minimizes the import of recent differences between the two nations, as "a problem of concepts and
disagreements in the definition of some terms." The
United States is ready, according to Pluntket, to
reestablish a continous dialogue for the benefit of both
countries.[118]

Likewise, Jose Carral, General Vice-President and
representative in Mexico of the Bank of America, has
been encouraged by signs of decreasing political and
economic tensions between the United States and Mexico,
due to Reagan's personal diplomacy, parallel to an
increment in foreign investments in Mexico and in the
general commercial relations between both countries.[119]

The American newspaper New Times has underlined the
divergencies in Mexican public opinion referent to ties
with the United States in the following terms: "The
government, bankers, and industrialists are pressuring
in favor of closer links with the United States, while
several opposition groups demand economic independence
for the country."[120] While this distinction may be too
sharply drawn, it does reflect some of the realities of
the response by politically aware forces in Mexico,
especially in light of the oil bonanza.

The increasing diversity and conflicting demands of
various political groups point to the fact that the

Mexican political system is becoming more open in terms of political competition. The process of political reform (<u>Reforma Política</u>), consolidated from 1976 to 1979 under former Secretary of the Interior Jesus Reyes Heroles, has allowed for an expansion in the number of registered political parties, their proportional representation in the Chamber of Deputies, and greater access to mass media, which the government strongly influences.[121]

At present there are, in addition to the PRI, eight registered political parties which were to present candidates in the 1982 elections. These include three groups that had enjoyed legal status previously to the <u>Reforma Politica</u>: the National Action Party (PAN); the Popular Socialist Party (PPS); and the Authentic Party of the Mexican Revolution (PARM). The five new parties include three that had participated in the 1979 congressional elections: the Communist Party (PCM); the Workers' Socialist Party (PST); and the Mexican Democratic Party (PDM). Two other parties have been legally recognized for the 1982 elections: the Trotskyte Revolutionary Party (PRTT); and the Social Democrat Party (PDS). Additionally, there is the Mexican Workers' Party (PMT), led by one of Mexico's best-known opposition leaders, Heberto Castillo, which the government has refused to register, as well as other minor groups.[122]

The National Action Party (PAN), created in 1939, is the largest and oldest political party in Mexico next to the PRI. To the right along the country's political spectrum, the PAN constitutes a pro-business force, ideologically committed to free enterprise and Catholic values. In spite of a continuous division among its upper echelon leadership, the PAN seems to have a unified policy thrust, which includes support for more domestic private involvement in the petroleum industry. PAN's candidate for President in the 1982 elections, Pablo Emilio Madero, was likely to be the runner-up after the PRI's candidate, former Secretary of Programming and Budget, Miguel de la Madrid Hurtado. Another alternative to the right of the PRI, and perhaps the most conservative of the registered political parties, is the Mexican Democratic Party (PDM), which wants to promote the collaboration between church and state and traditional family values.[123]

The Popular Socialist Party (PPS) and the Authentic Party of the Mexican Revolution (PARM), have traditionally been allies of the PRI. The PPS has attempted to rally supporters around the issues of land and income redistribution, while the PARM's views remain indistinguishable. Both parties have accepted, with token opposition, government policies for the petroleum industry. The role of both PPS and PARM is likely to be preempted by the entrance into the political arena of the new leftist parties.

Mexican leftist opposition parties have repeatedly argued against present government policies regarding petroleum production and exports. Since early 1978, the leaders of four Mexican parties of the left, the Communist Party (PCM), the Mexican Workers' Party (PMT), the Socialist Revolutionary Party (PSR), and the Mexican People's Party (PPM), have coincided in expressing the need to draw and implement an energy policy that would truly respond to the national interests, and have warned against the danger of continuing PEMEX's "handout policy." Present oil policy, according to this view, is totally opposed to that put into action by Cardenas in 1938.[124]

Heberto Castillo, head of the Mexican Workers' Party (PMT), has stood out in recent years with his acerbic criticism of the government's oil policy, both from an external and a domestic perspective. Externally, according to Castillo, present policies are bound to increase drastically Mexico's dependence on the United States. Internally, he says, petroleum exploitation is resulting in a dichotomous society, with two contrasting sectors: "one employed and benefiting from economic growth, and the other underdeveloped and relying on government handouts for survival."[125]

The announcement by the Mexican government early in 1977 of the construction of the gasduct to the United States, served as a catalyst for the various leftist opposition leaders to unite against it. Edward C. Williams has pointed out that even though the Mexican left failed to thwart the project, it did succeed in making the government effect a "strategic withdrawal." Under fire from critics, who advanced a scenario of increased economic dependence, pressures, and even U.S. occupation of Mexican oil fields, the government changed the emphasis regarding the objectives of the gasduct. The project, according to the revised official version, would be geared to improving Mexico's internal distribution system.[126]

More recently, Castillo has presented his view of the logic of increased petroleum exploitation in terms of a greater dependence of Mexico vis a vis the United States: "The U.S. needs our oil and Mexico is economically bound to that nation." Speaking early in 1981, Castillo pointed out that massive exports of petroleum have brought about the abandonment of various industries, and have aggravated unemployment problems in Mexico.[127] On the other hand, the Communist Party sees the issue in terms of "systematic pressures from imperialistic capital" to force Mexico to raise its oil exports level, enter GATT, and change its stand against intervention in Central America."[128]

In August, 1981, six leftist parties announced plans to unite for the 1982 elections. These included the Communist Party (PCM) and the Mexican Workers' Party (PMT), plus four other minor groups. The project attempted to form a new leftist alliance, to be called the Unified Socialist Party of Mexico, which could have become Mexico's second largest political force. However, by November 1981, the alliance had collapsed. The reasons for the quick end to the leftist challenge were mainly related to a personality conflict between Heberto Castillo, head of PMT, and Arnoldo Martínez Verdugo, head of PCM. More specifically, the issue referred to the preference by individual leaders to control their own groups rather than relinquish authority to a bigger organization, but also to the reluctance by Castillo to join forces with the Moscow-oriented PCM.[129]

Leftist groups in Mexico have usually relied on intellectuals and university students to strengthen their political demands. The student movement of mid-1968, which ended in a bloody confrontation with police and military forces on October 2 of that year, remains as a rallying point for leftist forces. At present the National University in Mexico City (UNAM), as well as other provincial universities, are footholds for Marxist ideology. However, leftist student groups have not recovered from the internal divisions that ensued following the 1968 debacle. On the other hand, the government provides most of the financial support for the public university system, and is directly involved in electing high administrators. Furthermore, it could be argued that the government perceives universities as providing and "escape value" for pressures from young urban sectors of the population. Nevertheless, the intelligentsia continues to be a strong source of criticism, some would say the "conscience" of Mexico's political establishment which, in turn, listens to its arguments.

Independent unionism represents another pressure group of particular importance, since it would seem to threaten the control of labor through official organizations such as the Confederation of Mexican Workers (CTM), one of the three sectors of the PRI, and the Congreso del Trabajo (Labor Congress). Dominguez has mentioned Mexican automobile industry unions as examples of these changes in labor's political role. Independent unionism would tend to have an impact on managerial practices, through a more frequent resource to strikes, and a more active attempt at participation in policy-making processes affecting production.[130]

Local peasant organizations in Mexico's southeastern states of Tabasco and Chiapas have attempted to retaliate against PEMEX, pressing for demands regarding compensations for their ruined or expropriated lands.[131] The takeover of some of PEMEX's installations has brought attention to the plight of the Mexican peasantry and, occasionally, the intervention of the army.[132] However, it is unlikely that these regional actions by the peasants, lacking real organizational strength, or a nationally established power base, can effectively challenge the control that the PRI exerts over that sector through the National Peasants' Confederation (CNC).

The various political uncertainties since 1968, which reached a high point in the mid-1970s with increasing urban guerrilla activity and terrorism, might be having a detrimental effect on one of the foundations of the Mexican political system: the nonpolitical role of the military. The limitation of the military's role in politics should not be automatically thought of as a permanently settled question for all time. As Martin Needler advanced in the early 1970s, "...rather than regarding the achievement of civilian control in Mexico as a definitive accomplishment, it is probably wiser to think of it as provisional."[133] If the government were to show steady signs of weakness and instability, or if it had to resort too often to the military to put down civilian discontent, such as it happened during the early 1970s with the guerrillas in the state of Guerrero, when close to 20,000 troops were mobilized there, the importance of the military in the political equation would be bound to increase.

In recent years there has been a substantial increase in the budget for military and police forces. According to a United Nations report on disarmament, Mexico's growing petroleum wealth has turned it into a "coveted prey" for weapons manufacturers. Mexico's military purchases had by 1979 risen to $780 million, the highest in the Caribbean and Central American area, with the exception of Cuba (which spent $1.065 billion approximately). Mexico's armed forces total 125,000 men, and the army is by far the most important branch, with 95,000 men. Still, in relation to its size, Mexico's military is one of the smallest in Latin America.[134]

The traditional low profile the Mexican military have kept in recent times may be giving way to a more assertive presence, mostly as a result of Mexico's new status as an increasingly important oil producer and exporter. In particular, the potential for difficulties arising from the political situation in the Central American area seems to be changing somewhat the priorities of the Mexican armed forces, to the southern Mexican states in terms of location and, in terms of functions, from basically social tasks to a truly self-defense force. The army's training centers increasingly on "regional tactical and counterinsurgency operations," and its arms purchases, mostly light armed vehicles and individual weapons, are geared to those objectives.[135]

In December 1980, as he directed the biggest
military maneuvers ever staged by the Mexican military,
in which 43,705 men from the various branches swept the
southern state of Chiapas, the Secretary of National
Defense, General Felix Galván López, declared that the
army has the obligation to prevent any groups from any
political tendency to enter Mexican territory and to
violate its sovereignty.[136] Some sources saw the maneuvers as a proof that Mexico's southern region was not
being used as a refuge by Guatemalan guerrillas and, most
important, as a means to quiet down rumors about violent
confrontations between Mexican forces, perhaps PEMEX's
"security" units, and groups of rural rebels.[137] For
1981, the Secretariat of Defense had a budget of 25,855
million pesos. The main objectives were the modernization of military equipment and an adequate level of
training and preparedness for the armed forces. Likewise, there are plans to accelerate the production of
war material, such as light weapons, mortars, and
rockets.[138]

Changes in the Mexican Political Establishment

The implications from petroleum exploitation are
permeating Mexican politics at all levels. Signs of
impending political change have come from the ranks of
Mexico's ruling political establishment. There has been
a displacement of the center of gravity of political
power, from traditional posts such as the Secretariat of
the Interior (Secretaría de Gobernación), the Secretariat of Agrarian Reform, and the Secretariat of Agriculture, towards more professional and technocratic
elites, located in the Secretariat of Programming and
Budget, the Secretariat of Patrimony and Industrial
Development, the Secretariat of the Treasury, and PEMEX.
As petroleum continues to be the lever of development,
and as the government tries to consolidate its reliance
on planning schemes, these latter agencies would seem
to be headed for growing political relevance.

The increase in political power of the Secretariats
associated with finances, planning, and energy, within
the context of the petroleum boom, leads to the issue
of the apparent process of technocratization of the
Mexican state. While in the extremely dynamic Mexican
development milieu, political approaches to problems
will certainly remain a must for the future ahead, a
growing reliance on economic growth and management,
fueled by the petroleum industry, is likely to manifest
itself in the rise of technicians and planners to the top
levels of national decision-making. Writing in the mid-
1970s, Rafael Segovia noted a progressive loss of power

by the traditional "caciques," i.e. "the men who use
their local implant and force to accede to national
power." Parallel to this,

> The new tendency seems to be that of a different
> cursus honorum to accede either to the Presidency
> of the Republic, or to the Cabinet....If this
> technostructure is the most visible and perhaps
> most important, the progressive and inevitable
> technification and bureaucratization of the state
> leads to the displacement of the traditional
> political class, limited more and more to functions
> that keep it away from the authentic centers of
> decision.[139]

This tendency seemed to be confirmed on September
25, 1981, when the PRI announced its candidate for the
July 1982, presidential elections, Miguel de la Madrid
Hurtado, Secretary of Programming and Budget. De la
Madrid, who was in charge of the Global Plan for Development, holds a graduate degree in Public Administration
from Harvard University, has a long record in economic
management, and is considered to have strong ties to
the business community.[140]

By mid-October 1981, just as de la Madrid was preparing to begin his campaign as official candidate, the
head of the PRI, Javier Garcia Paniagua, resigned
unexpectedly. He was replaced by Pedro Ojeda Paullada,
a close friend of President López Portillo who at the
time was Secretary of Labor. As the head of the PRI
directs and coordinates the campaign of the official
candidate, this move could be seen as a consolidation of
the political group closest to the President, and the
demotion of García Paniagua, who had presidential ambitions of his own. Likewise, it would seem to show
underlying tensions within the ranks of the PRI, between
the traditional politically-minded circles, and the
emerging groups of technicians and bureaucrats.[141]

The clash between the traditional, established
politicians, and the new technocratic groups, has been
brewing for some time, as a source of discontent and lack
of discipline within the PRI. These divergencies have
been underscored by the oil bonanza. A case in point
was that of Victor Manzanilla Schaffer, a PRI federal
deputy member of the CNC, from the state of Yucatan.
Agriculture and petroleum exploitation have been at odds
since the intensification of PEMEX's activities in 1977.
A rare act of dissent within the normally tightly knit
PRI was staged by Manzanilla, in October 1977, when he
voted against a constitutional amendment which gave PEMEX
broad powers to expropriate lands needed to proceed with
petroleum exploration and development. In effect, this

amendment, which was passed eventually, formally placed
the petroleum industry ahead of agricultural development.
After quite an upheaval in the PRI-controlled Congress,
caused by this unheard-of dissidence, Manzanilla finally
remained in his post and the controversy died down.[142]
Nevertheless, in 1977 this incident already reflected
subjacent tensions beneath the apparently unruffled
exterior of the government party apparatus, and may have
played a part in redirecting official attention to the
plight of the peasants and the agricultural sector in
general.

Parallel to these developments, a tug of war has
developed since the late 1970s, within the new professional and technocratic groups, directly related to contrasting views in regards to oil production and exports
plans. As Edward F. Wonder has pointed out,

> ...the bureaucracy itself is organized along
> lines that are more horizontal than vertical,
> with numerous agencies, often displaying quite
> different policy philosophies, involved in the
> same policy area, frustrating planning, and
> contributing to frequent shifts in policy
> emphasis, even during the same administration
> as the President seeks to hold together his
> coalition.[143]

A result of the previous situation was the dismissal
of Jorge Díaz Serrano as head of PEMEX, on June 6, 1981.
Since 1977, four Secretariats have been involved in
planning and implementing energy policy: Patrimony and
Industrial Development, Programming and Budget, Treasury,
and Commerce. These have often manifested diverging
viewpoints in the administrative councils of energy
industries. To this must be added the growing economic
and political importance of PEMEX, as the most dynamic
sector in the Mexican economy. The fact that PEMEX is
under the jurisdiction of the Secretariat of Patrimony
and Industrial Development, helps explain the rift that
developed between the head of the latter, Andrés de
Oteyza, and Díaz Serrano. While the former head of
PEMEX advocated an ever rising level of oil production
and exports, de Oteyza emphasized the need to curtail
expansion of the industry within the limits set by the
Energy Program.

Until shortly before his dismissal, Diaz Serrano
was considered to be the political figure closest to
President López Portillo, and a potential PRI candidate
for the 1982 Presidential elections. By mid-1980,
political rumors in Mexico were ripe concerning the
possible creation of a Secretariat of Energy, to be
headed by Díaz Serrano, and to comprise the petroleum,

electricity, nuclear, and coal industries.144 This did
not materialize. On the other hand, Díaz Serrano was
attacked by Mexican leftist forces for his alleged
association with U.S. political and business interests, 145 and for "invading the field of action of other
government officials."146

By November 1980, Díaz Serrano appeared to be
politically damaged by the presidential decision not to
raise the domestic prices of leaded gas and diesel, a
measure long advocated by the former PEMEX Director in
order to strengthen the financial base of the oil indus-
try.147 Nevertheless, in February 1981, Díaz Serrano
was designated as official speaker in the anniversary
ceremony of the enactment of the Mexican Constitution,
a fact that seemed to underline his aspiration to the
PRI's Presidential candidacy.148

However, everything came quickly unraveled for Díaz
Serrano as a result of the worldwide petroleum glut of
mid-1981. By April 1981, supplies were growing while
demand declined in the international oil market. Díaz
Serrano first reacted to the situation in late May, by
stating the PEMEX would maintain its prices, in spite of
oversupplies in the market.149 Then, suddenly, just a
few days later, Díaz Serrano announced that PEMEX, after
all, would have to reduce its prices in order to maintain its clients. PEMEX lowered its average price for
crude exports by $4 a barrel, from $34.60 to $30.60.150
On June 6 1981, Díaz Serrano presented his resignation
to President López Portillo.151

The official reasons for the dismissal of the PEMEX
Director were related to his disagreement with members
of the Mexican government's Economic Cabinet, especially
the Secretary of Patrimony and Industrial Development,
José Andrés de Oteyza, over the price reduction measures.
Other critics mentioned that PEMEX had turned into an
autonomous bureaucracy, and that petroleum policy had
been increasingly divergent from Mexico's national policy.
At the root of the disagreement was Díaz Serrano's persistent decision to continue raising oil production.152
The debate over petroleum and general development policy
in Mexico is bound to continue for the foreseeable
future.

The new Director of PEMEX, Julio Rodolfo Moctezuma
Cid, is a former Secretary of the Treasury and close
friend of President López Portillo. It was interesting
to note that the PRI candidate for the 1982 presidential
elections, Miguel de la Madrid Hurtado, had been Under-
secretary of the Treasury when Moctezuma Cid held the top
post. In any case, the change of directors in PEMEX did
not make Mexico immune to international market forces.
Attempts by Moctezuma Cid to restore the price of Mexican
oil during June and July 1981, led to an abrupt fall in
exports. Likewise, policies under the new PEMEX

administration did not seem to differ too much from previous guidelines, including the objective of diversification of clients and products. However, there would appear to be a greater willingness to conciliate views with respect to the pace of development of the petroleum industry.[153]

As a relevant group in the Mexican political establishment, PEMEX's workers union (STPRM)`, has benefited from the petroleum bonanza. There has been a change of guard in STRPM's leadership, from the men who belonged to the generation that participated in the nationalization of the oil industry, and traditionally opposed oil exports, to the United States in particular, to a younger group of leaders who see the fortunes of the union rising parallel to the rapid expansion of the petroleum industry. Thus, the petroleum workers' union is likely to support PEMEX's official policy, but not without proper compensation. According to Richard Mancke,

> In return for its consent, STPRM's primary conditions are that its members be guaranteed continued hikes in relative wages, and benefits, coupled with assurances of no layoffs.[154]

But the activities of the union, and of PEMEX in general, have traditionally been mired by corruption. Corruption is by no means a phenomenon exclusive of PEMEX but, rather, an endemic characteristic of the Mexican system. However, even in such a milieu, the situation in PEMEX has tended to be particularly serious. Some foreign assessments are indeed gloomy:

> Some critics suggest that PEMEX itself will have to be overhauled before there is any chance for wise use of Mexico's oil and gas...Riddled with nepotism, plagued by graft and corruption, the company is a model of inefficiency, spending $9 to get each $13 barrel of oil out of the ground (in August 1978). The Petroleum Workers' Union openly sells jobs, with the going rate for a permanent post in the oil fields about $3,500. And there are so many ghost workers on the PEMEX payrolls that roughnecks call them 'aviators'...'They only touch down here to get their checks.'[155]

The members of the STPRM constitute, in fact, an elite within Mexico's entire labor sector, and the oil boom is likely to reinforce their privileged position. As Edward C. Williams has succinctly advanced: "Corruption has always been a part of the PEMEX scene, but indications point to its increase as the economic pie expands."[156] The economic bonanza is bound to add fuel

to management-labor disputes over workers' benefits. So
far, the issue appears to have been solved through
increasing concessions to the union. For example, in
October 1977, as news of the construction of the gasduct
were spreading through the Mexican press, it was publicly
known that the STPRM would receive 2 percent of the total
investments on that project. Critics kept asking for
reasons as to "why the first beneficiary of said works
should be the powerful and corrupt petroleum syndi-
cate."157

Oxford specialist Lawrence Whitehead has pointed out
the dangers of excessive centralization of the oil industry in the following terms:

> To keep PEMEX as a state monopoly in the new
> conditions set by the boom, will permit the
> powerful and arrogant oil union to threaten the
> tranquility of domestic interests, and the
> security of the state itself.158

In the past, efforts to stamp out cases of corruption, such as auditing PEMEX's workers in order to stop
clandestine sales of fuel to sugar refineries and industries, have been turned down by union threats to
strike.159 Accusations of corruption have been thrust
not only at union workers, but at the highest levels of
PEMEX's management, by leftist groups as well as by the
independent National Petroleum Movement (MNP). The
latter, however, seems to lack any substantial support
within the industry. Allied to leftist political parties, the MNP has repeatedly denounced corruption in the
STPRM as a cancer that "threatens the independence of
the oil industry."160

There is official awareness of these problems. In
his fifth annual report of September 1981, President
López Portillo announced a new "Law of Responsibilities,"
geared to strengthen fiscal instruments and to supervise
the finances of high public officials.161 Previously,
in November 1980, the Mexican President had announced
reforms to the government's fiscal code, in order to
prevent tax evasion through the use of "name-lenders"
(presta-nombres).162

Political Tendencies

At present the state reigns supreme as the gravity
center of the Mexican political system. But the progressive democratization of the PRI, i.e. the expanding
number and sources of its components, as well as the
proliferation of outside political actors, might seem to
pose a threat to its stability. The Mexican President
is still, by far, the keystone of the system. But, in
spite of oil resources, both the institution of the

presidency, in its role as mediator between public and
private interests, and the PRI, as the main political
arena for such a debate, are under stress.   Jorge
Domínguez has appropriately described the present political crossroads, characterized by changes in its "internal
economic, social, ideological, and political factors:"

> ...Mexico has in the early 1980s a presidency
> less independent of economy and society than
> historical standards would suggest. The central
> organs of the state must respond to more diverse
> pressures within a context of persisting and at
> times rising bureaucratic and enterprise political
> rigidities. It is this state--relatively weaker
> than it had been, although it is still strong--
> that has had to face twin problems in its relations
> with the United States: greater real dependency
> on the U.S. in a political context of less support
> for such close relations. The needs of the Mexican
> economy require, for Mexican officials at least
> in the short run, such a deepened dependency, while
> the needs of Mexican politics require the opposite.
> Discoveries of hydrocarbon resources may have been
> the Mexican miracle of the 1970s. The 1980s
> may require a political miracle that is as yet
> not in evidence.163

It could be asserted that the conditions of a developing society such as Mexico's, i.e. population explosion, rapid urbanization, social dichotomy, economic
inequalities, and political flux, among others, are not
conducive to effective party competition, if the overall
objectives are political stability, sustained economic
growth, and social development in an evolutionary, rather
than a revolutionary, setting. The present political
system may be undergoing a transition, but new forms are
hard to visualize.

One of the main foundations of Mexico's ruling
party has been its flexibility, i.e. its ability to
accomodate different groups or political tendencies
within its organization. During the early and mid-1970s,
several factors contributed to strain this flexibility,
among them the reduction in the rate of economic growth,
with the consequent inability to satisfy fully the
demands of various groups, and the persistent deep inequality in the distribution of income. The continuing
question today is whether the PRI can handle the
increased pressures of the process of modernization,
originating to a great extend in the expansion of the
petroleum industry.

By March 1982, as a result of the international oil
glut and the devaluation of the peso, the role of the
Mexican president as a supreme conciliator seemed to be
under increasing strain. A clash ensued between the Confederation of Mexican Workers, which demanded emergency
wage increases and threatened a general strike, and the
private sector, reeling under the impact of the devaluation on its finances. The private sector cited its
economic difficulties as a deterrent to concessions to
labor. Burdened by a foreign debt of $2.3 billion, the
Alfa Industrial Group, Mexico's largest conglomerate,
had already withdrawn from activities in the petrochemical industry, shortly before the devaluation. However,
critics pointed out that the private sector, and not
labor, was the main beneficiary of the economic boom
from 1977 to early 1981. In response to protests by the
labor movement and opposition parties regarding the
inflationary effect of the devaluation, the government
promised to enforce price controls, and acceded to wage
increases, ranging from 10 to 30 percent according to
salary levels.[164]

The devaluation would seem to have set the stage for
a new economic strategy by Miguel de la Madrid Hurtado,
the PRI candidate. However, the social and economic
situation in Mexico, seen not from the beaming perspective of oil exports and income figures, but from that of
the living conditions of a sizable segment of the population, would seem to be deteriorating. There is a "critical limit," i.e. inflation, less consuming power, reach
of basic articles and services, beyond which an increasingly aware urban population will not remain calm. It
is impossible to foresee at what conjunction of economic
and social demands, on the one hand, and political awareness, on the other, this "critical limit" might be.

The possibility that the Mexican government will
carry on its programs in an atmosphere of political
order depends on the question of achieving a balance
between economic growth and social justice. Oil wealth
can give the government more time and resources to
stage needed reforms, but again, it might worsen the
situation. Revenues from petroleum exports could
aggravate corruption, inflation, and the inequality in
the distribution of income, and could easily be offset
if agricultural production were to decline again. On
the other hand, petroleum might offer new perspectives
to Mexico's political system, if resources are channeled in the proper direction: into the agricultural
sector, efficiently and with an emphasis on domestic
consumption; and into labor-intensive middle-scale
industries, to create more employment opportunities.
Thus, the internal impact of the oil bonanza still

remains to be seen. Oil wealth could lead to prosperity, or to a mirage.

James W. Wilkie has referred to the Mexican political system in terms of a situation of "permanent revolution," which draws deep from its very basis of sustenance, ideologically and politically. This would seem to give rise to a state of "permanent crisis," or political convulsion, in the midst of which the system finds itself periodically, with the danger of a final impasse. The previous situation underscores a basic feature of the Mexican system, i.e. the need for continous bargaining. In the end, says Wilkie, "the Mexican political system does not work smoothly."165

A parallel reflection on the issue would be the widely cited "pendulum effect," as Mexican leaders swing from side to side of the political spectrum, in search for stability. However, under the present accelerated process of social mobilization, Mexico's political establishment may be willing to dispense with abrupt political changes, notwithstanding the rationale for ideological renovation, and embark instead on a course of consolidation of more pragmatic, professional, and technocratic policies and styles of leadership. The selection of Miguel de la Madrid Hurtado as the PRI's Presidential candidate, who is likely to uphold the continuity of the present administration's policies, would tend to support this argument. Nonetheless, one must be cautious, for in the past predictions about the Mexican political process and presidential successors have proved to be a dubious enterprise.

GENERAL IMPACT OF OIL EXPLOITATION

The "Petroleum Syndrome"

The impact of the oil exploitation is determined by endogenous factors, i.e. government policy, and exogenous factors, i.e. world oil price levels. The euphoria about petroleum wealth has so far prevented to a certain degree an analytic criticism of potential pitfalls. For all its magnitude, the oil boom could become just a palliative, instead of a solution to basic structural problems, and could aggravate bottlenecks in the development process, such as corruption, inflation, and the distribution of income.166 In this respect, domestic critics have complained that Mexico's energy policy lacks an organic relation with the needs for profound changes in the country's socioeconomic structure, and that it is being increasingly incorporated to the U.S. global energy strategy.167 However, an impartial assessment of the overall impact would also have to

weigh in the fact that it is unrealistic to expect over-
night changes. In regard to a short-term outlook, U.S.
analysts in 1978 expressed the following:

> It does appear...that the major problems facing
> the Mexican government today will still be there
> in 1988, regardless of the level of petroleum
> output. Inflation will still be high, income
> distribution and geographic development will still
> be unbalanced, unemployment will still be high,
> and the country will still have difficulty pro-
> ducing domestically all its foodstuffs. To an
> extent, the continuation of these problems is
> simply an indication that 10 years is not a long
> time in the life of an economy."[168]

The most crucial question regarding Mexico's petroleum exploitation, since it could very well indicate the
future direction of México's development, is whether the
Mexican economy is becoming petroleum-bound. From the
evidence available in the early 1980s, it would seem
that petroleum tends to overshadow the remaining sectors
of the Mexican economy, and is having a substantial
impact on Mexico's social fabric. An article for the
August 1979, issue of the prestigious Mexican journal
Comercio Exterior, concluded that "for the first years
of the decade of the 1980s, Mexico could emerge as an
economy fundamentally dependent on its hydrocarbon
exports."[169]

In a subsequent issue of Comercio Exterior, of June
1980, Abel Beltran del Río, director of Diemex, an
econometric project for Mexico from the Wharton Econometric Forecasting Association at the University of
Pennsylvania, noticed the first symptoms of the "petroleum syndrome." Beltrán categorized oil rich countries
as hybrid in their process of development. That is,
their indices of inflation and their sectorial disequilibriums corresponded to those of less developed countries, while other signs such as a surplus in the balance
of payments, abundance of finance capital, high rates
of savings, and scarcity of labor, placed them in the
category of countries of medium development.[170]

According to Beltrán, the indicators of the "petroleum syndrome" in any given country include: high level
of petroleum production; an overwhelming participation
of oil as a percentage of their exports; a growing
surplus in their external balance of payments; a fast
and unbalanced growth of the petroleum sector, with the
subsequent bottlenecks; and accelerated inflation,
generated by excessive demand and currency converti-
bility vis-a-vis insufficient supply. Noneconomic

symptoms would include: politically, a more relevant
presence in the world scenario; socially, rising expectations and demands, as well as a get-rich-quickly and
speculative atmosphere; and culturally, the introduction
of foreign values and customs that clash with national
traditons.[171]

By 1979, says Beltrán, the first signs of the
"petroleum syndrome" were clearly detectable in Mexico,
albeit tempered somewhat by the fact that the process
was just beginning, and that Mexico has a good sized and
semi-industrialized economy. Some of these signs
included a growing participation of oil in Mexico's
exports, a high rate of economic growth based on the
exploitation of hydrocarbons, persistent inflation, congestion in Mexico's transportation and communication
infrastructure, land speculation, and growing foreign
investments.[172]

There seems to be a general awareness about the
negative effects of an excessively rapid exploitation of
oil. An editorial in the August 1979, issue of Commercio
Exterior warned against possible economic and social
distortions, i.e. the existence of two nations or economies within the same national territory, due to their
different degree of development. In this context, it
was necessary to avoid the destabilizing effect of excessive petro-funds, to prevent inordinate imports which
could eventually destroy Mexico's industrial sector, and
to control inflation.[173]

The main official instrument to manage Mexico's
petroleum industry has been the Energy Program, with its
production and exports platform. On February 4, 1981,
the Presidential decree approving the Energy Program and
ordering its implementation appeared in Mexico's
Official Diary. Thus, the Energy Program became a law.
The exports limit of 1.5 billion b/d until 1982, was
expected to prevent an excessive dependence on oil
exports.[174] Of course, by early 1982 the worldwide oil
glut was bringing about this same effect.

Some Mexican analysts emphasize the need on the
part of the public sector to reinforce its planning
mechanisms, as a means to condition the oil sector to
the global requisites of national development. In order
to avoid an excessive "petrolization," additional measures would include a deep fiscal reform, a more effective industrial diversification, and greater state
participation, not only in the design and control processes of industrial development, but in the production
process itself.[175]

Reflecting official concern, by September 1980, the
Secretary of Patrimony and Industrial Development,
José Andrés de Oteyza, stated as one of the basis of
Mexico's economic policy the need to guide development

along the path of greater equilibrium, and to diversify
the nation's economic structure away from an excessive
future reliance on oil. Petroleum resources should,
according to Oteyza: support PEMEX's expansion plans
in order for the industry to finance its own growth; be
channeled through taxes to finance government programs
in the fields of education, health, basic infrastructure, and general public sector productive projects;
and benefit the community through prices substantially
lower than those prevailing in the international market.[176]

There are indications that government policy is not
succeeding in avoiding the "oil syndrome." Out of the
official budget for 1981, PEMEX had one of the highest
shares, 377 billion pesos.[177] For 1981, Mexican exports
were expected to have a value of $25 billion. Of this
amount, non-petroleum exports would only account for
$6 billion. Hydrocarbon exports, that is, crude oil,
gas, refined products, and petrochemicals, were expected
to represent up to 82 percent of total Mexican exports.
Total manufactured exports, including petrochemicals,
would amount to only $3.5 billion.[178] Thus, it would
seem that Mexico's high rate of growth from 1977 to 1981
was to a great extent attributable to petroleum economics. In other words, the recovery of the Mexican
economy during those years would not appear to be extra-
ordinary at all, were it not for the sectorial impact of
the oil boom. Indeed, petroleum was the medullar center
of Mexican exports.[179]

In his fifth annual report of September 1981, President López Portillo vehemently denied that the Mexican
economy might be ineluctably tied to its petroleum
industry, citing that petroleum accounted for only 7
percent of Mexico's GDP, the public sector received only
28 percent of its income from petroleum, investments
from the oil sector represented only 12 percent of the
total, and only 38 percent of total foreign income was
derived from petroleum sales.[180] Likewise, Bancomer
(Bank of Commerce) pointed out that the Mexican economy
is quite diversified and does not depend on any single
product for its exports.[181] In this context, the preponderance of petroleum would be only a temporary phenomenon, as a result of the urgent need Mexico had in
the mid and late 1970s to expand its production quickly
to face the economic crisis.[182]

However, by February 1982, the devaluation had
driven home the detrimental effects of the excessive and
continuing reliance on petroleum exports. Referring to
the fundamental distortions of the Mexican economy, PRI
Senator and adviser to the President, Fausto Zapata
Laredo would state the following:

An economic policy relying mainly on oil also
generates unacceptable social risks...The inflation it creates, the rapid deterioration of other
sectors of the economy and the growing foreign
dependence comprise a syndrome that does not go
unnoticed by the Government."[183]

In this context, there would seem ·to be a relatively
positive element in the midst of the generalized oil
price drop which started in mid-1981, that is, a halt to
the process of higher reliance of the Mexican economy on
the petroleum industry and the corresponding awareness
of the limitations of an expansionist economic
policy.[184] Notwithstanding the fact that Mexico was
forced to reduce prices for its oil because of international market forces, by July 1981, this happenstance
had also allowed dissimilar political groups, i.e. the
PRI, leftist and rightist opposition parties, and all
concerned Secretariats, to coalesce around the banner of
reduced levels of petroleum exports, quite a feat which
illustrates the vagaries of Mexican political life.

Regional and Ecological Impact

Never before in Mexico's history has any single
economic sector, such as petroleum right at present,
been such a determining factor in the industrial location and organization of economic activities. According
to a Mexican analyst, the impact of oil activities affected only cities before, while now, the magnitude and
nature of their impact is such that it tends to "domin-
ate all the regional space, that is, all the forms of
zonal production..."[185] Some indications point to the
fact that the regional and ecological impact of petroleum exploitation so far has not been balanced at all.
In the Mexican states that are the center of the
present oil boom, Tabasco and Chiapas, PEMEX's activities have polarized conflicts such as the inequality in
income distribution and unemployment.[186] A social
dichotomy appears to be emerging, between the native
population, dedicated mainly to agricultural activities
and increasingly pushed out by oil projects, and PEMEX's
workers, who enjoy a substantially higher standard of
living.[187] Since 1979, there have been frequent clashes
between PEMEX and peasants in both states. In occasion,
groups of armed peasants have blocked PEMEX's installations. In January 1981, such an incident took place in
the petrochemical complex at Cactus, Chiapas, PEMEX's
industrial areas in Reforma, and various oil fields.[188]
Military patrols were called in to evict the peasants
and protect the installations.[189] PEMEX, for its part,
agreed in principle to pay an indemnization to the peasants for damages resulting from its activities.[190]

The problems seem to have started during 1977, when the reform to Article 27 of the Mexican Constitution transferred to the Secretary of Patrimony and Industrial Development the power to expropriate agricultural lands. Ever since, questions have been raised in regards to how well that Secretariat has fulfilled its role "to harmonize interests and in its case to indemnify."[191] The Secretary General of the League of Peasant Communities in Tabasco has denied that peasants oppose oil exploitation, but that such activities must be undertaken carefully, and just indemnizations paid to those who are affected by them.[192] On the other hand, PEMEX has stated that it does not have direct responsibility over the formation of "misery belts" in the southeastern regions of Mexico where it operates. Rather, there would be "prosperity belts" propitiated by PEMEX's activities.[193] In any case, President López Portillo declared in 1978 that Pemex's role is "to generate economic wealth, not to solve problems."[194]

Nevertheless, these problems are indeed multifaceted. There have been a number of accidents related to PEMEX's activities, significant both in terms of environmental degradation, and economic losses. These would tend to underline either the haste with which PEMEX has proceeded with its explorations, the lack of proper caution, or both. The Mexican magazine Proceso, in an August 1980, issue, was stating somewhat sarcastically that PEMEX was discovering oil and gas through accidents.[195] Such would have been the cases of the "Ixtoc I" well off in the Gulf of Campeche, and the "Giraldas 22" well, in the state of Chiapas. The Ixtoc well exploded on June 3, 1979, and spilled millions of barrels of oil into the waters of the Campeche Bay, one of the richest fishing zones in Mexico. According to Mexican scientists, the damages to the ecology of the zone, and thus to the fishing industry, have been irreversible.[196] Due to a "technical error," in August 1980, the explosion of the "Giraldas 22" well provoked the spill of thousands of barrels of oil and the burning of millions of cubic feet of gas, in an apparently unpopulated area of Chiapas.[197]

In both of these cases, there were economic losses to PEMEX that amounted to millions of pesos. But in some cases these losses are nothing compared to the damages to agriculture in the Mexican southeast. At present there is literally a clash between the petroleum and the agricultural industries in that region. Not only because of disasters such as those described, but through the noxious effects of the burning of gas, various crops such as corn, cacao, and bananas, as well as grasslands, are being destroyed. This is happening in some of the most fertile regions of a mostly arid country. According to a report of December 1980, by the

National Research Institute on Biotic Resources, the
tropical states of Tabasco, Chiapas, Oaxaca, Campeche,
and Quintana Roo are under ecological siege, and Mexico
is in danger of becoming an extensive desert.[198]
     Ixtoc I and Giraldas are not isolated accidents. In
July 1980, a huge fire at Salina Cruz refinery caused
damages for 200 million pesos. Seventy percent of the
population in that city lacks all types of services.[199]
In October of that same year, the "Corindon" well, in the
northern state of Tamaulipas, went out of control and
spilled oil and gas in an area 43 km. off Nuevo
Laredo.[200] The causes of most of these accidents have
not been satisfactorily determined. By mid-1980, peasant
communities in the Huasteca region of Hidalgo were brac-
ing themselves for the feared negative social and ecological effects of PEMEX's imminent exploitation of the
Chicontepec fields.[201] PEMEX has emphasized its commitment to undertake a dialogue with the officials of the
affected areas, in order to remedy the problems generated
by the accidents.[202] But a balanced assessment of the
relation between positive and negative impacts remains
to be made.
     The Mexican sociologist Rodolfo Stavenhagen, in
1978, foresaw three possible scenarios for Mexico's
development, based on the influx of petroleum resources.
The first scenario would lead to the exhaustion of petroleum reserves and a grave domestic crisis, with social
and political convulsions. The second, to a temporary
respite for the system, at least for a generation, until
the reserves are gone. And the third, to integral
development in the framework of democratic planning
with diminishing dependence and a more real autonomy for
Mexico as a nation. In this third scenario, prosperity
would be truly shared. Some of the key factors that
qualify the three scenarios would be: the degree of
dependence and vulnerability vis a vis the United States,
based on commercial transactions; the level of the foreign debt; the domestic destiny of the petroleum financial resources, leading to an improvement or a deterioration of the distribution of income; and the role of the
Mexican state, as a democratic and benefactor, or as an
authoritarian state.[203]
     The weight of evidence by the early 1980s points to
a process located somewhere around the second scenario.
Mexico has not been altogether successful in avoiding
the past pitfalls of other oil-producing countries. The
influx of funds from oil exports tends to have destabilizing social and economic effects with which the
Mexican government cannot quite cope. The fact that
Mexico's international financial position was considerably stronger than in the mid-1970s, could not hide the
domestic distortions due to the oil boom.[204]

164

However, at present this process would not seem to be irreversible. There is, for one thing, the awareness of government officials as manifest in their public expressions of concern. Also, there is the fact that Mexico's diversified economic infrastructure and plain market size, contrast favorably with those of most oil exporting countries. There is still a time margin available to Mexico, during which its government might devise effective means to deal with the effects of the expansion of the oil industry. The challenge consists in utilizing a viable resource in order to build foundations for a sustained, integral process of development in the future.

NOTES

1. Mario Ojeda, "Mexico ante los Estados Unidos en la coyuntura actual," in Continuidad y cambio en la política exterior de Mexico: 1977 (Mexico: El Colegio de Mexico, 1977), p. 41.
2. For a solid, more detailed analysis of the deterioration of the factors under consideration, see ibid., pp. 40-49.
3. José López Portillo, Primer Informe de Gobierno (September 1977), Cuadernos de Filosofía Política, No. 0, Secretaría de Programación y Presupuesto, Mexico, February 1980, pp. 8-9.
4. Ibid., pp. 12-13.
5. José López Portillo, "Discurso de Toma de Protesta como Presidente de la República," (December 1976), Cuadernos de Filosofía Política, No. 9, Secretaría de Programación y Presupuesto, Mexico, October 1978, pp. 7-8.
6. Plan Global de Desarrollo, 1980-1982, Secretaría de Programación y Presupuesto, Mexico, 1980, p. 84.
7. Ibid., p. 111.
8. José López Portillo, "Acto Conmemorativo de la Expropiación de la industria petrolera," Guadalajara, March 18, 1980, p. 172.
9. "Con la LFA no será ilusoria la justicia social: JLP," Excelsior, February 13, 1981, p. 1.
10. "Borrará el petroleo la miseria historica de los mexicanos," Excelsior, March 31, 1978, pp. 1, 17 & 22.
11. "Mexico's Oil, Foreign-Exchange Reserves Soar; President Cites Economic Recovery," The Wall Street Journal, September 5, 1978, p. 6.
12. Cautela en 79 o recaída; Petróleo, eje de Progreso: JLP," Excelsior, January 5, 1979, p. 1.
13. "Conferencia de prensa con corresponsales extranjeros," (January 26, 1978), in Cuadernos de Filosofía Política, No. 3, "Política Petrolera," Secretaría de Programación y Presupuesto, Mexico, February 1980, p. 14.

14. "Al termino de la salutación de año nuevo del Sindicato de Trabajadores Petroleros de la República Mexicana," Mexico, January 9, 1978, in ibid, p. 10.

15. "Estudio de Banamex: El Petróleo, recurso clave de Mexico," Uno mas Uno, May 12, 1978, p. 13.

16. "Segun Millán, de Consultores Internacionales, en 1981 la Economía Mexicana será una de las más dinámicas del mundo," Excelsior, February 5, 1981, p. 5-A.

17. "Conferencia de prensa con corresponsales extranjeros," Mexico, D.F., June 29, 1977," Cuadernos de Filosofía Política No. 3, op. cit., p. 24.

18. "Nueva estrategia para generar divisas: el Petróleo a segundo plano," Excelsior, March 14, 1979, p. 1.

19. "Hidrocarburos, Motor y Soporte del País; no petrolizan la economía; JDS," Excelsior, August 24, 1980, pp. 1 & 14-A.

20. Jean-Marc Kalfleche, Le Figaro, Paris, November 14, 1977, in "Nueva Saudiarabia, sin invertir mucho: Le Figaro," Excelsior, November 15, 1977, p. 1.

21. Frank Niering, Jr., The Petroleum Economist, in Carlos A. Mutto, "Mexico, el acontecimiento estimulante desde el embargo de 1973: The Petroleum Economist," Excelsior, April 3, 1979.

22. Among the publications: the conservative U.S. News and World Report, and the liberal New Times, see "El Petroleo hara a Mexico mas rico y estable," Excelsior, June 29, 1979, pp. 1 & 27.

23. Redvers Opie, "The Mexican Economic System," prepared statement for Recent Developments in Mexico and Their Economic Implications for the United States, Hearings before the Subcommittee on Inter-American Economic Relationships, of the Joint Economic Committee, Congress of the United States, Ninety-fifth Congress, January 17 & 24, 1977, U.S. Government Printing Office, Washington, 1977, pp. 35-37.

24. Ibid.

25. Rodolfo Stavenhagen, "Los Mitos del Momento," Uno mas Uno, February 11, 1978, p. 3.

26. Ibid.

27. Antonio Yunez Naude, "Política Petrolera y Perspectivas de desarrollo de la economía mexicana. Un ensayo exploratorio," in Las Perspectivas del Petróleo Mexicano, (Mexico: El Colegio de Mexico, CEI, 1979), p. 217.

28. Fernando Carmona, et al., El Milagro Mexicano, (Mexico: Editorial Nuestro Tiempo, S.A., 1970).

29. Enrique Padilla Aragon, Mexico: Desarrollo con Pobreza, (Mexico: Siglo XXI Editores, 1979), p. 56.

30. Ibid., p. 57.

31. Ibid., pp. 66-84.

32. Ibid., p. 85.

33. Ibid., pp. 99-105.

34. Roger D. Hansen, La Política del Desarrollo Mexicano, (Mexico: Siglo XXI, 1979), pp. 74-75.

35. "Cuestiona la inflación el progreso de Mexico, dice Washington," Excelsior, July 17, 1980, p. 26-A.

36. "Inflación, Costo de la Consolidación del Progreso: JLP," Excelsior, June 26, 1980, p. 1.

37. Alvin Kaufman, Gary J. Pagliano, and Susan J. Bodilly, "Mexico's Economic Problems and the Energy Plan," in Mexico's Oil and Gas Policy: An Analysis. Report prepared for the Committee on Foreign Relations of the U.S. Senate, and Joint Economic Committee of the U.S. Congress, 95th Congress, December, 1978, U.S. Government Printing Office, Washington, 1979, p. 35.

38. Hansen, op. cit., pp. 80-82.

39. Opie, op. cit., p. 24.

40. Mexico 1980, Compendio de Datos y Estadísticas de Mexico, Camara Nacional de Comercio de la Ciudad de Mexico, September, 1980, p. 94.

41. "Creció 34% la exportación por el petróleo, en 9 años; la agropecuaria, 23% menos," Excelsior, July 9, 1980, p. 1.

42. "Se cosecha en 1980 lo mismo que hace 15 años, señala el coordinador del SAM," Excelsior, July 5, 1980, p. 5-A.

43. "Al Campo se le regatean inversiones," El Heraldo, August 12, 1980, p. 1.

44. "Es inseguro el futuro alimentario de Mexico," Excelsior, August 10, 1980, p. 1.

45. "Empresas Mexicanas y Foráneas especulan con alimentos," Excelsior, August 20, 1980, p. 1., and "Propicia creciente irrupción externa la Reforma Agraria," Excelsior, May 7, 1979. p. 1.

46. "Por el desplome agrícola de 1979, en 1980 se hicieron las mayores importaciones de alimentos de la historia," Uno mas Uno, June 1, 1981, p. 17.

47. "Escasean los granos; lento paso de importaciones," Proceso, July 28, 1980, pp. 23-24.

48. "Deficit de 180 millones de dólares en la balanza comercial agropecuaria en 1980 por baja producción," Uno mas Uno, January 23, 1981, p. 12.

49. "Pese al aumento de la producción, Mexico seguirá importando cantidades significativas de granos," Uno mas Uno, January 5, 1981.

50. "El Petróleo no basta; sin alimentos, desarrollo a medias: JLP," Excelsior, October 26, 1978, p. 1.

51. "El SAM, esfuerzo totalizador," Uno mas Uno, August 6, 1980, p. 1.

52. "Oteyza: las petrodivisas, para alimentos," *Uno mas Uno*, December 10, 1980, p. 1.

53. V Informe de gobierno, *El Universal*, September 2, 1981, pp. 23 & 25. Also, Alan Riding, "Alarmed Mexicans Are Spending Heavily to Become Self-sufficient in Food," *The New York Times*, November 6, 1981, p. 6.

54. *Ibid*.

55. Raul Olmedo, "La Autosuficiencia es solo un medio," *Excelsior*, August 18, 1980, p. 4-A.

56. Raul Olmedo, "Ni producción ni demanda," *Excelsior*, June 30, 1980, p. 4-A.

57. "Desigualdad brutal en el Agro, no barbarie," *Excelsior*, November 29, 1980, p. 1.

58. "Limitado e incongruente, el PGD no alcanzará sus metas," *Proceso*, June 16, 1980, pp. 20-21.

59. V Informe de Gobierno, *op. cit.*, pp. 22 & 25. Victor L. Urquidi, "Not by Oil Alone: The Outlook For Mexico", *Current History*, Vol. 81, No. 472, February, 1982, p. 78.

60. Urquidi, *op. cit.*, p. 81. Alan Riding, "Mexican TV Preaches Birth Control", *The New York Times*, January 5, 1982.

61. Kaufman, *op. cit.*, pp. 36-37.

62. Alan Riding, "Mexico grapples with its oil bonanza," *The New York Times*, May 7, 1978, p. F-3.

63. "En dos años, deberán crearse 2,200,000 empleos o se frustará el PGD: SPP," *Excelsior*, December 8, 1980, p. 5-A.

64. Alan Riding, "Mexico's President at Midterm: Oil on Troubled Waters," *The New York Times*, December 12, 1979.

65. V Informe de Gobierno, *op. cit.*, pp. 22-23.

66. Luis de Cervantes, "Creará empleos el petróleo, no sustituirá los préstamos," *Excelsior*, September 28, 1978, p. 1.

67. See, for example, Heberto Castillo, "Mexico desmexicanizado," *Proceso*, August 25, 1980, p. 31, and "Mexico en el filo de la navaja," *Proceso*, November 10, 1980, p. 32.

68. "En 1980 las importaciones superarán en 7 mil millones de dólares los ingresos petroleros," *Uno mas Uno*, January 13, 1981, p. 2.

69. "Pagó Mexico 2 mil 88.4 millones de dólares de su deuda externa durante el segundo trimestre," *Uno mas Uno*, November 5, 1980, p. 3.

70. "Presupuesto de Egresos de la Federación para 1982," Secretaría de Programación y Presupuesto. Alan Riding, "Mexico's Road to Trouble is Coated With Oil," *The New York Times*, February 21, 1982.

71. Lawrence Rout, "Southern Storm: Mexico Weathers Float of Peso, but Problems Persist," *The Wall Street Journal*, March 19, 1982, p. 18.

168

72. V Informe de Gobierno, op. cit., p. 22.
73. "Mexico's Road to Trouble is Coated With Oil,"
op. cit. "Southern Storm: Mexico Weathers Float of Peso,
but Problems Persist." op. cit.
74. "Mexico Tries to Bolster Flagging Peso," The
Wall Street Journal, July 2, 1981, p. 25.
75. "Mexico: Economic Outlook After Currency
Devaluation," Latin American Index, Vol. X, No. 4. March
1, 1982, p. 15.
76. Alan Riding, "Mexico Devalues Peso 30%," The
New York Times, February 19, 1981, p.29.
77. V Informe de Gobierno, op. cit., p. 25.
78. "Mexico's Petroleum Hangover," Time, March 29,
1982, p. 50.
79. "Mexico: Economic Outlook After Currency
Devaluation," op. cit.
80. "Mexico Devalues Peso 30%," op. cit.
81. "Southern Storm: Mexico Weathers Float of
Peso, but Problems Persist," op. cit.
82. "Stabilizing Moves Set by Mexico," The New York
Times, February 22, 1982.
83. "En un año creció 230% el déficit de pagos con
E.U.," Uno mas Uno, June 8, 1981. Special Supplement,
pp. 1 & 6.
84. Ibid., Also, "La Inversión Extranjera se
duplicó el año pasado," Uno mas Uno, January 14, 1981.
85. Bo Anderson and James D. Cockcroft, "Control
and Co-optation in Mexican Politics," in James Cockcroft,
Andre Gunder Frank, and Dale L. Johnson, Dependence and
Underdevelopment: Latin America's Political Economy
(Garden City, New York: Doubleday, 1972), pp. 221-225.
86. Plan Global de Desarrollo, 1980-1982, op. cit.,
p. 23.
87. V Informe de Gobierno, op. cit., p. 22
88. Raymond Vernon, The Dilemma of Mexico's Development, (Cambridge, Mass: Harvard University Press,
1965), p. 23.
89. Opie, op. cit., pp. 22-23.
90. V Informe de Gobierno, op. cit., p. 23.
91. E.V.K. Fitzgerald, "The Fiscal Deficit and
Development Finance: A Note on the Accumulation Balance
in Mexico," Working Paper No. 35, Centre of Latin
American Studies, University of Cambridge, London, p. 17.
92. "Superavit Comercial de $2,032 millones
registró el Sector Público," Excelsior, July 21, 1980,
p. 28-A.
93. "El Estado rige la economía en Mexico," Excelsior, July 28, 1980, p. 26-A.
94. Marcos Kaplan, "Petróleo y Desarrollo: el
impacto interno," Foro Internacional, El Colegio de
Mexico, Vol. XXI, No. 1, July-September, 1980, p. 91.

95. Antonio Yunez Naude, "Política Petrolera y perspectivas de desarrollo de la economía mexicana," op. cit., p. 216.

96. Ibid., pp. 224-230.

97. V Informe de Gobierno, op. cit., p. 25.

98. Alan Riding, "Mexico's Alfa Tightens Belt," The New York Times, October 21, 1981, pp. 33 & 36.

99. Roger Bartra, "La República Fantasma," Uno mas Uno, January 23, 1981, p. 2.

100. In this context, see Edward J. Williams, Petroleum and Political Change in Mexico, Paper prepared for delivery at a Symposium on Mexican Politics, Harvard University, April, 1980, p. 2.

101. Richard B. Mancke, Mexican Oil and Natural Gas: Political, Strategic and Economic Implications (New York: Praeger Publishers, 1979), p. 112.

102. Ibid.

103. See Luis Angeles, "La Burguesía Necesaria," Uno mas Uno, December 9, 1980, p. 13.

104. Juan Antonio Zuñiga, "Fusión de banca e industria. Apoyados por el Estado, los empresarios concentran el poder económico," Proceso, No. 197, August 11, 1980, pp. 8-11.

105. Jose Carreño Canlon, "El Complejo burocrático-empresarial," Uno mas Uno, February 6, 1981, p. 9.

106. Cited in "El Grupo Monterrey en la élite del dinero mundial," Proceso, Año 4, No. 199, August 25, 1980, pp. 6-7. Also, Riding, "Mexico's Alfa Tightens Belt," op. cit.

107. Jorge I. Domínguez, "The Implications of Mexico's Internal Affairs for its International Relations," Centre for International Affairs, Harvard University, April, 1980, pp. 51-53.

108. Mancke, op. cit., pp. 113 & 114.

109. See "Pemex no acepto contratos de riesgo propuestos por consorcios privados," Uno mas Uno, December 8, 1980, p. 12.

110. Riding, "Mexico's Alfa Tightens Belt," op. cit.

111. "La entrevista JLP-Reagan decepcionó a líderes de la oposición; la IP espera relajamiento de tensiones," Uno mas Uno, January 6, 1981, p. 6. Also, "Las diferencias políticas y económicas con E.U. se superarán con la administración de Reagan," Uno mas Uno, January 22, 1981, p. 14.

112. Statement of Al R. Wichtrich, President, American Chamber of Commerce of Mexico, in Recent Developments in Mexico and Their Economic Implications for the United States, op. cit., p. 61.

170

113. Ibid., pp. 57 & 60.
114. Ibid., p. 63.
115. Ibid., p. 81.
116. Ibid., p. 82.
117. Domínguez, op. cit., p. 50.
118. "Buscamos recuperar respeto y prestigio, sin imponernos: John Pluntket, Presidente de la CAMCO," Uno mas Uno, January 14, 1981.
119. "Las diferencias políticas y económicas con E.U. se superarán con la administración de Reagan," op. cit.
120. Cited in José Ricardo Eliaschev, "El Petróleo hará a Mexico más rico y estable," Excelsior, June 29, 1978, pp. 1 & 27.
121. See George W. Grayson, "Oil and Politics in Mexico," Current History, February, 1980, pp. 53-55. For a detailed analysis of the reforma política, see John Foster Leich," Reforma Política in Mexico," Current History, Vol. 80, No. 469, November, 1981, pp. 361-363.
122. Ibid., Also, Alan Riding, "In Mexico, the Left's Dream of Unity Lies Dead Amid Un-Marxist Dialectic," The New York Times, November 9, 1981, p. 8.
123. Ibid. Also, Lawrence Rout, "Mexico's Also-Rans Influence Policy", The Wall Street Journal, March 3, 1982.
124. "Política petrolera, opuesta a la que planteó Cárdenas: líderes de partidos," Uno mas Uno, March 18, p. 3.
125. Alan Riding, "Mexican Concerned that Reliance on Oil May Aggravate Ills," New York Times, December 31, 1978, p. 23.
126. For an analysis of this topic, see Edward J. Williams, "Petroleum Policy and Mexican Domestic Politics: Left Opposition, Regional Dissidence, and Official Apostasy," a paper presented at the annual meeting of the Southern Economic Association, Washington, D.C., November, 1978, pp. 3-7.
127. "Legisladores mexicanos reiteran que Mexico debe acentuar su derecho soberano sobre sus recursos," Uno mas Uno, January 5, 1981, p. 6.
128. "La entrevista JLP-Reagan decepcionó a líderes de la oposición; la IP espera relajamiento de tensiones," op. cit.
129. Riding, "In Mexico, the Left's Dream of Unity Lies Dead Amid Un-Marxist Dialectic," op. cit.
130. Domínguez, op. cit., p. 51.
131. See, for example, "Grupos campesinos bloquean en Chiapas instalaciones de Pemex," Uno mas Uno, January 19, 1981, p. 1.
132. See, for example, "Protección militar a instalaciones de Pemex; Pláticas con inconformes," Excelsior, January 19, 1981, p. 15.

133. Martin C. Needler, _Politics and Society in Mexico_ (Albuquerque: University of New Mexico Press, 1971), p. 72.

134. Cited in Fernando Meraz, "Eleva Mexico compras de armas," _Excelsior_, September 9, 1980, p. 1.

135. _Ibid._

136. "Mexico comprará aviones de combate y equipo blindado a E.U. e Israel: Galvan," _Uno mas Uno_, December 11, 1980, p. 7.

137. Sol W. Sanders, "Mensaje Militar Mexicano a Centroamerica," _Business Week_, appeared in _Contextos_, Secretaría de Programación y Presupuesto, Mexico, Año 2, No. 7, 19-25 February, 1981, p. 49.

138. "La Secretaría de la Defensa Nacional ejercerá este año un presupuesto de 25 mil 855 millones," _Uno mas Uno_, January 19, 1981, p. 7.

139. Rafael Segovia, "Tendencias Politicas en Mexico," in _Las Fronteras del Control del Estado Mexicano_, (Mexico: El Colegio de Mexico, 1976), p. 9.

140. "Destapado Miguel de la Madrid!", _Diario de la Tarde_, September 25, 1981, p. 1. "M. de la M., Político y Revolucionario: PRI," _Ultimas Noticias_, September 25, 1981, p. 1. And "Mexican President Nominates Friend to Succeed Him in '82," _St. Louis Post-Dispatch_, September 27, 1981, p. 10-A.

141. "Mexico's Party Leader Resigns Unexpectedly," _The New York Times_, October 16, 1981, p. 7.

142. Edward C. Williams, "Petroleum Policy and Mexican Domestic Politics," _op. cit._, pp. 13-14; and Mancke, _op. cit._, pp. 112.

143. Edward F. Wonder, "Mexico, Oil Supply, and the Western Alliance," International Energy Associates Limited, Washington, D.C. Presented at the Conference on Energy and the Atlantic Alliance, Committee on Atlantic Studies, Courmayeur, Italy, October 8-11, 1981, p. 7.

144. "Control de Energéticos, con una nueva Secretaría, propone el SME," _Excelsior_, August 24, 1980, p. 4-A. Also, "Límite y control a ventas de petróleo. No habrá Secretaría de Energéticos," _Uno mas Uno_, November 19, 1980, p. 1.

145. See Heberto Castillo, "Mexico en el filo de la navaja," _op. cit._, p. 31. Also, Manuel Buendía, "Fuera Antifaces," _Excelsior_, February 4, 1981, p. 1.

146. Heberto Castillo, "Todos contra los piratas yanquis," _Proceso_, No. 194, July 21, 1980, pp. 31-32.

147. "En dos semanas, el aumento a la gasolina: DS", _Uno mas Uno_, November 18, 1980, p. 1; and "No habrá alza a la gasolina popular ni al diesel: JLP," _Excelsior_, November 21, 1980, p. 1.

148. "Mantendrá el Estado su derecho a conducir la economía, afirmó DS," Excelsior, February 6, 1981, p. 1. Also, "Señales," Excelsior, February 3, 1981, pp. 1-A & 9-A.

149. "Producción Inalterable Pese a la Decisión de OPEP: Pemex," Excelsior, May 28, 1981, p. 1.

150. "Tenemos que Abaratar el Petróleo Para Conservar Clientes," Excelsior, June 2, 1981, p. 1. "Baja Pemex el Precio del Crudo de Exportación," Excelsior, June 4, 1981, pp. 1 & 11-A. And "Cuatro dólares por barril, la reducción al precio del crudo," Uno mas Uno, June 4, 1981, p. 1.

151. "Renunció Díaz Serrano; Moctezuma Cid, Director de Pemex," Excelsior, June 7, 1981, p. 1.

152. Ibid., Also, see, Hector Aguilar Camin, "La era de Díaz Serrano," Uno mas Uno, June 8, 1981, p. 3, and Carlos Ramírez, "Díaz Serrano cavó su tumba al convertir en mercancia un recurso nacional," Proceso, June, 1981.

153. See "Se negocia un Aumento; Cancelan 310,000 Barriles al día," Excelsior, June 27, 1981, p. 1. And "Pemex Eleva 2 Dls. sus Precios," Excelsior, July 1, 1981, pp. 1 & 16-A.

154. Mancke, op. cit., pp. 113.

155. "Mexico's Oil Bonanza," Newsweek, August 14, 1978, p. 43.

156. Edward C. Williams, The Rebirth of the Mexican Petroleum Company, op. cit., pp. 117-119.

157. Ofelia Navarro, "Pemex: Inversiones y Corrupción," Excelsior, January 26, 1978, p. 7.

158. Cited in "Mantener el monopolio de Pemex hara todo poderoso al sindicato pertolero, Excelsior, July 9, 1978, p. 1.

159. "Paro de gasolineras, si Pemex no suspende auditorias," Uno mas Uno, March 11, 1978, p. 13.

160. Mario Garcia Sordo, "Líderes corruptos impiden la independencia de la industria petrolera: H. Vázquez Gutiérrez," Uno mas Uno, March 18, 1978, p. 5. See also, "Intermediarios Mexicanos hacen negocio con exportaciones de petróleo, Proceso, Año 5, No. 244, July 6, 1981, pp. 13-14.

161. V Informe de Gobierno, op. cit., p. 21.

162. "Iniciativa de JLP: Hasta 6 Años de Cárcel a Prestanombres," Excelsior, November 30, 1980, p. 1.

163. Domínguez, op. cit., p. 66.

164. "Mexico to boost salaries," The Sun, Baltimore, March 21, 1982. "Mexicans Gloomy Over Peso," op. cit. "Mexico Devalues Peso 30%," op. cit. "Stabilizing Moves Set by Mexico," op. cit. "Alfa suspende trabajos en petroquímica, por incapacidad financiera," Proceso, December 28, 1981, pp. 12-14.

165. James W. Wilkie, "Mexico: Permanent 'Revolution,' Permanent 'Crisis'", Los Angeles Times, December 5, 1976, in Recent Developments in Mexico and Their Economic Implications for the United States, op. cit., pp. 11-12.

166. See, for example, John Huey, "No fiesta Ahead. Despite Rising Wealth in Oil, Mexico Battles Intractable Problems," The Wall Street Journal, August 30, 1978, pp. 1 & 26.

167. Roberto Peña Guerrero, "Crisis: reajuste, hegemonía y dependencia," Relaciones Internacionales, Vol. VI, April-June, 1978, No. 21, CRI, UNAM, Mexico, p. 69.

168. Kaufman, op. cit., p. 44.

169. Roberto Gutiérrez R., "La balanza petrolera de Mexico, 1970-1982," Comercio Exterior, Vol. 29, No. 8, Mexico, August, 1979, p. 839.

170. Abel Beltrán del Rio, "El Síndrome del Petróleo Mexicano: Primeros Síntomas, medidas preventivas y pronósticos," Comercio Exterior, Vol. 30, No. 6, Mexico, June, 1980, pp. 557 & 558.

171. Ibid., pp. 558-560.

172. Ibid., pp. 560-569.

173. "El Reto del Petróleo," Comercio Exterior, Vol. 29, No. 8, August, 1979, pp. 835-838.

174. Decreto por el que se aprueba el Programa de Energía y se ordena su ejecución, Diario Oficial, Mexico D.F., February 4, 1981.

175. Clemente Ruíz Durán, "La Petrolización de Mexico," Nexos, No. 37, January, 1981, Mexico, p. 18.

176. "La Política Petrolera está al margen de presiones; Oteyza," Uno mas Uno, September 8, 1980, p. 1.

177. René Delgado, "2 billones 332,724 millones será el presupuesto para 1981," Uno mas Uno, November 28, 1980.

178. "El 82% de las exportaciones de Mexico corresponderán a la venta de petróleo," Uno mas Uno, February 10, 1981, p. 13.

179. "El Desafío de la Producción," Uno mas Uno, December 11, 1980.

180. V Informe de Gobierno, op. cit., pp. 23-24.

181. "Las exportaciones Mexicanas no se basan solo en un producto, señala Panorama Económico de Bancomer," in El Petróleo Hoy, Uno mas Uno, March 18, 1981. (Supplement), p. 6.

182. Jaime Corredor, "El Petróleo en Mexico," in ibid., p. 16.

183. Alan Riding, "Mexico's Road to Trouble is Coated With Oil," op. cit.

174

184. See "Paró la Petrolización de la Economía," Excelsior, June 4, 1981, p. 1. Also, "La Disminución de Ventas de Crudo-Petrolización," Excelsior, July 5, 1981, p. 5-A.

185. Angel Mercado, "Petróleo: Los nuevos espacios regionales," Uno mas Uno, December 9, 1980, p. 14.

186. Leopoldo Allub and Marco A. Michel, Industria Petrolera y cambio regional en Tabasco, Centro de Investigación para la Integracion Social, Mexico, 1980, mimeographed.

187. Marco Antonio Michel and Leopoldo Allub, "Petróleo y Cambio Social en el Sureste de Mexico," Foro Internacional, Vol. XVIII, No. 4, April-June, 1978.

188. "Grupos campesinos bloquean en Chiapas instalaciones de Pemex," op. cit.

189. "Protección militar a instalaciones de Pemex; Platicas con inconformes," op. cit.

190. "Se compromete Pemex a indemnizar a campesinos," Uno mas Uno, January 21, 1981, p. 2. Also, "Pemex se Compromete con la CNC al Pago Inmediato de Indemnizaciones," Excelsior, May 28, 1981, pp. 1 & 14-A.

191. Cecilia Tormo, Tabasco y el Auge del Petróleo, mimeographed, p. 9.

192. Victor Manuel Lozano, in the Reunión Estatal Conmemorativa del 50 Aniversario del PRI, March 2, 1979, in ibid., pp. 10-11.

193. "Rechaza Pemex responsabilidad directa en la formación de cinturones de miseria donde opera," Uno mas Uno, September 30, 1980, p. 2.

194. "Crear Divisas, no atender problemas, papel de Pemex: JLP," Excelsior, July 30, 1978, p. 1.

195. "A base de siniestros descubren petróleo y gas," Proceso, No. 198, August 18, 1980, pp. 23-24.

196. "Daños irremisibles: Ecólogos del IPN," Excelsior, June 17, 1979, p. 1.

197. "Se han quemado 600 millones de pies cubicos de gas en el Giraldas," Excelsior, August 24, 1980, p. 1.

198. "Mexico, en peligro de convertirse en gran desierto. Mermada en 50% la riqueza natural del país," Excelsior, December 13, 1980, pp. 1 & 10.

199. "Reanuda operaciones la refineria de Salina Cruz; 200 millones en perdidas," Excelsior, July 24, 1980, p. 1. Also, Salina Cruz, Ahogado por el Crecimiento Petrolero," Excelsior, May 27, 1981, p. 5-A.

200. "Pemex anuncia el descontrol de un pozo de gas en Tamulipas," Excelsior, October 14, 1980, p. 5-A.

201. "Temen en Hidalgo danos economicos y ecológicos por la explotación del crudo," Uno mas Uno, July 30, 1980.

202. For example, see "8,142 millones invertirá Pemex en plantas anticontaminantes," Excelsior, June 22, 1978, pp. 11 & 14.

203. Rodolfo Stavenhagen, "Escenarios de prosperidad petrolera," Uno mas Uno, March 18, 1978, p. 3.

204. See "Riesgo de que el auge petrolero lisie la economía mexicana," Excelsior, July 30, 1980, pp. 1 & 14-A. Also, "Irán y Mexico: historias que parecen converger," Proceso, Año 5, No. 211, November 17, 1980, pp. 17-18.

7
United States-Mexico Relations: Dimensions of the Debate

NATURE OF U.S.-MEXICAN RELATIONS

The "Special Relationship"

For some time now, both American and Mexican analysts have tended to approach the subject of relations between the United States and Mexico in the framework of what might be called a "special relationship." Regardless of periodic official disclaimers by both sides, the relationship between the two countries is indeed "special." Some key elements illustrate this fact. Mexico and the United States share an undefended 2,000-mile common border, through which people and goods have moved back and forth in an uninterrupted flux since the nineteenth century. The total value of trade between the two countries had risen to almost twenty-two billion dollars by 1980. The United States is Mexico's first commercial client, while Mexico is the third largest trading partner of the United States.[1] Additionally, a unique factor is the large and growing population of Mexican origin in the United States, which represents a permanent link that goes beyond the formal government relations. Mexico's petroleum boom is straining the scope of this traditional "special relationship."

David F. Rondfelt and Caesar D. Sereseres have defined the relationship between the United States and Mexico in regard to three concepts: interdependence, intermesticity, and the special reciprocal rights of bordering nations. The validity of the concept of interdependence can be ascertained by the close links between the two nations, both in societal and economic terms. In addition to trade, economic interdependence is underlined by the volume of U.S. investments in Mexico (about six billion dollars in 1980), exports of Mexican oil and gas to the United States, and purchases of American foodstuffs by Mexico. Intermesticity refers to the fact that, because of important, mutually shared problems, the usual distinction between the international and domestic sphere tends to wane. And, finally, these previous considerations add to the idea that neighboring nations have a right to a reciprocal special treatment.[2]

Rondfelt and Sereseres advance the proposition that these factors that tend to underscore a "special relationship" between the United States and Mexico, could likewise be applied to the relations between Canada and the United States. This initial conceptualization of two special bilateral relationships could very well be a stepping stone for a "trilateral" vision of North America, i.e. an interdependence between the United States, Mexico and Canada.[3]

If it is true that the United States and Mexico share many common problems derived at least partly from their "special relationship," such as unemployment, inflation, and environmental pollution, it is also a fact that their priorities are different. Calvin Pat Blair has referred to these differing perspectives in terms of a confrontation between a geriatric society, i.e. the United States, and a pediatric society, i.e. Mexico. The United States worries mainly about its access to energy sources and raw materials, and has to deal with an aging industrial base that renders it vulnerable to exports from foreign nations such as Japan, ready to encroach upon the U.S. domestic market. On the other hand, Mexico has an altogether different set of problems, such as a sharply unequal distribution of income, and must try to gain access to markets for its manufacturers, as well as for capital and technological imports, uphold the rights of its migrant workers, and diminish its dependence on oil exports. Furthermore, says Blair, whereas the United States lives in permanent fear of a radical leftist Mexico, the latter in turn dreads the possibility of U.S. policies such as stringent protectionist measures or an all out campaign to deport Mexican migrant workers.[4]

James W. Wilkie has summarized these conflicting national interests between the United States and Mexico in terms of a series of "dilemmas" facing both nations in their relations with each other. On the Mexican side, the structural dilemmas would be the following:

1. Mexico's national interest to encourage tourism vs. its national interest to develop industrialization.
2. Labor vs. capital intensive economic activity.
3. Need for U.S. investments vs. loans.
4. Need for diversified trading partners throughout the world, in order to achieve economic independence and protection against U.S. recessions vs. reliance on its northern

neighbor, especially during times of economic
crisis.
5. Need for urban food and export food vs. need
    to distribute land.
6. Need for an open U.S. border as an escape valve
    for excess labor vs. need to retain in Mexico
    the ambitious rural worker.

And, among the U.S. dilemmas:

1. U.S. national interest to have a cheap
    reserve labor pool vs. its national interest
    to close the frontier to "excessive" immigra-
    tion from Mexico.
2. Need to expand exports to Mexico vs. need to
    control imports from Mexico.
3. U.S. national interest to have a healthy,
    stable neighbor on its southern border vs.
    its national interest to keep Mexico
    politically and economically dependent upon
    the United States as it seeks to retain its
    role of world leader.[5]

In conclusion, Wilkie believes that "change within
and cooperation between Mexico and the United States
means that there are few 'solutions' to common problems."[6] Or, in other words, in what could be an unwill-
ing allusion to the impact of the oil boom in the relations between the two countries:

Historically, U.S.-Mexican relations have
involved the diplomatic resolution of common
border problems causing temporary tension
between the two countries, but with the advent
of the 1970's, new kinds of tensions that
reflect structural changes in the affairs of both
countries presage the rise of issues in the
1980's and 1990's that are not susceptible to
traditional diplomatic solutions that have
marked U.S.-Mexican relations in the past.[7]

There are at present varying opinions about the
special U.S.-Mexican relationship that reflect both an
acknowledgement of a de facto situation and an uneasiness
about it. On the whole, on the American side it is possible to appreciate a mixture of regard for Mexico's
needs, and an awareness of U.S. benefits from the relation. Mexican opinion, on the other hand, tends to be
qualified by apprehension about American intentions and
possible advantages.
    U.S. policies towards Mexico have often been
labelled by the latter as "inconsistent." In the view
of the U.S. Department of State these relations are,

rather, "very complicated."[8] Richard Nussio has pointed
at "bureaucratism" as one of the prevailing realities in
bilateral relations. There are, says Nussio, more than
200 U.S. government agencies participating in decisions
and matters pertaining to Mexico.[9]

Perhaps as a response to the increasingly complex
relations between the United States and Mexico, in
April 1979, the Carter administration decided to appoint
a special ambassador to Mexico, i.e. officially an
"Ambassador at large and U.S. Coordinator for Mexican
Affairs," directly dependent upon the President and the
Department of State. The new Ambassador, Robert Kruger,
was to assist the President and the Secretary of State
"in the development of effective national policies
towards Mexico and in the coordination and implementation of such policies." Likewise, Kruger was to serve
as chairman of a senior interagency group on U.S. policy
towards Mexico and as U.S. Executive Director for the
U.S.-Mexico consultative mechanisms. As coordinator,
Kruger was to be located in the Department of State,
while the director of the Office of Mexican Affairs in
the same department would serve as deputy coordinator.[10]

Carter's instructions on the subject of coordination of U.S. policy towards Mexico was delivered to his
entire cabinet, in an effort to assure the integration
of any overlapping entities into a coherent process of
policy development and formulation. The Presidential
Memorandum seemed to reflect an official awareness of the
"special relationship" with Mexico:

> In view of the increasing domestic and inter-
> national importance of our relations with
> Mexico, and of the intensity and complexity of
> those relations in the years ahead, I have
> decided to take steps to improve our ability
> to address effectively all issues which affect
> U.S. relations with Mexico....To ensure that
> all U.S. policies toward Mexico, and all actions
> directly or indirectly affecting Mexico, pro-
> mote basic U.S. national interests and are con-
> sistent with our overall policy toward Mexico,
> I ask: -that each of you accord a high priority
> to any and all matters within your jurisdiction
> affecting Mexico, consciously giving good rela-
> tions with Mexico a continuing high priority
> in your thinking and planning; and -that all
> proposed actions, which have an effect on Mexico,
> be carefully coordinated so as to be consistent
> with overall U.S. policy toward Mexico, and
> based on the fullest possible prior consultation
> with the Government of Mexico.[11]

A Mexican commentator, Joseph Hodara, viewed the designation of a "special ambassador" as a result of the strengths and weaknesses of Mexico's oil boom. The fact that Mexican affairs had been translated directly to the White House "reflected the strategic importance accorded by Washington to Mexico at present," since such consulting and decision mechanisms had been previously established only in the realm of detente and Middle East affairs.12

However, the appointment of an additional ambassador, albeit "at large," which in fact meant a duplication of some of the functions of the regular U.S. Ambassador in Mexico City, seemed to contribute to a situation of confusion and hesitation. Mexican government officials did not know precisely with whom to deal in the various areas of bilateral relations. By early 1981, the Reagan administration, congruent with its goal of streamlining policy making and eliminating excessive bureaucratization, initiated the dismantlement of this special agency. However, Reagan emphasized the importance he placed on the relationship with Mexico by meeting with López Portillo in Ciudad Juárez, in January 1981, breaking his previous promise not to confer with any foreign leaders before he assumed the presidency. The visit underscored the strategic and economic position of Mexico as the cornerstone of U.S. foreign policy towards Latin America. Additionally, Reagan stated that he personally would handle relations with Mexico, without need of any intermediaries.13

The views of other American officials and scholars have tended to reaffirm the existence of a "special relationship" with Mexico. For example, in 1978 former U.S. Ambassador to Mexico, Patrick Lucey, caused a stir by declaring that "there are not two nations on earth whose present and future are as closely intertwined as Mexico and the Unites States."14 James W. Wilkie has qualified the U.S. relationship with Latin America as a whole as "overdrawn and overdone," while affirming that this is altogether different in the case of Mexico, where the United States indeed has a special relation with its southern neighbor. In this context, says Wilkie, "...it is in the United States' best interest to make it easy for Mexico to solve its own problems."15 Edward H. Williams, David F. Rondfelt and Caesar D. Sereseres advance the opinion that, while there are particular obligations that fall on the United States, as a result of its "special relationship" with Mexico, such as a greater understanding and sharing of the problem of migrant workers, there has to be also a degree of Mexican reciprocity, in regards to supplying petroleum and gas to the United States.16 An official analysis for the U.S. Senate concludes that

Although some feel that the concept of "special relationships" is theoretically outmoded in this day of "global" perceptions of U.S. foreign policy, it remains a prominent concept to be considered in understanding United States-Mexican relations. The concept of "special relationship," in fact, could very well reach new prominence and importance under the new dimension of Mexican energy.[17]

Mexican official reaction tends to be one of suspicion towards the concept of a "special relationship." According to Rondfelt and Sereseres, the necessary incentives are not present for both countries to embark upon a new special framework for bilateral cooperation, and rather than upholding special bilateral guidelines. Mexico would seem to prefer to deal with the United States on the basis of legally accepted international principles and a multilateral framework of discussions.[18] This view would seem to reflect, not an open hostility to the idea of a "special relationship," but a disenchantment with it. Mexican Secretary of Foreign Relations, Jorge Castañeda, before his appointment and acting at the time as Ambassador at Large, declared in late 1978 that, as a whole, Mexico did not believe any longer that "there exists or can exist a special relationship with the United States." Castañeda's comment was inscribed within a general framework of Mexican official opinion that, as long as the United States proceeds to act unilaterally in areas such as trade and migration, a policy of "special relationship" is merely rhetoric.[19]

The concept of a "special relationship" is based to a significant degree on the existence of an economic interpenetration between the two countries. Hodara sees two possible results of a growing interdependence between the United States and Mexico, in the context of the latter's oil boom. A first scenario would have petroleum enhance the mutual benefits accruing from interdependence, thus contributing to solve accidental differences of opinion in regards to matters such as trade and fishing rights; beneath a facade of diplomatic rhetoric designed for public consumption, both nations would encourage more extensive commercial ties. A second scenario, however, would be qualified by an asymmetrical interdependence, which would lead to an irreversible Mexican subordination.[20]

Some Mexican analysts tend to visualize the second scenario. Carlos F. Rico plainly considers interdependence as a mechanism that reinforces U.S. hegemony and responds to the logic of its foreign policy objectives. A key objective here would be to transform Mexico into a trustworthy and influential partner of the United States in North-South negotiations.[21] Heberto Castillo contemplates a conspiracy by the Mexican government, which would be placing pro-United States and business officials in central administration posts and along the Mexican states bordering on the United States, in order to "create a border transition zone towards the eventual installation of an associate state."[22]

Olga Pellicer believes that the idea of a "special relationship," while not offering concrete solution to bilateral problems, has served to legitimize close links between the two nations.[23] By late 1978, Pellicer could discern an effort by American diplomats to reach an understanding with Mexico, under the slogan of interdependence, which would in reality strive to further U.S. priorities such as a steady supply of Mexican oil and gas. According to Pellicer, various political groups in the United States would be pressuring in favor of an "extraspecial relation" with Mexico, geared to propitiate the rapid exploitation of petroleum and its commercialization toward the United States.[24] In this context, adds Richard Fagen.

> The importance of Mexican petroleum at present... is not a simple function of its percentage contribution to world exports, but rather a very complex function related to Mexico's role as an exporter in rapid expansion which, at the same time, shares very close geographic, political, and economic ties with the biggest petroleum consumer in the world.[25]

By June 1980, the Mexican Secretary of Foreign Affairs, Jorge Castañeda, was emphasizing that Mexico does not wish a special treatment from the United States but, rather, "...a relation based on mutual benefit, taking into account the relative degree of economic development of both countries."[26]

Perhaps it would be pertinent, in order to clarify Castaneda's statement, to inscribe it within a conceptual framework developed by Victor S. D'Souza. D'Souza distinguishes between three types of international relations: domination, interdependence, and common interest. In the first type, the principal means to carry out policies on the part of the more powerful nation would be to threaten the weaker country. In regard to interdependent relationships, the powerful nation would offer help to solve a particular problem of the weak country, inasmuch as it affects the interests of the former. And, in relations based on common interests, the objective would be to pay attention to the basic problems of the weak county, among which the particular problems affecting the powerful nation would be only aspects of the overall framework. In this last type of relationship the developed nation would leave aside its role as a "powerful nation," and behave instead as a "worried partner.[27]

D'Souza's classification would seem to cover quite appropriately the attitudinal spectrum in U.S.-Mexican relations. While the Mexican position tends to react against domination and suspect interdependence, it does seem to coincide strikingly with the basis of a "common interest" relationship.

Linkages

The concept of a "special relationship" between the United States and Mexico is intimately tied to the global nature of their relations. Even though petroleum permeates the entirety of the complex amalgam of U.S.-Mexican relations, it is but one of many issues, such as migrant workers, trade, and environmental degradation. In the past, the Mexican government has preferred to deal with all these problems in terms of a linkage, viewing them as a whole, while the United States would rather treat them individually.

Petroleum may be changing the U.S. perception towards the concept of "linkage." For example, in March 1979, a joint commission in Congress asked the federal government to take into account, together with the issue of imports of Mexican oil and gas, the problems of bilateral commerce and migration, "in the context of a spirit of comprehension and cooperation between the two nations."[28] Calvin Blair has stressed that the various topics in the agenda of U.S.-Mexican relations must be, by necessity, considered as a package, which would tie the key themes and allow both coutries to obtain advantages in economic agreements. Mexico will insist, say, Blair, on tying petroleum matters, so important to the United States, to those which are important to Mexico, such as Mexican manufactured exports, access to American technology, and the treatment of Mexican migrant workers.[29]

The offical Mexican position towards linkage is especially relevant in regard to the theme of migrant workers. Early in his administration, President Lopez Portillo stressed that migratory policies should address the causes, and not just the effects, of the problem. That is, to the extent that Mexico achieves an economic equilibrium, it will be able to generate more employment opportunities. But the situation is connected with the economic relations and commercial exchanges with the United States. In this context, the Mexican president has emphasized that, in the short run, the U.S. government should relax its migratory laws in order not to aggravate domestic problems in Mexico. In the long run, however, it is necessary to solve the disparities in the balance of trade between Mexico and the United States, as a means to foster employment creation in Mexico.[30]

For its part, the Reagan administration has proposed a number of initiatives to deal with migration into the United States, which would include: a strengthening of enforcement of existing legal authorities; a prohibition on hiring illegal aliens; the establishment of an experimental temporary worker program for Mexican nationals, under which, during a two-year trial period, up to 50,000 workers would be admitted annually for stays of nine to twelve months; granting limited legal status to illegal aliens present in the United States prior to January 1, 1980; and cooperating with Mexico in regulating immigration of third-country nationals and smuggling practices through the border area. Additionally, in January 1982, the Reagan administration proposed doubling to 40,000 a year each the number of legal immigrants to the United States from Mexico and Canada, as a means to improve relations with neighboring countries. However, during that same month, a Mexico-U.S. immigration policy dispute had developed in regard to the "Silva letter," a temporary permit to remain in the United States held by approximately 150,000 Mexican workers, and which according to an announcement by the Department of State, was to be revoked in some cases.[31]

According to Mexico's view, the situation of migrant workers is closely tied to the issue of trade. For example, reaffirming a crucial "linkage" between trade and oil sales, the Mexican Secretary of Foreign Relations declared in June 1980:

>...would it not be useful for those who influence
>on the definition of policies in the United States
>to begin to consider the relation that exists
>between Mexico's economic development, sales of
>crude oil and gas to the United States, and the
>growing need we have of access to that nation's
>market on a less restrictive basis, so as to export
>the production from that industrial infrastructure
>that we are creating.[32]

From this perspective, Mexico maintains that lesser trade restrictions on the part of the United States would contribute to Mexican development and employment creation, and would slow down illegal migration to the United States. Thus, from the Mexican viewpoint, trade would seem to be the cornerstone of the global nature of U.S.-Mexican relations. As López Portillo declared early in his administration:

>...We are extremely concerned that Mexican exports
>are confronted by a large number of restrictions
>applied by our northern neighbor. We think the

trade problem should be viewed in its entirety,, in terms of its impact not on individual interests but on the U.S.-Mexican relationship as a whole.[33]

One of the most important recent trade issues for Mexico has been the debate over membership in the General Agreement on Tariffs and Trade (GATT). President López Portillo has defined Mexico's potential entrance to GATT as basically a "substantial modality of commerce with the United States, since 70 percent of our foreign commerce is with that nation."[34] In other words, the liberalization of trade barriers would take effect mainly vis a vis the United States. In March 1980, when the Mexican government decided not to join GATT, the official reaction from the United States was one of the disenchantment, not to say anger. Robert Kruger, at the time Special Coordinator for Mexican Affairs, described U.S.-Mexican commercial relations as in a state of uncertainty. Kruger emphasized that trade between the two nations, which in 1979 had reached the record level of 18.7 billion dollars an increase of 46 percent in a year, would expand at a slower pace. The United States, said Kruger, was anxiously looking forward to Mexican proposals regarding bilateral commercial relations, but negotiations to that end would be prolonged.[35]

The reasons behind Mexico's refusal to enter GATT were closely tied to its petroleum exports. On the one hand, given the recent decline in Mexico's non-oil exports, membership in GATT might have hurt Mexico's protected domestic industry. Petroleum also has given Mexico's political leadership the necessary self-confidence to try to pursue trade advantages without affiliating to GATT. Furthermore, the decision was also meant to be for domestic consumption, quieting a considerable nationalistic uproar.[36] But there was another important consideration. Mainly because of the availability of oil, Mexico would not be accorded guarantees within GATT pertaining to less developed countries. In other words, "it is not feasible to obtain a preferential and differentiated treatment (for Mexico) within GATT."[37] Thus, the likelihood of a disruption of the Mexican economy, at least in terms of increased dependence on the United States, seemed to loom large in the minds of Mexico's political decision makers.

In regard to trade, President López Portillo has emphasized that Mexico is pursuing "global agreements of bilateral cooperation," i.e. bilateral arrangements that encompass various issues.[38] It seems likely that for the near future Mexico will refrain from joining multilateral trade accords such as GATT, concentrating instead on bilateral trade packages. However, although Mexico refused to enter GATT, in 1980 it lowered tariffs and imports permits in all activities in which domestic supply was deemed to be insufficient.39

The commercialization of natural gas clearly illustrates the volatility of U.S.-Mexican relations, in the framework of the petroleum boom. As PEMEX increased its activities in Mexico's southeast, there were growing volumes of available natural gas that could not be used domestically. By mid-1977, PEMEX signed a letter of intent to sell the gas to six U.S. private distributor companies, at a price of $2.60 per thousand cubic feet (MCF). The means to transport the gas to the United States was to be a gasduct, from Cactus, Chiapas, to Reynosa, Texas, which began to be built in October 1977. There were compelling economic arguments in favor of the pipeline. In short, the cost for the project was estimated to be 1.5 billion dollars, and the construction time twenty-four months; at the outset, the pipeline would represent earnings in foreign exchange at the rate of 3.3 million dollars a day. However, as the duct neared completion, the U.S. government, acting on the specific recommendations of Secretary of Energy James Schlesinger, refused to allow the companies to buy the gas at the price they had previously agreed with Mexico. The argument of the Department of Energy centered on the fact that the United States could not pay Mexico forty-four cents more than Canada for an MCF. Also, there were fears that Congress would not approve the $2.60 price tag, while American gas producers were only paid up to a ceiling of $1.75, according to Carter's energy bill.40

Reaction in both sides of the border was swift, and seemed to coincide in deploring the failure of the deal, with its subsequent detrimental repercussions on U.S.-Mexican relations. In the United States, The Wall Street Journal, among other major newspapers, harshly criticized the lack of a more enlightened approach to the problem on the part of U.S. government authorities.[41] Mexican reaction was twofold. On the one hand, the Mexican government proceeded to redirect the pipeline to distribute and use the gas domestically. On the other, Mexican officials took advantage of every opportunity to denounce the lack of frankness and finesse manifest in U.S. actions concerning the deal. The gas fiasco was the main factor that darkened the talks between López Portillo and Carter in Mexico in February 1979. During Carter's visit, López Portillo lectured the American president on what he saw as a U.S. practice of treating Mexico with a "mixture of interest, disdain, and fear," and added:

> Among permanent, not casual neighbors, surprise moves and sudden deceit or abuse are poisonous fruits that sooner or later have a reverse effect. No injustice can prevail without affronting decency and dignity.42

In June 1980, the Mexican president still remembered vividly the gasduct fiasco. At that time, López Portillo expressed his opinion that "the ties between Mexico and the United States have deteriorated lately, with respect to what they were in 1977." And, again, he recalled how his good faith had been betrayed by the U.S. government when it cancelled abruptly the deal between PEMEX and the American gas companies.[43]

After protracted, off-and-on negotiations, which in all amounted to seven rounds of talks, on September 21, 1979, the two governments issued a joint announcement to the effect that an understanding had finally been reached. The agreement called for the sale of 300 million cubic feet per day of natural gas by PEMEX to U.S. purchasers, starting as of January 1980, at an initial price of $3.625 per million btu, subject to reconsideration if the price for natural gas from comparable sources were to exceed that amount prior to the starting date.[44] By November 1979, the Department of Energy received an application to import Mexican natural gas by the consortium Border Gas, Inc., made up of six U.S. energy companies,[45] and gave it final clearance by late December 1979, after an order issued by the department's Economic Regulatory Administration (ERA), which was responsible for approving imports and exports of natural gas.[46] DOE officials stated that "these approvals (were) a further step in establishing closer relations between the U.S. and Mexico,"[47] a doubtful proposition considering the bitterness of the preceding exchanges.

A case with serious environmental consequences also affected U.S.-Mexican relations. From June 1979 to March 24, 1980, when it was finally capped, the Mexican oil well Ixtoc I blew out and spilled millions of barrels of oil into the waters of Campeche Bay in the Gulf of Mexico. Eventually, ocean currents carried the oil to the Texas coast, affecting close to 200 miles of beaches. This environmental disaster affected the relations between the two countries, and resulted in damages to sea life, beaches, tourism, and property in still unknown proportions.[48]

The Ixtoc I disaster gave rise to a series of public accusations and discussions between the two governments in regards to delineating responsibilities. By February 1981, the U.S. government was trying to determine the effect on its relations with Mexico of a possible lawsuit against PEMEX for the damages caused in 1979 as a result of the Ixtoc I oil spills. Lawsuits were filed by the U.S. federal government, the government of Texas, and private concerns against PEMEX and the firm Permargo, a subcontractor in charge of drilling the well when the disaster took place. However, a direct suit against PEMEX would involve the Mexican government itself, with the possibility that general relations between the two countries would deteriorate.[49]

In Mexico the Ixtoc I case aroused nationalistic
sensibilities. Following his trip to Washington late
in September 1979, President López Portillo declared
that Mexico rejected liability damages, and compared the
issue to that of the salinity of the Mexicali Valley in
northwestern Mexico, where the United States has never
paid for damage to Mexican agriculture from the high
salt content of the waters of the Colorado River.
Although Ixtoc I was a serious foreign policy issue for
both countries, the fact that other issues of greater
importance might suffer, i.e. the question of linkage,
has contributed to keep the problem from going beyond
certain limits of diplomatic propriety.50

From the preceding discussion, it would appear that
a mutually binding package which takes into account the
overall set of issues between the two countries is
perhaps rather unfeasible. Both governments would ultimately be opposed to such an agreement, albeit from a
different rationale. The United States remains committed
to global policies and multilateral accords, and the
American political system itself is not conducive to
"package" deals, due to the multiplicity of government
agencies and lobbying interests operating in the context
of U.S.-Mexican relations.51 From the Mexican perspective, nationalism and the ever present theme of increased
dependence on the United States constitute a formidable
opposition to a permanent "package" arrangement. However,
the interrelationship between numerous issues also underlines the fallacy of trying to approach them on an
individual basis. In this respect, Alfred Stepan has
advanced the need for a "more integrated bargaining
framework:"

> ...a bargaining framework that recognizes the
> complete range of issues at stake, and one in
> which the United States, precisely in order to
> advance its overall interests, would aggres-
> sively seek out new formulas for responding to
> Mexico's special needs, especially in the areas
> of migration and trade.52

A North American Common Market?

For some time now, various public and private
sources in the United States have seemed to advocate as
a logical extension of that nation's "special relationship" with Mexico and Canada, a North American Common
Market. For example, Redvers Opie has developed this
point, in terms of a "geographical division of labor:"

> Canada, the United States, and Mexico are in many
> respects complementary rather than competing
> economies; and perhaps especially Mexico and

the United States are complementary. These two
countries have a mutuality of interest in protecting harmonious development together.[53]

Clark Reynolds, in a somewhat deterministic assessment of the situation, advances the idea that there is
a "silent economic integration" between the United
States, Mexico, and Canada. This process could be
furthered, says Reynolds, by formalizing closer economic
links through mutual safeguards in regards to labor
migration, and the establishment of standing commissions
to deal with the ample spectrum of problems likely to
arise between neighbors.[54] Reynolds suggests, in order
to promote the idea of a common economic region, that the
United States should act as a partner, rather than as
an overwhelming leader:

> I feel that the United States would be well
> advised to reconsider the possibility of
> regarding the entire North American Continent
> as an economic region in which it is one
> important participant and in which it can play
> an increasingly relative role rather than an
> absolute or dominant role.[55]

Specifically in regard to energy, in a 1979 study
called "A Proposal for a Common Market Between Canada,
Mexico and the United States," Kenneth E. Hill talks in
terms of a crucial need for the United States to foster,
within a maximum time lapse of ten years, a trinational
alliance between these countries with the objective of
solving U.S. energy needs. Among the mutual benefits of
such an alliance, says Hill, there would be U.S. guarantees to buy Mexican and Canadian fuels and stabilize
prices, and to purchase agricultural and manufactured
products from Mexico, free of trading restrictions, as
well as a solution to the problem of Mexican migrant
workers, through an elimination of some of the present
migratory barriers. The Mexican and Canadian currencies
would continue to be tied to the fluctuations of the
dollar. Furthermore, the United States would guarantee
the military security of this economic community which
would extend its operations into the Caribbean.[56]
From the American perspective, there would seem to
be sound economic incentives for such a common market.
By mid-1980, U.S. business circles acknowledged that,
while a broad trade alliance among the United States,
Canada, and Mexico was not likely yet, pacts for specific
industrial sectors might be possible. One candidate for
agreement would be petrochemicals, and the effects would
be profound.[57] By August 1980, in a series of meetings
of policy committees of the U.S. Senate and the Working
Group of North American Commerce of the National

Association of U.S. governors, the need was stated for reciprocity on the part of Mexico and Canada, in regard to allowing the access of U.S. products to their domestic markets. The discussions, which included the participation of the president of the American Chamber of Commerce in Mexico, had as their main objective the delineation of strategies relative to the establishment of a North American Common Market.58

President Reagan has expressed his support for an integration of the economies of the three countries in terms of a North American Common Market. However, Mexico and Canada have both turned down the idea as a scheme that would be mostly favorable to the United States.59 In April 1979, Jesus Puente Leyva, President of the Energy Commission of the Mexican Congress, went public in denouncing the U.S. goal of interdependence, or North American Common Market, as contrary to Mexican interests.60 In mid-1980, during a visit to Canada, President López Portillo tried to put an end to speculations in Washington regarding a North American accord, by declaring that Mexican energy sources would not be used to maintain the high standards of living of other nations.61

From the Mexican perspective, progress on this issue seems to be precluded by the disparity in levels of development and income between the United States and Mexico, which would foreordain, apparently, American predominance over Mexico. The resulting asymmetrical relationship would lead to an institutionalization of dependency, through which the United States would gain access to Mexican energy sources and abundant cheap labor, while Mexico would be hindered in its efforts to promote exports and foster its domestic industry. Nationalism underscores the Mexican position in its objective of regulating foreign investments. This is especially true of the state-owned petroleum sector, in which direct foreign investment is prohibited altogether, while limited to 40 percent in certain firms within the secondary petrochemical industry.62 For example, back in October 1978, as a reply to the interest manifested by Exxon and Texaco to participate in the direct exploitation of Mexican hydrocarbon resources, PEMEX stated categorically that Mexico would not allow any such intervention by American oil companies.63

GEOPOLITICAL AND STRATEGIC CONSIDERATIONS

Mexico and the United States share the same geopolitical space, i.e. the Caribbean and Central American Basin. There are common, as well as contradicting, elements, values, and goals, in the Mexican and American approaches towards this vast area. The Mexican position

has been reinforced by its new status as an oil-rich
nation. Just as this latter fact has impelled the U.S.
government to seek closer relations with its southern
neighbor, Mexico has perceived, in its role as an oil
producing and exporting country, a propelling factor for
imprinting a new dynamism into its foreign policy. This
situation is shaping a scenario fertile for joint initiatives, but also fraught with potential conflict
between the two governments, in regards to a series of
security and strategic points of contention.

Security and Strategic Questions

In 1976, the Pentagon prepared a report on "Energy
Geopolitics, 1976-2000," which could be considered to be
one of the antecedents for present U.S. policies regarding the establishment of a close energy relation with
Mexico, Venezuela, and Canada. According to the document, the bases for this relationship were to be found
in the fact that the United States is the natural market
for oil exports from those countries, and the source of
financial and technological assistance. The authors of
the study, Melvin Conant and Fern R. Gold, believed that
Canada would accede to such an association rather willingly. However, Mexico and Venezuela posed a problem
derived from their nationalistic sensitivities. Thus,
the United States should act with caution in its
approaches to those governments, in order to avoid any
appearances of exploitation.[64]
Specifically in regards to Mexico, Conant and Gold
concluded that, politically, it would be the most difficult case. In order to appease Mexican opposition, a
"special treatment" should be developed, related not
only to energy issues, but also to other bilateral matters such as trade and investments. In this context,
access to energy resources would be determined by a complex assortment of geographic factors and governmental
policies, as well as by political and economic vari-
ants.[65]
By mid-1981, the Reagan administration was pursuing
the objective of an association with Mexico, Venezuela,
and Canada. Following an American initiative, the foreign ministers of the four nations met in Nassau, at the
Bahamas, to study the possibility of launching a joint
program of economic assistance for the countries of the
Caribbean and Central America.[66] Commenting on the
Nassau conference, President López Portillo praised the
efforts to achieve cooperation in fostering economic
development in the region, as long as the right of the
Central American and Caribbean countries was respected,
"to decide for themselves the forms of government and
social organization to which they aspire."[67]

In the present world energy context, the consolidation of a closer relationship between Mexico and the United States, from the perspective of the latter, is seen in terms of national security. In other words, Mexico represents a secure source of energy for the United States. According to Richard B. Mancke, two matters of consideration threaten the national security of the United States: the disparity in political and economic perspectives vis a vis a small group of countries, mainly located in the Middle East, that control most of the world's exportable oil; and the fact that this problem of distant sources is compounded by growing Soviet naval strength. Thus,

> Increased imports of crude oil and natural gas from Mexico's Reforma and Campeche fields would permit a political, economic, and geographical diversification that would, in part, alleviate these threats and enhance the energy security of the United States.[68]

Besides these security objectives, i.e. prevention of political threats and geographic diversification, Mancke has underlined the military-security benefits in case of conventional, limited, and undeclared naval wars, in which Mexican oil could become a life-saving link for the United States. As an energy source, Mexico would be relatively secure from terrorist activities, because of shorter transportation routes and the possibility of bilateral arrangements for the protection of Mexican oil fields.[69] In a late 1981 interview, asked about accessibility to Mexico's oil for the United States, in case of an international emergency such as a war in the Middle East, President López Portillo declared that it was not a matter of "conflict of interests but a convergence of purposes... We live in such proximity and interrelation that assuredly there would be an understanding..." Still, the Mexican president did not foresee such extreme cases for which there were no contingencies in Mexico's energy plans.[70]

Offficial awareness in the United States about the security implications of Mexican petroleum has been manifest in the last few years. Even in early 1979, in the midst of the controversy over the gas deal, President Carter recognized their strategic value on a long-term basis, especially in case of war.[71] By September 1980, the U.S. Secretary of the Treasury recommended to pay careful attention to bilateral relations with Mexico and Canada as a means to assure a future supply of oil and gas. The report concluded that "Mexico will probably be the primary source of petroleum and gas imports by the U.S. during the next decade."[72] In October of that same year, the American Ambassador to

Mexico, Julian Nava, openly described Mexico as a "key part of the U.S. security strategy."73

The Rand Corporation, in a late 1980 study titled "Mexican Petroleum and U.S. Policy: Implications for the 1980s," stressed the need for a greater emphasis on U.S.-Mexican interdependence, not only in regard to energy questions. According to the study, greater cooperation would be enhanced by a number of initiatives related to the field of energy, including:

1. A long-term energy agreement to insure continued exports to U.S. markets.
2. The establishment of an Energy Common Market, which would also include Canada.
3. Hemispheric coordination in the production of energy and commerce with these two nations plus Venezuela, and Caribbean and South American countries with refining capacity.74

The Rand Corporation has depicted two alternative policy concepts for future relations between the United States and Mexico. The first places emphasis on "internationalism," that is, Mexico would be treated much like any other developing country emerging as a "middlepower." The second underlines the concept of "community," in which Mexico would be viewed as a special partner in the long-range development of North America. According to Rand, the first approach assumes that Mexico's development would make it more independent than interdependent vis a vis the United States, and would result in restrictions to the process of integration of both economies and societies. This approach would be congruent with Mexico's desires to reaffirm its sovereignty and diversify its foreign relations and to conduct its dealings with the U.S. on the basis of international principles.75

However, the "internationalist" approach would imply a weakening of the "special relationship" between the United States and Mexico. In other words, the more independent Mexican development is, the greater its economic competition with the United States, with the subsequent added bilateral tensions. Thus, Rand would suggest the second alternative, by means of fostering U.S. policies based on the concepts of community, partnership, and interdependence. According to Rand, if Mexico were to futilely persist in ignoring this possibility, this would lead to a reinforcement by the U.S. government of policies geared to prolonging Mexico's role as an increasingly weaker and dependent client.76

A work group created by President-elect Reagan in December 1980, with the task of examining the conditions of supply of strategic minerals to the United States, warned of the precarious and vulnerable state of national

security, and recommended economic integration strategies
and political alliances with exporting countries that are
geographically closest to the United States, i.e. Mexico,
Canada, and other Caribbean and Central American countries. Another recommendation suggested the creation of
a national strategic reserve of thirteen basic minerals,
eleven of which are already supplied by Mexico to the
United States.[77]

In this context, Mexico has been selling crude oil
for the U.S. strategic petroleum reserve since 1978.[78]
By August 1981, the U.S. Department of Energy reached an
agreement with PEMEX to purchase 106 million barrels of
oil over the next five years for the strategic reserve.
The agreement included 200,000 b/d of oil at $31.80 per
barrel from September 1, 1981, until the end of that
year. Afterwards, deliveries would be reduced to 50,000
b/d of oil, and the price renegotiated.[79] It should be
underlined here that most of the Middle Eastern producers
have refused to sell oil for the strategic reserve. On
the other hand, the deal guaranteed Mexico secure sales
at a time when it was still recovering from the lost
revenues that resulted from the worldwide oil glut.

There is yet another angle to the U.S. problem of
national security, intimately tied to Mexico's internal
processes. This is, according to Richard R. Fagen, the
"time bomb" of Mexican development, with profound implications for U.S. strategic concerns. In other words, a
distorted process of development in Mexico, i.e.
economic growth without improvements in the distribution of income, could eventually bring about grave domestic repercussions in Mexico and destabilize the country's
political system, with the subsequent multifaceted
impact on the United States.[80]

In a scenario of uncontrolled social and political
disturbances, the U.S.-Mexican border would be but a
symbiotic membrane, bringing unrest to both sides.
Apparently aware of this possibility, the Rand Corporation has suggested that Mexico should perhaps be a conservative petroleum country, albeit with a calculated
strategic perspective: even though it might restrict
its total oil output for reasons of domestic stability,
Mexico would, nonetheless, widen its extraction, transportation, and exports capacity. This excess production
capacity could be incorporated rapidly during a sudden
international energy crisis.[81] Another report titled
Petroleum Geopolitics, prepared for the Energy and
Natural Resources Committee of the U.S. Senate, under the
director of James Z. Pugash, has also recommended that
the United States should encourage Mexico to create such
an excess production capacity, for strategic reasons.
The need is underlined for a "mutually beneficial association that includes Mexican energy development."[82]

However, these potential arrangements would seem to run counter to the national goals of Mexico's Energy Program.

Geopolitics

There are a number of questions that could be inscribed within the framework of the Mexican oil boom, and are at the heart of a process of geopolitical reaccommodation under way at present, between the United States and Mexico.

Historically, a key point of the U.S. strategy for its immediate sphere of influence in the Caribbean has been a transisthmian means of transportation and communication between the Pacific and the Atlantic oceans. Even though the strategic value of the Panama Canal has diminished somewhat in the nuclear age, it remains a crucial link in military and political terms. For some time in the XIX century, the isthmus of Tehuantepec in Mexico was considered by the United States as an alternate and cheap means of communication. Due to the prospect of saturation in naval traffic of the Panama Canal, by February 1980 the Mexican government initiated work for the project Alfa-Omega, with the objective of linking overland the ports of Coatzacoalcos in the Gulf of Mexico, and Salina Cruz in the Pacific. Parallel to the oil ducts that cross the isthmus, various types of cargo, including American goods, were to be transported in "containers," i.e. large metal and wooden boxes, through 300 kilometers of Mexican territory. The cost of the investment was estimated to be around one billion pesos.[83] These works constitute a new factor in the closely connected U.S. and Mexican commercial interests, and additionally, a new potential point of geopolitical contention.

Another matter pending resolution between the two nations pertains to the jurisdictional boundary limits in the Gulf of Mexico and in the Pacific. On May 4, 1978, the governments of the United States and Mexico signed a draft treaty which, according to U.S. geologists, resulted "in (the) giving away (of) some 25,000 square miles of potential, albeit deep-water, petroleum areas in the Gulf of Mexico." It appears that the west-central part of the Gulf of Mexico is a promising geological region, in terms of oil deposits, lying between the fields of the Texas-Louisana coast, and those of the Campeche-Reforma region in Mexico.[84] By September 1980, faced with a petition from the U.S. Petroleum Geologists Association, the U.S. State Department had postponed the ratification of the treaty. However, according to a spokesman of the state department, new "negotiations could fail, since it is very difficult to make the Mexicans change their way of thinking."[85]

Early in 1981, a study by the U.S. geological survey indicated that the deeper areas of the Gulf of Mexico whose jurisdiction has not been established yet could contain more than nine billion barrels of oil and more than eighteen billion cubic feet of natural gas. It is expected that new technology will be developed so that the oil industry may be able to operate at depths in excess of 10,000 feet, where more than 75 percent of the potential wealth would be located.[86] Geologist John Hunt, from the Woods Hale Oceanographic Institution, has emphasized that the Gulf of Mexico as a whole could be one of the three major areas in the world in terms of oil potential (the other two would be Alaska and the USSR), once exploration and drilling techniques develop further.[87] These facts explain the delay in the ratification of the treaty on Maritime Boundaries with Mexico. In any case, by April 1981, Mexico's Secretariat of Foreign Relations was still officially awaiting the ratification by the U.S. government.[88]

But, by far, the main geopolitical issue that threatens to perturb U.S.-Mexican relations is the situation in Central America and the Caribbean. Mexico regards the area as a natural region for its own commercial expansion and, albeit not officially acknowledged, political influence and leadership. Undoubtedly, petroleum has given Mexican foreign policy an added ingredient of self-assurance and dynamism. In this respect, from Mexico's position, petroleum serves somewhat as an equalizer in its dealing with the United States. Mexico does not share the U.S. government's apprehension with respect to communism. This could be partly related to the fact that the Mexican government traces itself back to a revolution. It is pertinent to remember that Mexico never broke relations with Cuba, and helped Salvador Allende's regime in Chile until its overthrow in 1973. Likewise, Mexico sympathizes with the Sandinista government in Nicaragua, and the rebel groups in El Salvador. Conversely, it views with suspicion American political and military overtures in the Caribbean and Central America.

Needless to say, U.S. perception of the situation in Central America and in the Caribbean, as well as actual policies, tend to clash with Mexico's. According to a December 1979 report by Radio Liberty Research, Mexico is the Soviet Union's ultimate target in Central America, and the disturbances in the area could determine a scenario quite dangerous for U.S. national interests and national security:

...Soviet-Cuban nibbling in Central America and the Caribbean may well set the stage for a major effort to shift Mexico's political and ideological orientation towards the Communist

world...growing Soviet-Cuban influence in
Central America and the Caribbean is capable
of constraining the flow of Mexican oil to
the U.S. at a time when anti-American forces
already exercise a potential stranglehold on
the oil-rich Persian Gulf.[89]

Lewis A. Tambs sees as a backdrop of the situation
a "grand geopolitical game plan" by the Soviet Union.
According to this view, the USSR would be applying the
classical principles of geopolitics, i.e. encircle,
isolate, and overrun, to the Caribbean area, in order to
interrupt American access to strategic minerals and
petroleum supplies. In this context, "even the oil
fields of Mexico are under long range attack."[90] For
it part, Moscow dismisses the "Soviet threat" to the
Caribbean as a propaganda veil the United States uses to
disguise its attempt to control the world's hydrocarbon
reserves.[91]

In any case, the Reagan administration would seem to
agree with the need for greater U.S. efforts to counter
radical influences in the region. With Reagan's election
in November 1980, some political observers foresaw a
definite shift in the balance of forces in Central
America, towards the conservative side, as the United
States intensified its involvement in that convulsing
region.[92] By late January 1981, official spokesmen for
the State Department were talking about the Caribbean as
the "third border" of the United States.[93]

It was highly significant that one of the first
foreign visitors to Reagan's White House was Edward
Seaga, Prime Minister from Jamaica, who defeated leftist
Michael Manley in that island's 1980 election, and was
singled out by the Reagan administration as a source of
hope for the beleaguered region. In regards to
Nicaragua, by late 1981 Secretary of State Alexander Haig
declared that "the hours (were) growing rather short"
to prevent the Sandinista government from turning their
country into "a totalitarian state like Cuba." Haig
accused the Sandinstas of staging a huge military
buildup through Cuban assistance, and supporting the
insurgents in El Salvador. White House counselor Edwin
Meese, as well as Haig, did not rule out any particular
action, such as a naval blockade, that might be taken
against Nicaragua.[94]

A Specific point of contention is Cuba, visited by
López Portillo in 1980, and with which the Mexican
government has increasingly identified itself. Since
January 1981, during his confirmation audiences in the
U.S. Senate, confronted by a question related to Mexico's
possible defense of Cuba if that island were attacked by
the United States, Secretary of State Haig opted for
avoiding any confrontation, and declared his intention

not to enter into a dispute with López Portillo. The issue remains a stumbling block in U.S.-Mexican relations, as the Reagan administration sees Cuba as the main focus of terrorist activities in the Caribbean area, and has even threatened to resort to military action to stop Cuba's meddling.[95]

Geopolitical contention between the United States and Mexico could be fueled, additionally, by the apparent existence of substantial hydrocarbon deposits in Belice, which obtained its independence from Great Britain in September 1981, and where PEMEX is undertaking exploratory works, together with other international oil companies.[96] Additionally, the intended construction of an interoceanic petroduct through Guatemala by an American petroleum consortium, as well as indications that there are significant deposits of petroleum in the Peten region of Guatemala could likewise fully incorporate that Central American country into U.S. political-military schemes and create another source of friction with Mexico.[97]

There is no likelihood for an early agreement between the United States and Mexico in regards to a mutually accepted modus vivendi in these various foci of potential geopolitical confrontation. As if to emphasize his views on matters related to Central America and the Caribbean, and in a comment obviously directed at the United States, in March 1981, President López Portillo declared that "for Mexico the danger does not reside in ideologies, but in intervention," and went on to add that Mexico cannot stand by passively in regards to such intervention in the Central American and Caribbean countries. Said the Mexican president: "(Mexico) wants a rational alternative, and not an hegemonic fate."[98]

Mexico's official support for revolutionary movements in Central America and the Caribbean could have an internal implication, too: the insulation of Mexico from that very same turmoil. In other words, Mexican foreign policy would respond to domestic political needs. However, this is not an all-encompassing explanation. There is also an element of genuine revolutionary consciousness and tradition permeating the actions of a government such as Mexico's, born of revolution. According to Washington analysts, Mexico believes in the inexorable course of revolutions.[99] In other words, Mexican society is the result of a revolutionary process, similar to that under way in Central America at present.

Some American analysts perceive a missing element in the logic of the Mexican position, determined by the breach between rhetoric and socioeconomic reality, i.e. Mexico's own vulnerability to contemporary revolutionary tendencies. Despite the wealth and multifaceted expectations to be derived from its energy resources, the

potential for social unrest remains high in Mexico, due
to factors such as the precarious distribution of income,
and high birth rates. U.S. worries in regards to Central
American turmoil could be possibly explained, as much in
terms of Soviet-Cuban meddling, as in relation to a
Mexican indulgency apparently not quite justified by its
domestic situation.[100]

In this respect, Jeanne Kirkpatrick, U.S. Ambassador
to the United Nations and one of the key Latin American
experts in Reagan's administration, has lumped Mexico
together with the rest of the Caribbean and Central
American countries, as governments with various degrees
of institutional deficiencies and "vulnerable and dependent economies." "All these countries," says Kirkpatrick,
"find themselves in permanent risk of revolutionary
destabilization."[101]

In this context, the Mexican pluralistic model, seen
by some Mexican officials as an alternative between U.S.
capitalism and Cuban marxism, i.e. in Mexican terms "the
institutionalized revolution," would be a unique consequence of historical processes that cannot be
repeated.[102] In any case, it remains to be seen whether
Mexico's activist foreign policy in Central America and
the Caribbean may be able to induce viable models of
government that emulate some of the characteristics of
the Mexican system.

Under certain conditions, the Mexican position could
be undermined by the meaning of its energy wealth to U.S.
national security. During a late 1980 visit to Mexico,
Clyde Mark, Assistant to the Foreign Affairs Division of
the U.S. Congress, declared openly that if Mexico were
to critically limit its supply of oil to the United
States, or if this supply were subject to domestic and/or
external threats, Washington would likely send military
forces to gain control of Mexican wells. If such a
military occupation were to take place, said Mark, a
subsequent return of the wells to Mexico would be most
unlikely.[103]

Olga Pellicer has somewhat substantiated the previous assessment, by suggesting that Mexico's oil wealth,
as well as its foreign policy towards Central America
and the Caribbean, presage an open interventionist tendency on the part of the United States over the Mexican
state.[104] According to Pellicer, the reasons are plain
to see:

> Independently of whether the Mexican project
> toward Central America is aggressive or not,...
> the fact is that its foreign policy has become
> an obstacle to the advancement of the project
> sponsored by other countries in the Continent.[105]

As a sequence to the previous situation, Joseph Hodara has delineated three possible scenarios, related to Mexico's emergency as an oil-rich country. The first would be the "finlandization" of Mexico, based on the overwhelming control of the means of information and intelligence by the United States, which would result in an intermittent diminution of Mexico's freedom of action. The second alternative would be for Mexico to "selectively disentangle" itself progressively from the strategic project of the United States. The third scenario would be, simply, a frank, reasoned, and "technologically and intellectually guided" process of negotiation between the two nations.106 In any case, the path to either scenario seems to be, at present, tortuous and fraught with potential convulsions.

PETROLEUM AND MEXICO'S FOREIGN POLICY

The Bases of Mexico's Foreign Policy

Petroleum policy is not, obviously, the equivalent to foreign policy. Mexico has a long tradition with respect to certain principles of international conduct. Nevertheless, its new role as one of the world's leading oil producing and exporting countries is having a definite impact on Mexico's formulation and implementation of its foreign policy. Specifically, oil wealth is serving as the propelling factor for the apparent consolidation of a more aggressive, self-assured role in international forums. The continuance and coherence in the objectives of Mexico's foreign policy are ascertained in the Global Plan for Development, 1980-1982. Mexico's foreign policy is geared towards:

> ...preserving our sovereignty, strengthening
> our independence vis a vis the rest of the world,
> practicing international solidarity, supporting
> domestic efforts at development, and participat-
> ing in the conformation of a world order that
> guarantees these objectives and allows the
> development of all peoples in this same inter-
> national sovereignty, equality, security, and
> justice that we wish for ourselves.107

Within this framework, some key principles can be clearly underscored:

1. The respect for national sovereignty, non-
   intervention by one or more foreign states
   in the internal affairs of another, and the
   principle of self-determination.

2. The peaceful solution of controversies.
3. The renunciation of the use of force or threats in international relations.
4. The legal equality of states.
5. International cooperation.[108]

Mexico has traditionally practiced a basically defensive foreign policy. The reason for this attitude is to be found in a historical precedent, i.e. the proximity of the United States, which has tended to neutralize Mexico's potential for an independent foreign policy. According to Mario Ojeda, various interventionist experiences throughout Mexican history, during the XIX and into the XX century, which resulted in the loss of territory, temporary occupations of national territory, and interference in Mexico's domestic affairs, have resulted in "an attitude of repudiation to contacts with foreign nations and isolationism....self-determination and non-intervention became the fundamental concepts of Mexican foreign policy." These basic principles have also been reflected in the Mexican objective of trying to avoid foreign domination as a fundamental requisite for domestic economic development.[109]

Since the beginning of the 1940s, mutual understanding and cordiality in the relations between the United States and Mexico seemed to leave behind the tensions and conflicts of the revolution and post-revolutionary period in Mexico, which climaxed with the oil expropriation in 1938. There were obstacles, related to issues such as trade and migration, but both countries, on the whole, tried to reduce their frictions to a minimum. To the United States, Mexico became a trustworthy neighbor, with a predictable behavior. From the Mexican perspective, the postwar period of relations with the United States seems to have been qualified by a feeling of "geographic fatalism," springing from the fact of a continuous border with the most powerful nation in the world, from whose economic and political influence it was impossible to escape. It was during this period that the concept of a "special relationships" took hold of the imagination of leaders in both governments.[110]

By the mid-1960s, Mario Ojeda could perceive a gradual shift in the conduction of Mexico's foreign policy, from the traditional passive, defensive, and isolationist attitude, towards a more dynamic presence in the international scenario. This change, which seemed to have started during the Lopez Mateos administration (1958-1964), was a result of the maturity achieved by Mexico, on the basis of sustained economic growth and political stability. As the capacity of Mexico to resist foreign pressures was enhanced, there was also a gradual subsidence of the fear of domestic subversive movements.[111] In conclusion, said Ojeda:

...it could be stated that Mexico's foreign
policy is in a transition stage...from a passive defense and isolationist attitude, Mexico
is passing into a more dynamic and internationalist phase in its foreign relations....But
this transition is taking place gradually. The
country seems to be proceeding pragmatically,
testing the possibilities of a new international
status. The general conclusion would then be
that it is not to be expected that the country
adopts an active role of importance in the near
future.[112]

However, during Echeverría's administration, from
1970 to 1976, Mexico did attempt to conduct an extremely
active foreign policy, based on a Third World activism
that brought it into conflict with the United States.
Domestic difficulties and an adverse international
economic juncture turned the experiment into a failure.
By the mid-1970s, some Mexican analysts foresaw the
imminence of a return to "bilaterality" in Mexico's foreign relations, vis a vis the Unites States, due to the
critical weakness of the country's economic-political
system at the time.[113] According to Ojeda, the effort
to diminish unilateral dependence on the United States
had resulted, paradoxically, in a much more dependent
country, and a drastic weakening of the structural bases
needed to follow a more independent course in foreign
policy matters.[114] Another Mexican analyst, Eugenio
Anguiano, while lamenting the frustrated experience,
suggested nonetheless its continuing viability:

In the end, it would be very costly, in political
and economic terms, to abandon the reformist
efforts of the last two decades, only because
of the need to solve the short-term crisis.
The Mexican state has sufficient human and
material elements, as to continue to pursue
multilateral relations, without impairing
bilateral relations (with the U.S.).[115]

Indeed, Mexico would find these elements, mainly in
the form of petroleum resources. As early as February
1977, during his first official visit to the United
States, President López Portillo confidently declared
that "Mexico is not bankrupt...I did not come to ask for
help."[116] Petroleum would come to be the crucial element
in trying to renew the search for a more independent
Mexico, domestically and in regard to foreign relations.
By late 1978, The Economist could assert that petroleum
was bringing about a "...fundamental change in the equilibrium of power in the Western hemisphere. It is a
sudden change so big and new that neither the Carter

administration nor Mexico itself have understood it
yet."117

The initial fiasco in the gasduct negotiations seems
to have marked a turning point in the attitude of the
López Portillo administration towards the United States.
In any case, by 1978 rhetoric had hardened in regards to
the inevitable new relationship with the neighbor to the
north. In October of that year, expressing his awareness that neither Mexico nor developing countries in
general have the priority nor the respect they deserve
from industrialized nations, López Portillo would declare
that, on the basis of Mexico's natural resources, there
would no longer be a "master-client relation" vis a vis
the United States, but an equal partnership.118 Petroleum, he would say during an interview with the tele-
vision network CBS in February 1979, "is for Mexico, not
for the convenience of the U.S." And, again, at that
time López Portillo criticized the wheeling-dealing of
the U.S. government as the main reason behind the failure
of the gas negotiations.119 Shortly after the 1980
presidential election in the United States, the Mexican
president would emphatically comment that "Mexico's
destiny is above the political fluctuations in the United
States."120

Parallel to the previous pronouncements, Mexican
analysts were underlining the need for a coordination
between Mexico's petroleum and foreign policies.
Mexico's oil strategy, stated Samuel Berkstein in mid-
1980, must be geared towards an increments of three basic
criteria in the evaluation of foreign policy: security,
welfare, and prestige. The objective of such a strategy
would be to project into international relevance the
political dimension of the petroleum policies of the
Mexican state.121

By mid-1980, the Secretary of Foreign Relations,
Jorge Castañeda, could state that in ten years Mexico's
presence amidst the community of nations had enlarged
appreciably. At the time, Mexico maintained relations
with 138 countries, and was the source of various initiatives in international forums in favor of a more just
and peaceful international scenario. In spite of renewed
external pressures, especially in the case of petroleum,
Mexico's foreign policy was more active, and had gained
elements for negotiations that made it less dependent
on subjective appreciations such as sympathy and con-
veniences.122

Specially, in regard to relations with Washington,
Castañeda emphasized that Mexico had attempted to tread
a middle course, conciliatory to the United States but
at the same time definite about the objective of a
greater autonomy for Mexico. Castañeda acknowledged that
"the principal element of Mexico's foreign policy (was)
the nature and degree of its relations with the United

States," because of obvious multiple causes, i.e. geography, multiple exchanges, and the global importance of the United States, something that "cannot be denied by past problems or historical experiences, it is simply a fact of life." Parallel to this, however, Castaneda underlined the idea that Mexico had abandoned the "cautious and up to a degree defensive attitude" that tended to characterize its foreign policy, and had begun to play an increasingly active role in international affairs, in order to uphold traditional principles and to defend specific interests.[123]

In other words, the fact that relations with the United States are the key component of Mexican foreign policy, does not mean a passive acceptance by Mexico of political, economic, and cultural dependence. The United States, according to Castañeda, is a key element, an important factor, but not a "factotum" in Mexico's foreign policy. Thus, for example, for Mexico economic diversification represents an essential national goal, and not an action directed against the United States.[124] In this context, petroleum constitutes an invaluable ally:

> ...petroleum...must be sen not only as a simple product to be sold at the going world price, but rather as something in such demand that an additional value could be affixed to it. This could consist -as it happens with other nations- of an extra cash price. But in our case it has a much more essential character.[125]

U.S. and Mexican Mutual Expectations

Mario Ojeda has correctly noted that Mexico's strategic value for the United States increases in periods of political crisis in the world and, particularly, in the Western Hemisphere. The United States, sayd Ojeda, has usually:

> ...recognized and accepted the need for Mexico to dissent with North American policy in all that is fundamental for Mexico, even though for the United States it may be important, but not fundamental. In return, Mexico gives its cooperation in all that is fundamental or even important for the United States, and not so for Mexico.[126]

Ongoing processes, in particular those in Central America and the Caribbean, may be changing this set of perceptions, as Mexico emerges as a "middle power," with a growing influence on the national and international policies of the United States. Petroleum would

be seen as the key factor in a scenario for U.S.-Mexican
relations, qualified by a mainly technical and strategic
perspective of matters by the United States, in contra-
position to a vision by Mexico in agreement with nationalistic priorities and tested principles of international
behavior.[127] Some American analysts believe that
Mexico's new assertive foreign policy carries a number of
ominous implications for the United States, especially
in regard to the situation in the Caribbean and Central
America, and that the stage would seem to be set for a
potential clash between the contrasting interests of
Mexico and the United States.[128]

The Reagan administration perceives the crisis in
Central America and the Caribbean as an East-West confrontation. Thus, the socioeconomic situation of the
countries in the area must be subordinated to the exigen-
cies of the global U.S.-Soviet conflict. From this
view, American foreign policy should be geared, primarily, to containing Soviet-Cuban expansionism through
military assistance to friendly governments such as that
in El Salvador. There seems to be an urgency to prevent
the "domino effect," according to which revolutionary
movements akin to Cuba's would extend their field of
action from Nicaragua to Mexico itself. Indeed, by
November 1981, the Pentagon announced the formation of a
new U.S. military command for the Caribbean, whose area
of responsibility would include waters and islands of
the Caribbean Sea, Gulf of Mexico, and portions of the
Pacific Ocean bordering Central America. Pentagon officials declared that the move "reflects the continuing
U.S. interest in the vital Caribbean areas."[129]

However, as the American mood towards the crisis in
the Caribbean Basin turns increasingly aggressive, the
means to carry out a tougher policy are not clearly dis-
cernible. Alfred Stepan has noted a deterioration of the
traditional instruments of U.S. foreign policy in the
area. For example, U.S. military assistance programs in
Latin America, which flourished during the 1950s, were
by 1979 barely in effect anywhere in the region.
Bilateral economic assistance to Latin America, which
under USAID programs played an important role in the
1960s, had been discarded by the late 1970s by "middle
income" countries such as Brazil and Venezuela. U.S.
military intervention faces significantly greater
obstacles in the 1980s than in previous decades. Stepan
also emphasizes the "domestic dimension" of U.S. policies
towards Latin America, i.e. the seventeen to twenty-two
million Hispanic Americans, largely Mexican Americans,
who are close to become the largest minority in the
United States, and are reaching for growing political
power. Finally, there is the fact of the emergence of
new power centers in Latin America, of which Mexico is
possible the most relevant due to its oil wealth, which

are bound to significantly shape American foreign policy in the region.[130]

Mexico is opposed to a reprise of U.S. reliance on military means to achieve its objectives in Central America and the Caribbean. By mid-November 1981, President López Portillo declared that it would be a "gigantic error" for the United States to stage military actions against Nicaragua or Cuba.[131] The Mexican government sees the crisis in Central America in terms of a North-South dimension, i.e. development. Socioeconomic conditions are primarily the cause for the upheaval and, thus, only a political and not a military solution is feasible. There is a difference of approach between the Mexican and the American positions, more noticeable now that Mexico has come out of its shell in foreign policy matters. Simply, whereas U.S. policymakers believe that conservative, old-fashioned regimes would be more convenient for its interests in Central America, Mexico seeks to strengthen its role as a regional power through the support of more progressive governments.[132]

Nevertheless, both the Mexican and the U.S. governments realize that they must work together. During the years of the Carter administration, an important factor that led to a deterioration in the relations between the two countries was the subjective dimension of leadership perception. López Portillo and Carter were definitely incompatible in character, and they developed a mutual animosity that was to be reflected at the wider level of bilateral relations. With the advent of the Reagan administration, this personal equation of politics has improved greatly. The personal chemistry between Lopez Portillo and Reagan is, indeed, warm and both leaders feel at ease with each other. This fact is contributing to create a new, improved climate for negotiations. The Mexican president, as previous Mexican leaders sensitive to nationalistic motivations, believes that mutual respect and dignity must pave the way for a better understanding. "The problems are the same," has said Lopez Portillo, "but the attitude toward them has changed radically, and this means that treatment of them is possible."[133] For his part, Reagan is seeking to personally gain the sympathy of the Mexican leaders, through personal charisma as well as through well geared publicity.[134]

From the American perspective, U.S. overtures towards Mexico must seem somewhat as a component of a tug-of-war. Whereas Mexico is pulled by its self-conception as part of Latin America, and as a developing country member of the Third World, i.e. the South, fundamentally in agreement with the non-aligned movement, the Reagan administration believes that Mexico's ties with the United States and plain, basic geopolitics are

bound to solidify its identification with U.S. policies
and objectives.

An important element that would tend to underscore
this latter reasoning is the role of Mexico's private
sector in bilateral relations. The Latin American policy
of the Reagan administration, following the norm of previous Republican governments, reflects a symbiosis
between the interests of the public and private sectors
in the United States. According to this appreciation,
U.S. policy must be closely coordinated with private
American business interests in the region, and by extension with the latter's liaison with Latin American private concerns.[135]

Former Ambassador to Mexico, Robert H. McBride, has
noted that the relationship between Mexico's private
sector and its U.S. counterpart is thriving. According
to McBride:

> ...there seems to be a harmony of objectives and
> an ability to work together on the part of U.S.
> and Mexican industry and banking which are absent
> from government-to-government relationships.
> The powerful business groups in Monterrey have
> been closely associated with major U.S. corpora-
> tions for most of the post-World War II period,
> as have most of the Mexico City business groups,
> the banking groups of Banamex and Bancomer, and
> others. The intense desire of the Mexican govern-
> ment to diversify its investments sources in
> order to prevent "dependence" on the U.S. does
> not seem to be reflected in attitudes of the
> private sector.[136]

Mexican analysts concur that, indeed, the Reagan administration is placing its trust on U.S. entrepreneurs to
reach a better understanding between the private sectors
of both countries, which would be expected to have a
beneficial impact on governmental circles as well.[137]

McBride has underlined the special situation prevailing along the border, which is bound to foster a
growing association of interests from both sides, stem-
ming from factors such as trade, commerce, and the
maquiladora program.[138] Among the various plans to
propitiate cooperation, there is the Agreement for the
Exchange of Electric Energy signed in May 1980, as well
as joint projects regarding agricultural transactions.
Olga Pellicer sees as the obvious attraction of these
projects for the United States "the possibility to transfer the political handling of relations between the two
countries from the federal government to local governments."[139] According to Pellicer:

This permits to find, on the Mexican side, inter-
locutors less reluctant to the open acceptance of
greater Mexican-U.S. ties. The lesser responsibility of local political leaders in the maintenance of a defensive and nationalistic ideology,
allows them to proceed, without great political
costs, on an openly friendly dialogue with their
American counterparts.[140]

On a broader scale, the reemergence of Mexico as an
oil-exporting nation has underscored its economic bonds
with the United States. Trade between the two countries
is soaring. By 1980, new investments had surpassed the
billion dollar mark, up from 374 million dollars in 1978.
Projections for 1981 indicated that, only in the manufacturing sector, new U.S. investments would be well
above the billion dollar mark, geared mainly towards the
automobile industry.[141] In short, the economic panorama
would seem to bear implications for closer political
relations between the two nations.

In this context, U.S. expectations of Mexico's role
in Central America and the Caribbean would appear to be
especially high in regard to diffusing the politically
explosive situation in the area. The Mexican government
seems to be willingly pursuing this role, too. The
differences between the respective positions, of course,
spring from the degree of independence of Mexico's foreign policy, and the diverging appreciations of issues
by the two governments.

The previous proposition is not new. McBride has
noted that in earlier U.S. administrations the Department
of State had envisaged a greater Mexican presence in
Latin American affairs. Specifically, it was thought
that Mexico could play a part in hemispheric "bridge-
building," regarding the Central American region.[142]
By mid-1981, indeed, the Mexican government was apparently trying to carve a niche of its own for its potential role as a "common communicator" in international
relations.[143] For example, in reference to the view by
the U.S. government of the situation in Central America
and Cuba, Mexico believes it can ultimately help to narrow the gap in perceptions and lessen misunderstandings.
President López Portillo maintains that

> ...because we have open and frank relations, these
> relations could be useful in communicating with
> two parties that frequently do not communicate,
> provided there is political goodwill to relax
> the area.[144]

By November 1981, during Secretary of State Haig's
official visit to Mexico City, Mexican officials reiterated their opposition to any precipitate action by the

United States against Nicaragua. Mexican Secretary of
Foreign Relations, Jorge Castañeda, underscored that
"anti-interventionist" feeling was widespread throughout
Latin America, and added that "a sharp response (to
Nicaragua) could be counterproductive." However, Mexico
was ready to act as a "communicator" in order to improve
relations between Washington and Managua.[145] For its
part, a spokesman for the Department of State declared
that the United States and Mexico "...clearly do not have
identical views but they share a common concern in the
search for ways of dealing with the problems of Nicaragua."[146]

Petroleum as an Instrument of Mexico's Foreign Policy

The suddenness with which Mexico has been catapulted
into a prominent position as an oil-producing and exporting country raises a number of questions. There is the
suspicion that the "discovery" of the petroleum fields
in the southeast during the mid-1970s may have been
merely the official announcement of a fact already known
by the inner circle of top Mexican government officials.
One of the explanations for the secrecy would be related
to the fact that President Echeverría, who apparently
had ambitions to become Secretary General of the United
Nations, viewed the announcement of the existence of
huge oil deposits as indirectly harming his candidacy
with respect to OPEC countries, which might then have
seen Mexico as a relief source for oil imports by the
United states and Western Europe.[147]

On the other hand, in 1977 PEMEX's Director Díaz
Serrano underlined the technical difficulties which had
to be overcome in order to undertake drillings to 5,000
meter deep as to locating the new deposits. Only through
these operations could the finds be confirmed.[148]
According to information obtained by France's Le Figaro,
the secrecy was maintained because Mexico wished to avoid
an excessive oil consumption as in the Middle East
countries, and to conserve its hydrocarbon resources.[149]
In this respect, President López Portillo declared in
March 1978, that PEMEX's technicians had deliberately
withheld information pertaining to the new deposits,
because of fear of squander by Mexican politicians.[150]
It is pertinent to remember that the Mexican political
system itself tends to secrecy, and neuralgic issues are
not openly discussed. Additionally, an obvious reason
for the reluctance to divulge information about oil
reserves could have been wariness of growing economic
and politicial pressures by the United States.

In any case, the economic crisis of 1976, and the
subsequent need to court external and internal confidence
in Mexico's process of development, led to a complete
turnabout in the previous policy. The administration of

López Portillo aimed to augment and verify the claims
concerning PEMEX's reserves.

In general terms, Mexican policy orientations are
significantly conditioned by U.S. strategy and, in
certain cases, are a direct response to that strategy.
The actions by the Mexican government on the issue of
oil reserves illustrate this causal relationship. U.S.
sources were among the first to publicize the existence
of sizable hydrocarbon deposits in Mexico. Whereas by
May 1978, the Energy Commission of the Mexican Congress
had tried to disprove what it deemed to be an exaggerate
estimate of Mexico's oil reserves by the CIA, in contradiction with PEMEX's lower figures,[151] a year later
PEMEX's Director Díaz Serrano was busy disclaiming "a
campaign in the United States to underestimate Mexico's s
petroleum reserves."[152] By November 1980, Díaz Serrano
once again denied assertions by the U.S. Department of
Energy that questioned PEMEX's figures.[153]

The previous scenario serves as a background for the
role of petroleum as an instrument of Mexico's foreign
policy. It is a scenario qualified by restraints, as
well as by increasing flexibility for Mexican initiatives.

Constraints. Olga Pellicer has analyzed Mexico's
foreign relations in terms of two possible outcomes. interdependence with the United States, or a national project of development. In the process of redefinition of
its foreign policy, Mexico faces a series of conditions
set by the expansion of the petroleum industry, such as
incoming pressures from the United States, and the
contrasting policies of domestic groups in regard to the
possibilities of further integration with that country,
or the pursuit of a national project. From the American
perspective, interdependence would seem to be the most
appropriate path. And here is found a net source of
conflict between the two countries, that springs from
nationalistic feelings commonly expressed in Mexico
through an anti-American attitude.[154] Nationalism
remains, indeed, the most powerful political ideology in
Mexico, closely tied to the fortunes of the petroleum
industry.

But the search for a nationalistic course of action
in Mexican foreign relations must take into account a
series of structural limiting factors. Jorge Domínguez
has aptly referred to a "triple dependency" that constraints Mexico's overtures:

Considerable continuities are shown in the international implications of Mexican internal affairs.
There are remarkable continuities in economic
structure, especially in the economy's general
vulnerability and in its links to the U.S.....

> There has also been a deepening of a triple
> dependency well beyond historical standards.
> Mexico relies increasingly on the export of a
> single family or products (hydrocarbons), on a
> single country for its international economic
> relations (the United States), and on a declin-
> ing number of regions within Mexico for such
> relations....The autonomy of foreign policy
> consequently declines. To an unparalleled degree,
> Mexican foreign policy must serve internal
> economic needs, and non-economic foreign policy
> objectives must be subordinated to serve them....
> The more Mexico relies on petroleum exports to
> meet its internal economic needs, the more
> important it will become to the U.S., and the
> more likely that there will be conflicts over
> new issues between the two countries.[155]

In sum, says Domínguez, "the deepening of Mexico's triple
dependency has constrained the independence of the
Mexican government in the conduct of foreign policy."[156]
The constraints on petroleum as an instrument of Mexico's
foreign policy are well illustrated by the convulsions
of the industry since mid-1981, as a result of the worldwide oil glut, which has had domestic, as well as external repercussions.

By late 1980, PEMEX was actively embarked on a
course of increasing levels of oil exports, and higher
sales prices. In December of that year, PEMEX raised
prices for its exports even above the levels then prevalent in most OPEC countries. At that time, the crude
denominated "Istmo" was selling at a price of $38.30 per
barrel, and the "Maya" crude at $34.50 per barrel. Most
of the Mexican reserves correspond to these two types
of oil: "Istmo," which is a light crude of 34° API[157]
and 1.8 percent sulfur content; and "Maya," a heavier
crude of 23° API and 3.42 percent sulfur content.
Increasingly, production has corresponded more to the
"Maya" crude, extracted mostly from the Gulf of
Campeche.[158] Likewise, PEMEX was successfully continuing
its policy of markets diversification. By January 1981,
PEMEX exported, or had plans to export oil to nineteen
countries.[159]

By April 1981, the international petroleum market
was feeling the impact of lower levels of demand, and a
growing surplus in supply. The big western importers
had been successful in reducing consumption, at the same
time that Saudi Arabia raised its production in order
to pressure other OPEC countries to agree to a common
price level.[160] This situation unleashed, in rapid succession, a series of events which were to demonstrate
the degree of vulnerability of Mexico's economy and
polity to international market forces. By late May 1981,

PEMEX announced that it would not alter its program of production and exports, nor its price structure, in spite of OPEC's decision to reduce output.[161] Shortly afterwards, by early June, PEMEX Director Díaz Serrano had reconsidered the matter, and acknowledged the need for PEMEX to lower prices in order to retain its clients.[162] At the time, the Secretariat of the Treasury estimated that Mexico would have to contract an additional external debt for 1,200 million dollars, to compensate for lost reserves.[163] The reduction in prices, of four dollars per barrel, was expected to bring about a loss of revenues of more than five billion dollars for 1981, in relation to previous projections. By early June, exports were down to 1.4 million b/d, 560,000 "Istmo" and the rest "Maya."[164]

The decision to lower prices, albeit perhaps unavoidable from an economic standpoint, was politically explosive. On June 6, 1981, Diaz Serrano presented his resignation as director of PEMEX. The decrease in prices had not been, apparently, unanimously approved by the Economic Cabinet. Behind the dismissal of Díaz Serrano loomed the fact of PEMEX's independent course of action vis a vis other Secretariats, and the continuing debate over production levels. The pursuance of bureaucratic autonomy and an ever increasing petroleum output ultimately cost Diaz Serrano his post.[165] Commenting retrospectively on the episode, President López Portillo would express his belief that "a precipitate action reduced the exports price of our crude, with a chain reaction over the world's oil market."[166]

By mid-June 1981, the Mexican president was attempting to restore stability to the petroleum industry, by declaring that the production goals would be kept, as delineated in the Energy Program, and that the sudden drop in prices would be corrected.[167] The Secretary of Patrimony and Industrial Development, Jose Andres de Oteyza, reiterated the objective of revaluating the price of crude oil, even if it meant a "depuration " of PEMEX's list of clients.[168]

The new PEMEX Director, former Secretary of Treasury Julio Rodolfo Moctezuma Cid, was soon to realize the difficulties of trying to manage a product such as petroleum, subject to the fluctuations of the international market, according to considerations of national interest. Moctezuma Cid proceeded to prepare a program to overcome the crisis. The proposal included a more dynamic and flexible commercialization policy, in order to obtain more favorable prices and sales conditions and to uphold the production goals in the Energy Program, and a greater coordination between production, commercialization, infrastructure, and operation of facilities.[169]

By late June 1981, PEMEX announced it intended to raise prices back to their former level, and that the possibility of reducing exports was under consideration.[170] On July 1, as a step in recuperating from the economic effects of the drop in revenues, PEMEX proceeded to increase its prices by two dollars per barrel of oil.[171] This move resulted in a series of cancellations of purchases by a number of clients. The French Petroleum Company, which had been buying 100,000 b/d from Mexico, notified PEMEX that it would reduce its purchases by half.[172] Companies from other countries, i.e. United States, the Philippines, Sweden, Yugoslavia, and India, also cancelled orders, bringing the total of lost sales to 310,000 b/d. This meant financial losses of 230 million pesos daily.[173] By early July, the previous cancellations had become official. These included four U.S. petroleum campanies: Exxon, Ashland Oil, Charter Oil, and Clark Oil and Refining Company. Lost sales continued to mount to 550,000 b/d.[174]

Parallel to the previous developments, on July 1, in San Francisco, PEMEX had signed an agreement with eighty-two banks from eleven countries, in order to obtain credit for four billion dollars, the highest amount ever contracted by any country during a single operation. The Bank of America was to be the agent and twenty other banks, including seven from Japan, would administer the operation. The Japanese banks were to contribute 1,200 million dollars, thirty U.S. banks were responsible for 1,500 to 1,600 million, and twenty-eight European banks would accout for the remainder. PEMEX officials declared that the loan was a transitory measure, while payments for exported oil arrived. Likewise, part of the credits was to be destined to acquire additional exploration and drilling equipment.[175]

According to Alicia Girón, in a study for the Economic Research Institute of Mexico's National University, by early July 1981, PEMEX's foreign debt amounted to more than thirteen billion dollars. Between 1970 and early 1979, PEMEX's debt increased from 438.6 million to 6.213 billion dollars. Shortly before the record four billion credit operation, the total had surpassed the nine billion dollar mark.[176]

Faced with the possibility of financial disaster, the Mexican government retaliated against France, which had been purchasing 100,000 b/d of oil from Mexico since February 1979. By early July 1981, the French Petroleum Company communicated to PEMEX its intention to cancel purchases altogether for the rest of the year. Apparently the French were applying one of the clauses of the contractual agreement with PEMEX, which allowed any of the two parties to suspend operations for a trimester, if disagreements developed over price levels.[177] In any case, on July 4, 1981, the Mexican government proceeded not only to suspend the petroleum deal, but to eliminate all French companies from participation in Mexico's projects of national development, as a reaction against France's cancellation of oil purchases.[178]

Nevertheless, negotiations between PEMEX and the French Petroleum Company were resumed shortly afterwards, with the personal intervention of President Francois Mitterand, who stated that it was essential for France to deepen relations with Mexico.[179] By mid-July 1981, both sides had announced that the oil contract remained in effect, and that France would continue to buy Mexican crude, pending further negotiations.[180]

In the end, the episodes of mid-1981 demonstrated to the Mexican government the high volatility and unpredictability of the international oil market, and the corresponding obstacles to relying on petroleum for domestic development and activism in foreign policy matters. The storm subsided as quickly as it had arrived. By early August 1981, PEMEX was able to announce that it had recovered its petroleum market. Sales were up to 1.250 million b/d, at an average price of $31.25 per barrel. This latter figure was the combination of sales prices of $34 for "Istmo" crude and $28.50 for "Maya" crude. PEMEX's production schemes were geared to a 50 percent mixture of each of these two basic types of oil.[181]

In spite of the turmoil, total sales for 1981 were expected to amount to more than fifteen billion dollars, i.e. an increment of up to 50 percent, over the 1980 income of 10.4 billion dollars. In retrospect, events resembled a cycle, from euphoria to deception back to euphoria.[182] As a result of OPEC's new price structure, agreed upon by November 1981, Mexico raised the price of its light "Istmo" crude by one dollar to thirty-five dollars per barrel, and held the price of its heavy "Maya" crude steady at $28.50.[183] By September 1981, President López Portillo could speak of the drop in prices as a "transitory phenomenon."[184]

Nevertheless, the fluctuations of the international oil market are not likely to cease soon. Faced with continuing instability in sales levels, by April 1982, PEMEX doubled credit limits to its customers, to sixty days, which translated into a price reduction of forty cents a barrel.[185] In spite of this easing of purchase terms, Mexico was struggling to maintain its crude oil exports at a level of a million b/d. Exports of oil to the United States had fallen by 40 percent, to 450,000 b/d, and other customers were reducing purchases from 15 percent to 40 percent less than contracted. By April 1982, it appeared increasingly unlikely that PEMEX would reach its projected level of seventeen billion dollars in export revenues for 1982.[186]

The Mexican government remains wary of potential future developments. There has been a proportionally quicker increment of production and reserves of heavy "Maya" oil, especially from the wells off the Gulf of

Campeche, over the ligher "Istmo" crude from Tabasco and
Chiapas.187 This fact could strain the flexibility of
refining facilities in customer countries, which might
be an obstacle to growing Mexican petroleum exports,
under soft international market conditions.

In his 1981 annual report, President Lopez Portillo
summarized Mexico's tentative initial steps in the world
of the big oil exporters:

> The expectations raised by petroleum and our
> sudden presence in the world of its conflicts,
> took us by surprise, and we do not yet fully
> understand its meaning. We graciously accepted
> the upwards price movements, and at the first
> downwards change became discouraged and bitter....
> this resource (will)...give us the opportunity
> for progress if we know how to administer its
> abundance; if we organize work.188

The selection of Miguel de la Madrid Hurtado as the
PRI candidate for the 1982 presidential election would
seem to indicate that Mexico will slowly but steadily
try to increase petroleum production and exports, albeit
attentive to the need for planning and efficiency in the
midst of uncertain international market conditions for
the rest of the decade. Conversely, market realities
are bound to act as a constraint to the determination of
the Mexican government to continue utilizing petroleum
as a key level to spur domestic development, and to
substantiate the projection of Mexico's foreign policy
objectives.

Mexican Initiatives. In spite of the built-in constraints, petroleum constitutes a formidable element in
policy formulation and implementation. Based on its
petroleum wealth, Mexico has embarked upon a highly ambitious course in its foreign policy, which has both points
of continuity and contrast in regard to previous stances.

According to Olga Pellicer, the foreign policy
project of the Lopez Portillo administration has followed three basic directions, clearly manifest since
1980: in the first place, towards a diversification of
its foreign relations, both economic and political, on
the basis of the negotiating power afforded by petroleum;
secondly, a somewhat more discreet solidarity with
"Third World" positions, parallel to a selective
strengthening of relations with key countries in terms of
regional influence and prestige, such as Sweden, Canada,
Brazil, and India, and a more solid presence in international forums such as the U.S. Security Council, where
Mexico accepted a post after thirty years of declining
participation there; and thirdly, contrasting with the
pragmatism of the two previous lines, support for

ideological pluralism and a maintenance of the commitment to its revolutionary origins, through its support of
revolutionary regimes such as those in Cuba and Nicaragua. Thus, says Pellicer, there is a mixture of pragmatism and revolutionary tradition in Mexico's foreign
policy, with petroleum as the basic pillar for its
actions.189

Officially, Mexico has denied any attempts at exert-
ing a subregional, or Latin American leadership, but
this seems to be an impending role. Mexican analysts
abound in the concept of a "sleeping giant," to describe
Mexico's leadership potential.190 According to Edwin
Deagle, from the Rockefeller Foundation, the Reagan
administration must recognize the status of Mexico as an
"emerging leader."191 The President of Costa Rica,
Rodrigo Carazo, has openly acknowledged that Mexico
exerts "in a certain way a leadership role in Central
America, at the time economically."192

This leadership, or at least the potential for it,
is demonstrated by a series of actions on the part of the
Mexican government, that confirm the efforts to deline-
ate a more assertive foreign policy. In regard to the
objective of economic diversification, the achievements
would seem to be substantial. In 1976, Mexico sold all
its hydrocarbon exports to the United States. By
January 1981, PEMEX was exporting oil to eleven countries, and had plans to extend the list to eight more.193
By July 1981, the following were its most important
clients: the United States, Spain, Japan, France,
Israel, Brazil, Canada, Sweden, Great Britain, the
Philippines, and Yugoslavia.194

Some additional factors illustrate the attempts to
diversify exports markets and operations. By January
1981, PEMEX announced that it had acquired a total of
34.29 percent of the stock of the Spanish refining
company Petronor, with facilities in Bilbao, Spain.
This action not only strengthened PEMEX's operations in
Spain, but also gave it a firm vantage point to consolidate and expand its European operations.195

In November 1980, President-elect Reagan invited
PEMEX to establish itself in U.S. territory, and to
compete with its products in the American market.196 The
Mexican government received the proposal in a positive
way, and PEMEX announced that Mexico would commercialize
its gasoline and petrochemicals in the United States
through independent producers rather than through the big
U.S. refineries.197 By early 1981, PEMEX had plans to
establish plants of its own to distribute gasoline and
diesel fuel in California, Arizona and Texas. These
operations were expected to compensate for the problem
caused to PEMEX by the fact that up to 40 percent of the
total volume of gas and diesel it sends to the Mexican
northern states, along the border with the United States,

is acquired by American citizens who cross the border.198
    An aspect of PEMEX's expansion plans that has
resulted in misunderstanding with the U.S. government is
that related to dealings with Cuba. In 1978, during his
visit to the Soviet Union, President Lopez Portillo
raised the proposal for a triangular oil supplying agreement, through which the Soviet Union would supply petroleum to a Mexican client, Spain, while Mexico would
supply it to Cuba. By May 1980, the idea had been discarded, due to the fact that Cuba would have to pay substantially higher prices, since the Soviet Union sells
oil to the island at discount prices.199
    However, Mexican cooperation with Cuba has con-
tinued. By December 1980, PEMEX announced that through
a protocol on cooperation agreed upon by both countries,
Mexican technicians would explore Cuba's sea platform
in search for oil.200 In February 1981, the Chicago
Tribune published news in regard to a "secret agreement"
between Mexico and Cuba, through which the former would
supply Castro's regime with petroleum machinery manufactured in third countries. PEMEX emphatically denied
this version.201
    President López Portillo has acknowledged that dis-
agreements between Mexico and the United States possibly
lie in the diverging orientation towards certain critical
countries in Central America and the Caribbean, such as
Cuba and Nicaragua. But the Mexican president believes
that

> Mexico's friendship with Cuba is not a condition
> (that interferes with) friendship between Mexico
> and the United States. The United States has
> friendships with many countries of the left...with
> practically all of them except Cuba, which makes
> one suppose that there are very special reasons
> for it, and not ideological one....But Cuba and
> Mexico have been united since the sixteenth cen-
> tury.202

However, increased cooperation on petroleum and general
matters between Mexico and Cuba is bound to underline
U.S.-Mexican differences over approaches to the problems
of the Caribbean and Central American region.
    The Mexican government has repeatedly underscored
its vital interest in the Caribbean and Central America.
In February 1981, the Secretary of Foreign Relations,
Jorge Castañeda, in a specially arranged meeting with the
Mexican ambassadors to the countries in that region,
emphasized the "maximum priority" accorded to the situation there.203 In regard to the mid-July 1981, Nassau
meeting between the foreign ministers of Mexico, the
United States, Venezuela, and Canada, to define programs

of cooperation for the development of Central America and
the Caribbean, the Mexican government strongly made the
point that any form of assistance must be free of political and/or military components.[204]

The Mexican government has emphasized the need to
deal with three "knots" of tension in the region: relations between Washington and Managua; relations between
Washington and Havana; and insurgency in El Salvador.
In February 1982, during a visit to Managua, President
López Portillo unveiled a peace plan which included
negotiations among the warring factions in El Salvador,
and a rapprochement among the United States, Nicaragua,
and Cuba. Mexico would act as a conduit in facilitating
negotiations. At the time, the Mexican President underscored that the initiative could be the "last opportunity" to avoid a "conflagration" in the region.[205]

The Reagan administration reacted coolly to the
Mexican proposal. However, under pressure from numerous
members of Congress, and faced with the endorsement of
the plan by several of the interested parties in the
Caribbean and Central American region, by March 1982, the
Department of State nominally agreed to pay attention to
the scheme for negotiations, albeit in a lukewarm
fashion. The question remained as to the depth of commitment by the Reagan administration to the Mexican plan.
At various points, U.S. government spokesmen tended to
underscore the need to assuage Mexican sensitivities, to
demonstrate the fallacy of cooptation as a means to dif-
fuse the crisis, and to preempt Soviet support for
Mexico's mediation offer.[206] These counterproductive
expectations have brought about an appeal from various
American public opinion circles, for the Reagan administration to seriously support negotiations and peaceful
diplomacy, as well as the Mexican role as mediator. As
the New York Times emphasized in an editorial of mid-
March 1982, "In fact, without Mexican involvement, there
can be no Central American policy worthy of the name."[207]

Part of the Reagan administration's reluctance to
accept the Mexican peace plan at its face value springs
from a distinct set of perceptions towards the Caribbean
and Central American situation, in terms of a security
threat by Soviet and Cuban interference.[208] This was
underscored by President Reagan's Caribbean Basin Initiative, enunciated in February 1982. The program professed
to encourage economic and political reform, through
measures such as duty-free status on Caribbean goods
imported to the United States, and guarantees plus tax
incentives to American investors.[209] However, it was
strongly tinted by warnings regarding the military
dangers posed by Cuba and Nicaragua. Reagan proceeded
to virtually consign the Sandinista government of
Nicaragua to the Soviet camp, and did not exclude military intervention and escalation by the United States as

means to achieve peace and security in the area.[210]
There seemed to be a contradiction between socioeconomic
initiatives and belligerent rhetoric. Indeed, there was
a noticeable gap between an apparent readiness for confrontation on the part of the United States and an emphasis on the need for compromise by Mexico. American
allies within the European Common Market have also
stressed economic problems and social inequalities as
the roots of political violence.[211]

Nonetheless, by Mid-March 1982, as a result of
representations made to both countries by Mexico, the
United States and Nicaragua had apparently agreed to
hold negotiations on all issues, including American
charges of Sandinist arms shipments to the rebels in
El Salvador, and Nicaragua's fears of U.S. aggression.[212]
But procrastination was likely to underscore the
fragility of these diplomatic overtures. Meanwhile,
Mexican support for the Sandinista government was not
only diplomatic and political, but included measures of
economic assistance, as well as the presence of about
400 Mexican technicians providing expertise in areas
such as agronomy, medicine, and petroleum engineering.[213]

The Mexican position has been particularly forceful
in the case of El Salvador, where its objective has been
to promote a political solution among the warring factions. Mexico pointed out that elections, given the turmoil and instability, were unlikely to be conclusive, and
might even prolong the conflict. Late in August 1981,
the Mexican and French governments issued a joint statement recognizing the rebels in El Salvador as "a representative political force." The document emphasized that
a negotiated solution among the various factions, including the rebels, was the only way out of the conflict.
The U.S. government expressed anger and indignation at
the French-Mexican initiative. For the United States,
the elections were the key to legitimize the reformist
and pro-U.S. Christian Democrat government. Likewise,
several Latin American nations reacted unfavorably. In
early September 1981, Argentina, Colombia, and Venezuela
had issued a statement supporting El Salvador's government, and criticizing Mexico and France for interfering
in that country's internal affairs.[214] These actions
raised the possibility of an attempt to isolate Mexico
diplomatically, if the Mexican government were to harden
its views on the matter.

By late March 1982, after the elections in El
Salvador were finally held, the logic of the Mexican
position became clear. The elections, far from elucidat-
ing the political situation in that country, made it
increasingly explosive, by undermining the democratic
center of Salvadoran politics, and the possibility for
deep-seated reforms. Rightist factions were the ultimate
winners, strengthened beyond their real level of popular

appeal, due to the peculiarities of the election process, i.e the absence of other centrist and leftist groups. In control of the Constituent Assembly, these rightist forces were likely to pressure for a military solution to the civil war and a phasing out of the most significant points of the reform program of the Chistian Democrats. Likewise, the elections seemed to prop up conservative, anti-reform sectors of the army. Finally, the outcome was bound to convince the guerrilla groups of the need for unity and continued fighting, perhaps with increased outside assistance.215

Thus, in spite of the euphoria of some U.S. officials, the election results were likely to bring about a polarization and an intensification of the conflict in El Salvador. In this context, attention to the socioeconomic roots of the crisis would diminish, and U.S. foreign policy would be forced to support and ally itself with groups that ultimately are unresponsible to the urgent need for reforms. On the other hand, the possibility still remained, of a negotiated solution along the lines of the Mexican proposal, to a basically stalemated civil war.

In his annual report of September 1981, President López Portillo reiterated his government's support for Cuba, Nicaragua, and the leftist insurgents in El Salvador, in the following terms:

> ...during the last year we have centered our action on the nearest area, geographically and politically, to our own essence: Central America and the Caribbean holding high the banner of nonintervention. We have, on repeated occasions, made clear publicly, privately and in many ways, our disagreement and opposition to all types of interterence in the area, especially by the superpowers.... By further tightening the links of friendship and cooperation that bind us with the revolutions of Cuba and Nicaragua, we have underscored Mexico's attachment to the political principle of the free determination of peoples... because of sympathy and affinity with the essence of their struggle-social justice-(Mexico) has helped them and will continue to do so.216

A key component of Mexico's foreign policy is the Energy Cooperation Program for Central America and the Caribbean, i.e. the San Jose Pact, created by Mexico and Venezuela in August 1980. The program provides approximate 160,000 b/d of oil to nine countries, at 70 percent of the going market rate, and the rest payable through long-term, low-interest loans.217 For President López Portillo, this program of easy oil terms for developing countries represents a solid step "in the construction

of a new economic order not dominated by the superpowers." Mexico also intended to set an example for
Venezuela's fellow OPEC members.[218] In August 1981,
Mexico and Venezuela renewed the accord for another
year. At that time the countries benefiting from the
program were: Barbados, Costa Rica, El Salvador,
Guatemala, Honduras, Jamaica, Nicaragua, Panama, and the
Dominican Republic. Savings for these countries represented a total of one billion pesos per year.[219]

The San Jose Pact must be inscribed within the context of Mexico's strategy to promote a global energy
agreement. On September 27, 1979 in his address to the
United Nations, President López Portillo unveiled a nine-
point World Energy Plan, which would guarantee the sover-
eignity of the participating states and create an agency
to finance the energy needs of hard-pressed developing
countries.[220] The objective of the plan would be "to
insure an orderly, progressive, integral, and just transition between two epochs of humanity," i.e. the era of
petroleum and that which will be based on new energy
sources.[221]

This proposal followed the international objectives
of former President Echeverría's "New Economic Order,"
based on more equal and just economic exchanges between
developed nations and "Third World" countries, which
Mexico has tried to promote through its sponsorship of
the "Charter of Rights and Duties of the States." In
November 1979, 113 developing countries (the Group of
77), presented in the United Nations a project for international economic cooperation that included the World
Energy Plan as a medullar part. Industrial nations
accepted the project as an adequate framework for
negotiations.[222]

In September 1980, the United Nations proclaimed a
new international strategy for development during the
1980s, which included a restructuring of the global
energy market, on the basis of the Mexican World Energy
Plan.[223] However, opposition to the plan developed from
some OPEC members, since it could diminish the bargaining
power of petroleum vis a vis the industrial nations.[224]
Mexican initiatives in the field of energy have included
regional schemes as well. By early April 1981, the
Mexican and Venezuelan governments proposed the formation
of a Latin American Multinational Petroleum Enterprise,
which would refine and distribute all the crude contributed by both countries, according to the terms of the
San Jose Pact.[225] Since late 1980, the Canadian government has expressed its interest in participating in the
Mexican-Venezuelan petroleum cooperation program towards
Central America and the Caribbean.[226]

By mid-1980, as a result of President López
Portillo's visit to Brazil, commentators in both nations
believed that the energy crisis and Mexico's willingness

to cooperate with Brazil, were likely to bring a complete turnabout of previously cold relations between "the two most developed Latin American countries," in what could be on a long range "the most important step taken in the last years towards Latin American integration."[227] In October 1981, Mexico, Brazil, and Venezuela officially announced the signing of a joint agreement on Latin American potential oil extraction and exploration projects. This trilateral effort is designed to promote schemes of technical and financial assistance to western hemispheric countries. The accord is to be carried out through the participation of PEMEX, the Brazilian Petroleum Corporation (Petrobras), and Venezuelan Petroleum, Inc. (PDVSA).[228]

An analysis of Mexican initiatives must include the International Meeting on Cooperation and Development, informally known as the North-South Conference, which took place at Cancún, Mexico, in October 1981. Under the sponsorship of the Mexican and Austrian governments, leaders of eight industrialized and fourteen developing nations met to discuss international problems related to issues of food, energy, trade, and finance. Third World countries would like to obtain more favorable terms of trade, a stronger voice in the World Bank and the International Monetary Fund, and in general better bargaining conditions.[229]

The position of the United States on these issues, as expressed by President Reagan at Cancun, relies on free trade and free enterprise as the key to development. Reagan emphasized that discussions must remain within the framework of international agencies, contrary to the wish of delegates from developing countries of consolidating the debates into a single forum, ideally the United Nations General Assembly.[230] By contrast, President López Portillo stressed the need to move towards a transfer of resources from the north to the south, and to establish guaranteed prices for raw materials and easier access to finance.[231]

Specifically, one of the key demands of developing nations, since their economies are strapped by the high cost of imported oil, refers to the establishment of an energy agency connected to the World Bank, with a thirty billion dollar fund to promote exploration and development of energy resources. Mexico strongly supports this scheme. At the end of the Cancún conference, spokesman reported a "near consensus" in favor of the creation of the energy affiliate. However, the Reagan administration opposed this idea, emphasizing rather the efforts by private enterprise.[232]

In the end, even though no specific agreements were reached concerning energy, nor in regard to food distribution, financing and trade, the conference was unanimously hailed as constructive and positive. The presence

of President Reagan at Cancun pleased and encouraged
Third World delegates, and a vague compromise appeared to
develop, as well as the apparent decision to meet again
in the future. As host to the meeting, Mexico reaped
very definite diplomatic rewards.233 President López
Portillo, in September 1981, referred to the North-South
Conference at Cancun as

> the most important international action attemped
> by Mexico during the last year, and that which
> best reveals the active and dynamic character
> of its realistic policy to influence events and
> not only to invoke principles.234

Mexican policies are increasingly important not only
in regard to North-South, but also South-South relations.
This is clearly illustrated by Mexico's stand vis a vis
the Organization of Petroleum Exporting Countries.
There are several points worth mentioned here. PEMEX has
considered OPEC's prices as the basic reference for
adjustments in its price and exports levels. In this
respect, the presence of Mexico in the international
petroleum market could be argued to represent a stabilizing factor, as long as Mexico follows a policy consonant
with that of OPEC.235

On the other hand, PEMEX's growing exports since the
mid-1970s have tended to diminish the bargaining strength
of OPEC. Mexico has refrained from selling its oil in
the "spot" market, where immediate delivery plans determine prices according to the supply and demand of crude
outside official national and international controls.
However, in July 1981, the OPEC Bulletin, the official
publication of that organization, denounced that PEMEX
was, in fact, selling "Istmo" crude directly to companies
and governments, in Rotterdam, London, and New York. The
"spot" market is anathema to OPEC since it lessens that
organization's control over the market. PEMEX insists
that it has sold oil only through bilateral accords,
and that no significant volumes of Mexican oil have been
detected in the "spot" markets.236

Some Mexican analysts argue that Mexico should join
OPEC, as a measure of solidarity with Third World countries, and in order to strengthen the position of that
organization in questions such as international trade and
financing.237 While indirectly supporting the price
levels out by OPEC, the Mexican government has been
reluctant to enter that organization. The reasons for
this attitude are to be found in the traditional Mexican
policy of self-reliance and independence in foreign
matters. Furthermore, in the past Mexico has publicly
criticized the "oligopoly commercialization practices"
prevailing in OPEC, especially as they have adversely
affected the development programs in poor countries.238

However, by May 1982, as yet another effect of the world
oversupply of oil, Mexico agreed to accept "observer"
status in OPEC, in a move that could be a step towards
full membership. Additionally, as a demonstration of its
endorsement of OPEC's policies of restricting production,
Mexico lowered its exports ceiling to 1.25 million b/d.
These signs seemed to indicate a change of policy by the
Mexican government vis a vis OPEC.[239]
Mexico is delineating a coherent connection between
its regional and global policies. In September 1981,
President López Portillo explained the reasons for
Mexico's greater attention to international relations:

> ...(there is) the clear conscience of an active
> interaction between domestic and international
> affairs. Much of what occurs in the rest of the
> world affects us decisively, and a great part
> of the principal solutions to our problems lies
> outside.[240]

In his fifth annual report, President López Portillo
underscored Mexico's opposition to "a new and unacceptable bipolarity," based on a huge weapons buildup by the
superpowers. Likewise, he lamented the apparent demise
of the Salt II treaty as a return to Cold War conditions,
and singled out the ominous noutron bomb as an added
threat to mankind. In regard to Mexico's traditional
support for non-intervention, the Mexican president
demanded the withdrawal of foreign troops from
Afghanistan and Cambodia, and a peaceful resolution of
the Middle East crisis, according to the United Nations
resolutions. He also expressed the support by the
Mexican government of the independence of Belice, which
Guatemala does not recognize as a sovereign state, and
the censure of South Africa's occupation of Namibia and
its apartheid policies.[241]
As Mexico pushes on with a more vigorous foreign
policy, it would appear that growing differences with
Washington might undermine U.S.-Mexican relations.
Mexican stands on certain worldwide issues and regional
questions are at odds with those of the Reagan administration.[242] The Mexican government has made friendly
gestures towards the Soviet Union which, according to
some American observers, means that "Mexico is more fearful of the United States," due to geographical
proximity.[243] The Mexican position on Central America
has echoed in NATO, as several European allies of the
United States, i.e. Greece, Denmark, and the Netherlands,
have supported the French-Mexican resolution urging the
ruling junta in El Salvador to negotiate with the guerrilla forces there. [244]
However, visible areas of dispute may obscure the
underlying fact that, ultimately, both the United States

226

and Mexico share views on the need for political stability as the basis for peaceful development. In this
regard, President López Portillo has expressed that, "the
relations between Mexico and the United States must
transcend their traditional mold and look for shared
criteria and solutions."[245]

NOTES

1. Only behind Canada and Japan.
2. David R. Rondfelt and Caesar D. Sereseres,"Un
nuevo marco político para las relaciones de Mexico con
Estados Unidos," Foro Internacional 74, Vol. XIX, No. 2,
October-December 1978, El Colegio de Mexico, p. 249.
3.. Ibid.
4. Calvin Pat Blair, Petróleo y desarrollo, algunas
políticas para E.U. y Mexico, cited in "Precipita el
petróleo el cambio en las relaciones Mexico-E.U.," Uno
mas Uno, February 3, 1981, pp. 1-2.
5. James W. Wilkie, "Conflicting National Interests
between and within Mexico and the United States,"
Prepared Statement for Recent Developments in Mexico and
their Economic Implications for the United States, hearings before the Subcommittee on Inter-American Economic
Relationship of the Joint Economic Committee, Congress
of the U.S., 95th Congress, 1st Session (Washington:
U.S. Government Printing Office, January 17 & 24, 1977),
pp. 6-10.
6. Ibid., p. 11.
7. Ibid., p. 6.
8. "Muy complicada, no inconsistente, la relación
de Estados Unidos con Mexico: Departamento de Estado,"
Uno mas Uno, July 31, 1980, p. 7.
9. Ibid.
10. Memorandum from the President, The White House,
Washington, April 26, 1979.
11. Ibid.
12. Joseph Hodara, "Hacia la finlandización de
Mexico?" Vuelta, No. 51, Vol. 5, February 1981, Mexico,
p. 22.
13. In this context, see, for example, Robert
Leiken, "Como ganar la amistad de Mexico," Vuelta, Vol.
5, No. 53, April 1981, p. 26, and Olga Pellicer de Brody,
"La Política de Reagan Hacia Mexico," Uno mas Uno
(Special Supplement), 1981, date not available.
14. "No existen en la tierra dos naciones tan
estrechamente entrelazadas," Proceso, 1978, p. 6.
15. Wilkie, op. cit., pp. 5-6.
16. Edward J. Williams, The Rebirth of the Mexican
Petroleum Industry (Lexington, MA: D.C. Heath and Co.,
1979), p. 60; Rondfelt, op. cit., pp. 252-253.

17. Barry A. Sklar and Gary J. Pagliano, Energy and Future U.S.-Mexican Relations," in Mexico's Oil and Gas Policy: An Analysis. A report prepared for the Committee for Foreign Relations, U.S. Senate and the Joint Economic Committee, Congress of the U.S. by Congressional Research Service, Library of Congress, 96th Congress, 2nd Session, December 1978 (Washington: U.S. Government Printing Office, 1979), p. 52.

18. Rondfelt, op. cit., p. 248.

19. Washington Post, November 7, 1978, cited in Sklar, op. cit., p. 52.

20. Hodara, op. cit., pp. 19 -20.

21. Carlos Rico, "Las relaciones Mexicano-norte-americanas y la retórica de la interdependencia," Proceso, February 1978, pp. 8 & 10.

22. Heberto Castillo, "Mexico socio preferente de E.U.," in ibid., p. 8.

23. Olga Pellicer de Brody, "La política de los Estados Unidos hacia Mexico en la coyuntura actual: una relación muy especial?," Working Paper No. 7, Latin American Program, Woodrow Wilson International Center for Scholars, April 1978, p. 4.

24. Pellicer, "La Política de Estados Unidos hacia Mexico: la nueva perspectiva," Foro Internacional 74, op. cit., pp. 202 & 214.

25. Richard R. Fagen, "El Potróleo Mexicano y la Seguridad Nacional de Estados Unidos," in ibid., p. 222.

26. Jorge Castañeda, "Mexico y E.U.: El Próximo Decenio," Comercio Exterior, Vol. 30, No. 6, June 1980, Mexico, p. 618.

27. Victor S. D'Souza, "La Transformación de las sociedades: una perspectiva para las relaciones entre los paises desarrollados y los que están en vías de desarrollo," Social Action, Vol. 26, No. 2, April-June 1976, New Delhi, India.

28. "Carter debe tomar en cuenta problemas de comercio e ilegales," Excelsior, March 20, 1979, pp. 1 & 13-A.

29. Blair, op. cit., pp. 1 & 12.

30. "Trabar exportaciones no resolvera el bracerismo: JLP," Excelsior, February 8, 1979, p. 1. Conferencia de Prensa del presidente de Mexico ante el Club Nacional de Prensa de E.U., El Sol de Mexico, February 16, 1977, pp. 1 & 12. "Mexico: The Road Back to Confidence," Time, February 21, 1977, pp. 16-22.

31. "U.S. Policy on Mexican Immigration," Current History, November 1981, p. 385. "Reagan Plan Asks New Alien Quotas," The New York Times, January 26, 1982, pp. 1 & 9. Sylvia Ann Hewlett, "Coping with Illegal Immigrants," Foreign Affairs, Winter, 1981-1982, pp. 355-378. "Mexico-U.S. Immigration Policy Dispute," Latin American Index, Vol. X, No. 1, January 15, 1982, p. 1. "E.U. no Presiona a Mexico con la Carta Silva,"

228

<u>Excelsior</u>, January 9, 1982, p. 1.

32. Castañeda, <u>op</u>. <u>cit</u>., p. 18.

33. "The time to look to the future," <u>Time</u>, February 21, 1977, p. 22.

34. "Conferencia de prensa al finalizar la visita del Presidente Carter," Marzo, 1979, in <u>En Torno a la visita del Presidente Carter a Mexico</u>, Cuadernos de Filosofía Política No. 17, Secretaría de Programación y Presupuesto, Mexico, p. 29.

35. "Será lento el Comercio con Mexico: Kruger," <u>Excelsior</u>, June 27, 1980, pp. 1 & 11-A. And "Incertidumbre en el Comercio de Mexico y E.U. por el Rechazo al GATT: Kruger," <u>Excelsior</u>, July 23, 1980.

36. See Edward Williams, <u>Petroleum and Political Change in Mexico</u>, Harvard University, April 1980, pp. 48-49.

37. Armando Labra, "Introducción al Acuerdo General sobre Aranceles Aduaneros y Comercio," in <u>Las Relacions Mexico/ Estados Unidos/1</u>, UNAM, Editorial Nueva Imagen, 1980, p. 159.

38. V Informe de Gobierno, <u>El Universal</u>, September 2, 1981, p. 26.

39. Robert Gutiérrez M., "Planeación energética y política económica," in <u>El Petróleo Hoy</u> (Supplement) <u>Uno mas Uno</u>, March 18, 1981, p. 11.

40. For a precise, detailed account of the gasoducto affair, see Richard R. Fagen, <u>Mexican Gas: The Northern Connection</u>, Working Paper No. 15, the Latin American Program, Woodrow Wilson International Center for Scholars, March 1978.

41. See, for example, <u>The Wall Street Journal</u>, "The Mexican Gas Fiasco," September 1978, and "Mexico's Plan to Sell Natural Gas to the U.S., beset by problems, is cancelled by Pemex," September 15, 1978.

42. "The Battle of the Toasts," <u>Time</u>, February 26, 1979, p. 16.

43. "Franqueza y Respeto, Necesarios," <u>Excelsior</u>, June 27, 1980, p. 1.

44. U.S.-Mexican Joint Announcement, The White House, Office of the White House Press Secretary, September 21, 1979.

45. "DOE receives application to import Mexican Natural Gas," <u>DOE News</u>, U.S. Department of Energy, Office of Public Affairs, November 21, 1979.

46. Importation of Mexican Natural Gas - 1979. Order approving in part an application of Border Gas, Inc., to import Natural Gas into the U.S. from Mexico. DOE, Economic Regulatory Administration, December 29, 1979.

47. DOE gives final clearance to import of natural gas from Mexico," DOE News, <u>op</u>. <u>cit</u>., December 29, 1979.

48. For an account of various estimates on damages in the U.S., see <u>Blowout of the Mexican Oil Well Ixtoc I</u>,

Hearings before the Committee on Merchant Marine and Fisheries and the Subcommittee on Water Resources of the Committee on Public Works and Transportation, House of Representatives, 96th Congress, 1st Session, on the Impact of the Blowout of the Mexican Oil Well Ixtoc I and the resultant oil pollution on Texas and the Gulf of Mexico, Corpus Christi, Texas, September 8-9, 1979 (Washington: U.S. Government Printing Office, 1980).

49. "El Gobierno de E.U. estudia la posibilidad de demandar a Pemex, pero teme las repercusiones," Uno mas Uno, February 3, 1981, p. 14.

50. For a detailed study of the effect of the Ixtoc I blowout on U.S.-Mexican relations, as well as possible solutions to the issue, see Robert D. Tomasek, "United States-Mexican Relations: Blowout of the Mexican Oil Well Ixtoc I," American Universities Field Staff Reports, 1981/No. 20, Hanover, NH.

51. Alfred Stepan, "The United States and Latin America: Vital Interests and the Instruments of Power," Foreign Affairs, Vol. 58, No. 2, 1980, pp. 665-668.

52. Ibid., p. 668.

53. Redvers Opie, State, in Recent Developments in Mexico and their Economic Implications for the U.S., op. cit., pp. 18 & 20.

54. Clark Reynolds, Statement, in ibid., pp. 38 & 43.

55. Ibid., p. 77.

56. See Kenneth E. Hill, "Three Nations together on Energy," The New York Times, March 23, 1979, relative to this study dated January 1979.

57. Earl V. Anderson, "North American Trade Alliance Gains Support," Chemical and Engineering News, Vol. 58, No. 28, July 14, 1980, pp. 12-22.

58. "Estrategia para persuadirnos a integrar el Mercomún del Norte," Excelsior, August 8, 1980, pp. 1 & 14.

59. See, for example, "Reagan's Mexican Overture," Newsweek, January 12, 1981, pp. 6-7.

60. "Provocación, el Mercomún que pretende E.U.," Excelsior, April 19, 1979, pp. 1 & 9-A.

61. "Alan Riding, The New York Times, in "Mexico da a Canada unas lecciones sobre como tratar a E.U.: NYT," Excelsior, July 6, 1980.

62. Bruce Bagley, "Mexico in the 1980s: A New Regional Power," Current History, November 1981, p. 356. Paul E. Sigmund, "Latin America: Change or Continuity?" Foreign Affairs, Vol. 60, No. 3, 1982, p. 648.

63. Riding, op. cit., p. 668.

64. Melvin Conant and Fern R. Gold, "Geopolitics of energy," Committee on Interior and Insular Affairs, U.S. Senate, Energy Publication, No. 95-1, Washington, January 1977, p. 5.

65. Ibid.

230

66. Tad Szulc, "An Interview with Mexico's President Jose Lopez Portillo," Parade, St. Louis Post-Distatch, October 4, 1981, p. 7.

67. V Informe de Gobierno, op. cit., p. 26.

68. Richard B. Mancke, Mexican Oil and Natural Gas (New York: Praeger Publishers, 1979), p. 125.

69. Ibid., pp. 124-131.

70. Szulc, op. cit., p. 4.

71. "No urgen a E.U. los hidrocarburos de Mexico, dice Carter," Excelsior, January 18, 1979, p. 1.

72. "Debe E.U. cuidar sus relaciones con Mexico," Excelsior, September 18, 1980, p. 1.

73. "Mexico, pieza clave en la estrategia de seguridad de E.U.: Nava," Excelsior, October 10, 1980, p. 1.

74. David Rondfelt, Richard Nehring, and Arturo Gandara, "El Petróleo de Mexico y la política de E.U.: Implicaciones para la década de los ochenta," Rand Corporation, cited in "Estados Unidos debe incrementar la interdependencia con Mexico sin limitarse al área de los energéticos," Uno mas Uno, October 6, 1980, p. 14.

75. Cited in "Más acuerdos bilaterales con Mexico proponen a E.U. Ambas naciones son interdependientes: Rand Corporation," Excelsior, October 22, 1980, pp. 1 & 18.

76. Ibid.

77. "Proponen asesores de Reagan Asegurar minerales con Mexico," Excelsior, December 9, 1980, p. 3-A.

78. See, for example, "Pemex venderá al Pentagono 1,400,000 barriles este mes. Destino: la reserva estratégica," Excelsior, June 6, 1978, p. 1

79. "Latin American Petroleum Survey, Part I," Washington Report on the Hemisphere, Vol. 2, No. 4, Council on Hemispheric Affairs, November 17, 1981, p. 6.

80. Richard Fagen, "The Realities of U.S.-Mexican Relations;" Also see John Saxe-Fernandez, Petroleo y Extrategia, Mexico y E.U. en el contexto de la política global (Mexico: Siglo XXI Editores, 1980), especially his concept of "strategic dependence," pp. 160-171.

81. Rand Corporation, Document R-2510-DOE, prepared for the Department of Energy, The White House, cited in "Condicionará E.U. sus acuerdos con Mexico, al abasto," Excelsior, November 19, 1980, pp. 1 & 19-A.

82. "Recomendación para que Estados Unidos aliente la creación de una sobrecapacidad petrolera mexicana," Uno mas Uno, May 9, 1981, p. 1.

83. Juan Antonio Zuniga, "Alternativa barata del Canal de Panamá," Proceso, Ano. 4, No. 173, February 25, 1980, pp. 6-8.

84. Letter by Hollis D. Hedberg, August 20, 1980, published as "The Great Gulf of Mexico Giveaway," The New York Times, September 7, 1980.

85. Aplaza E.U., "el tratado de límites de aguas," Excelsior, September 18, 1980, pp. 1 & 8.

86. "Enorme yacimiento de petróleo en el Golfo," Uno mas Uno, April 29, 1981, p. 1.

87. "En Mexico, un Quinto de la Reserva Petrolera Mundial," Excelsior, May 8, 1981, p. 1.

88. "Espera la SRE que E.U. ratifique el tratado de límites marítimos," Uno mas Uno, April 27, 1981, p. 1.

89. Marian Leighton, "Mexico, Cuba and the Soviet Union: Ferment in the U.S.'s backyard," Radio Liberty Research, FL 1/80, December 27, 1980, pp. 1 & 10.

90. Lewis A. Tambs, "Crisis in the Caribbean," SAFF Position Paper, Vol. 2, No. 24, 1979.

91. Yuri Gvozdev, "El Apetito de E.U. por el Petróleo, la Explicación de su Política Exterior," in Excelsior, July 15, 1981, page not available.

92. See Alan Riding, "Reagan Impact Felt in Central America," The New York Times, November 16, 1980, p. 8.

93. "El Caribe, 'tercera frontera' de E.U.: Departamento de Estado," Uno mas Uno, January 28, 1981, pp. 1 & 9.

94. "Haig Warns 'Hours Are Growing Short' on Nicaragua," The New York Times, November 23, 1981, p. 8.

95. Ibid., also, "Haig al Senado: no se desea una disputa con López Portillo," Uno mas Uno, January 14, 1980, p. 1.

96. "El Petróleo, potencial tesoro y amenaza a la independencia belicena," Proceso, June 30, 1980, pp. 18-19.

97. "Oleoducto en Guatemala," Uno mas Uno, May 24, 1978, p. 8. Also, "Guatemala, Nueva Fuente Petrolera para Estados Unidos: NYT," in Excelsior, May 29, 1981.

98. Intervencionismo, no ideologías, el peligro real: JPL," Excelsior, March 10, 1980, p. 1.

99. Christopher Dickey, The Washington Post, September 7, 1980.

100. See, for example, "La peligrosa indulgencia de Mexico," The Washington Post, in Contextos, Ano 2, No. 7, 19-25 February 1981, pp. 54-55.

101. "Mexico y Centroamerica, 'en riesgo permanente de desestabilización revolucionaria,'" Proceso, Año 5, No. 216, December 22, 1980, Mexico, pp. 11-14.

102. See sol W. Sander, "Mensaje Militar Mexicano a Centroamerica" Business Week, in ibid., pp. 49-51.

103. "Mexico podria ser invadido militarmente por E.U. si le limitara el suministro de petroleo: Clyde Mark," Uno mas Uno, December 11, 1980, p. 5.

104. "Preve Olga Pellicer una escalada de intervencion de Estados Unidos en Mexico," Proceso, Año 5, No. 219, January 12, 1981, p. 11.

105. Ibid., p. 13.

106. Hodara, op. cit., pp. 20-23.

107. Plan Global de Desarrollo, 1980-1982, Secretaría de Programación y Presupuesto, Mexico, 1980, p. 120.

108. Ibid., p. 121.

232

109. Mario Ojeda, "Mexico en el ámbito internacional," Foro Internacional, El Colegio de Mexico,
Vol. VI, No.s 2-3, October-December 1965, January-
March 1966, pp. 247-257.
110. Olga Pellicer de Brody and Esteban L. Mancilla,
"El entendimento con los Estados Unidos y la gestación
del desarrollo estabilizador," Historia de la Revolución
Mexicana 23, Periodo 1952-1960, El Colegio de Mexico,
1978, pp. 85-96.
111. Ojeda, "Mexico en el ámbito internacional,"
op. cit., pp. 264-265.
112. Ibid., pp. 264-265.
113. In this context, see Rosario Green, "Deuda
externa y política exterior: la vuelta a la
bilateralidad en las relaciones internacionales de
Mexico," in Continuidad y Cambio en la Política exterior
de Mexico: 1977, CEI, El Colegio de Mexico, 1977,
pp. 63-89.
114. Ojeda, "Mexico ante los E.U. en la coyuntura
actual," in ibid., pp. 40-41.
115. Eugenio Anguiano, "Mexico y el Tercer Mundo:
racionalización de una posición," in ibid., p. 227.
116. "Mexico no está en quiebra; no fui a pedir
prestado, declaró JLP," El Sol de Mexico, February 18,
1977, p. 1.
117. "Mixed feelings about Mexico," The Economist,
December 30, 1978.
118. "No mas nexos amo-cliente con E.U.; socios
iguales, JLP," Excelsior, October 14, 1978, p. 1.
119. JLP: Petróleo para Mexico, no para conveniencia
de E.U.," Excelsior, February 12, 1979, p. 1.
120. "El destino de Mexico ajeno a vaivenes políticos
de E.U.," Excelsior, November 6, 1980, p. 1.
121. Samuel Berkstein K., "Mexico: estrategia
petrolera y politica exterior," Foro Internacional, El
Colegio de Mexico, Vol, XXI, No. 1, July-September 1980,
pp. 65-82.
122. "Mantendrá su linea conservadora la extracción
petrolera," Excelsior, September 10, 1980, pp. 1 & 16-A.
123. Castañeda, op. cit., pp. 615-616.
124. Ibid., pp. 616-617.
125. Ibid., p. 617.
126. Mario Ojeda, Alcances y Límites de la Politica
Exterior de Mexico (Mexico: El Colegio de Mexico, 1976),
pp. 93-94.
127. See, for example, Mexico's petroleum and U.S.
policy: implications for the 1980's (R-2510-DOE), Rand
Corporation, June 1980, cited in "Retador Nacionalismo
Mexicano" and "Deben pesar igual crudo e interdependencia
Mexico-E.U.," Excelsior, November 17-18, 1980.
128. See Daniel James, "Mexico, Problema para
U.S.A.," The Washington Quarterly, and Christopher
Dickey, "El papel independiente del Mexico petrolero,"

The Washington Post, in Contextos, Secretaría de Pre-
supuesto y Programación, Año 1, No. 13, Mexico, 16-22
October 1980, pp. 6-21 and 24-26.
    129. "Pentagon Creates Caribbean Force," The New
York Times, November 24, 1981, p. 8. Also, see Olga
Pellicer de Brody, "La Política de Reagan Hacia Mexico,"
Uno mas Uno, date not available.
    130. Stepan, op. cit., pp. 659-662.
    131. Alan Riding, "Mexicans Caution Haig on Nicara-
gua," The New York Times, November 24, 1981, p. 7.
    132. Pellicer, "La Política de Reagan Hacia Mexico,"
op. cit.
    133. Szulc, op. cit., p. 9.
    134. See Pellicer, "La Politica de Reagan Hacia
Mexico," op. cit.
    135. See Luis Maira, "Los Supuestos Básicos de la
Política Latinoamericana de Reagan," Uno mas Uno, date
not available.
    136. Robert H. McBride, "The United States and
Mexico: The Shape of the Relationship," in McBride
(ed.), Mexico and the United States, The American
Assembly, Columbia University (Englewood Cliffs, NJ:
Prentice-Hall, Inc., 1981), pp. 6-7.
    137. Pellicer, "La Politica de Reagan Hacia Mexico,"
op. cit.
    138. McBride, op. cit., pp. 7-8.
    139. Pellicer, "La Política de Reagan Hacia Mexico,"
op. cit.
    140. Ibid.
    141. Ibid.
    142. McBride, op. cit., p. 3.
    143. Szulc, op. cit., p. 9.
    144. Ibid.
    145. Riding, "Mexicans Caution Haig on Nicaragua,"
op. cit., p. 7.
    146. Ibid.
    147. Jean Marc Kaelfeche, Le Figaro, Paris, November
14, 1977, cited in Carlos Alberto Mutto, "Nueva Saudiarabia, sin invertir mucho: Le Figaro," Excelsior,
November 15, 1977, pp. 1 & 14-A.
    148. Ibid., p. 14-A.
    149. Ibid.
    150. "Datos petroleros ocultos por años. Los
técnicos negaban información: JLP," Uno mas Uno, March
31, 1978, pp. 1 & 6.
    151. "Los datos de Pemex, únicos validos, opinan
diputados," Uno mas Uno, May 7, 1978, pp. 1 & 5.
    152. "Confia en Pemex la Banca Mundial; los ataques,
sin datos. Adivinanzas en la prensa de E.U.," Excelsior,
May 25, 1979, p. 1.
    153. "Hay 60,000 millones de barriles, reitera
Pemex," Excelsior, November 17, 1980, p. 1.

234

154. Olga Pellicer de Brody, "Relaciones Exteriores: Interdependencia con Estados Unidos o Proyecto Nacional," Mexico Hoy (Mexico: Siglo XXI Editores, 1979), pp. 372-384.

155. Jorge I. Domínguez, The implications of Mexico's internal affairs for its international relations, Center for International Affairs, Harvard University, April 18, 1980, pp. 1, 7, & 14.

156. Ibid., p. 20.

157. API degrees indicate the quality of petroleum, according to a scale developed by the American Petroleum Institute.

158. "Eleva Pemex sus tarifas de exportación," Uno mas Uno, December 24, 1980, pp. 1 & 14.

159. "Reduce Pemex su Dependencia de Mercado con E.U.: Díaz S.," Excelsior, January 28, 1981, pp. 1 & 8.

160. "Producción Inalterable Pese a la Decisión de OPEP: Pemex," Excelsior, May 28, 1981, p. 1.

161. Ibid.

162. "Tenemos que Abaratar el Petróleo Para Conservar Clientes," Excelsior, June 2, 1981, p. 1.

163. "Mexico tendrá que contratar una deuda externa adicional," Uno mas Uno, June 2, 1981, p. 1.

164. "Baja Pemex el Precio del Crudo de Exportación," Excelsior, June 4, 1981, p. 1. Also, "Cuatro dólares por barril, la reducción al precio del crudo," Uno mas Uno, June 4, 1981, p. 1.

165. "Renuncio Diaz Serrano; Moctezuma Cid, Director de Pemex," Excelsior, June 7, 1981, p. 1. Also, see "Las finanzas de Pemex a punto de estallar, por corrupción e incapacidad," Proceso, Año 5, No. 238, May 25, 1981, pp. 6-10.

166. V Informe de Gobierno, op. cit., p. 24.

167. "Se corregirá la baja precipitada al precio del crudo: JLP," Excelsior, June 12, 1981, p. 1.

168. "Se Revaluará el Crudo; Mexico no Propiciará Despilfarros," Excelsior, June 17, 1981, p. 1.

169. "Programa Energético de Cinco Puntos Para Superar la Crisis," Excelsior, July 27, 1981, p. 15-A.

170. "Considera Mexico Reducir Ventas de Petróleo, no Precio," Excelsior, June 23, 1981, p. 1. And, "Menos Producción y Precio más Alto, Desde Julio: Pemex," Excelsior, June 24, 1981, p. 1.

171. "Pemex Señala a sus Clientes las Bases Para Acordar el Alza," Excelsior, June 29, 1981, p. 1. And, "Pemex Eleva 2 Dls. sus Precios," Excelsior, July 1, 1981, p. 1.

172. "Francia Desea Bajar a la Mitad sus Compras de Crudo a Pemex," Excelsior, June 23, 1981, p. 1.

173. "Se negocia un Aumento; Cancelan 310,000 Barriles al dia," Excelsior, June 27, 1981, p. 1.

174. Cancelan 9 clientes, Pero se Negocia: Pemex, Excelsior, July 3, 1981, p. 1.

175. "Convenio de Pemex y 82 Bancos," Excelsior, June 30, 1981, pp. 1 & 14.

176. Cited in "13,000 Millones de Dolares, la Deuda de la Empresa; Sigue la Linea del FMI: IIEUNAM," Excelsior, July 3, 1981, pp. 1 & 8.

177. "La CFP, con Derecho a Suspender Compras," Excelsior, July 5, 1981, p. 1.

178. "Elimina Mexico de Todo Proyecto a Empresas Francesas," Excelsior, July 5, 1981, p. 1. Also, "A su Tiempo, Detalles de las Cancelaciones a Francia: JLP," Excelsior, July 6, 1981, p. 1.

179. "Francia, Dispuesta a Llegar a un Compromiso con Mexico," Excelsior, July 7, 1981, p. 1. "Pide la CFP Reanudar Negociaciones Sobre el Petróleo," Excelsior, July 8, 1981, p. 1. "Esencial, Ahondar las Relaciones con Mexico: Mitterand," Excelsior, July 9, 1981, p. 1.

180. "Francia continuará comprando el petróleo mexicano," El Universal, July 17, 1981, p. 1.

181. "Venderá Petróleos Este mes 1.2 Millones de Barriles Diarios," Excelsior, August 4, 1981, p. 1.

182. Raul Olmedo, "Después de la Tormenta," Excelsior, August 1981.

183. Thomas L. Friedman, "Oil Price Rise Put a 40¢ a Barrel," The New York Times, November 10, 1981, pp. 27 & 36.

184. V Informe de Gobierno, op. cit., p. 24.

185. "World Oil Output Falls," The New York Times, April 1, 1982, p. 47.

186. "Mexican Sales of Oil Decline," The New York Times, April 13, 1982, p. 41.

187. See Luis Angeles, "Petróleo: un camino pesado," Uno mas Uno, April 21, 1981, p. 13.

188. V Informe de Gobierno, op. cit., p. 24.

189. Olga Pellicer, "Pragmatismo y tradición revolucionaria en la política exterior de Mexico," Proceso, Año 4, No. 195, July 28, 1980, pp. 13-14.

190. See, for example, R. Perez-Ayala, "Mexico, líder impasible," Excelsior, July 24, 1980, pp. 7-8.

191. Cited in "EU debera considerar a Mexico como lider emergente de America Latina," Uno mas Uno, December 2, 1980, p. 14.

192. "En Centroamerica, liderazgo mexicano: Carazo," Uno mas Uno, December 5, 1980, p. 1.

193. "Reduce Pemex su dependencia de mercado con EU," Excelsior, January 28, 1981, pp. 1 & 8-A.

194. "Pemex Eleva 2 Dls. sus Precios," op. cit.

195. Report of the Director General, Petroleos Mexicanos, March 18, 1981, pp. 25-26. Also, "Pemex ya es socio mayoritario de la empresa hispana Petronor," Uno mas Uno, January 13, 1981, p. 13.

196. "Invita Reagan a Pemex a competir en el mercado estadounidense," Excelsior, November 15, 1980, p. 17-A.

197. "Pemex en platicas para competir en EU," Uno mas Uno, November 19, 1980, p. 1. And "Mexico comercializará su propia gasolina en EU," Uno mas Uno, November 21, 1980, p. 14.

198. Marcela Serrato, "La Expansión de Pemex," in El Petróleo Hoy (Supplement), Uno mas Uno, March 18, 1981, p. 4.

199. Miguel Granados Chapa, "Petróleo para Cuba," Uno mas Uno, July 31, 1980, p. 4.

200. "Pemex explorará en busca de petróleo en la plataforma marina de Cuba," Excelsior, December 4, 1980, p. 4-A.

201. Cited in "Antojadiza versión sobre el protocolo Mexico-Cuba," Uno mas Uno, February 3, 1981, p. 9. Also, "Ningun acuerdo secreto entre Pemex y Cuba; no se transfiere maquinaria estadounidense," Excelsior, date not available.

202. Cited in Szulc, op. cit., p. 7.

203. "Reune a los embajadores en Centroamerica la SRE," Uno mas Uno, February 10, 1981, p. 1.

204. "Promoverá Mexico Ayuda a CA sin Condiciones Políticas," Excelsior, June 28, 1981, p. 1. And "Definirán Mexico, EU, Venezuela y Canada la Ayuda a CA," Excelsior, July 1, 1981, p. 1.

205. "Mexico's Bold Initiative," Washington Report of the Hemisphere, Vol. 2, No. 12, March 9, 1982, p. 3. "Mexican Peace Plan Takes Root," Washington Report on the Hemisphere, Vol. 2, No. 13, March 23, 1982, p. 1. Alan Riding, "López Portillo Urges Talks on Region," The New York Times, February 22, 1982, p. 4.

206. "U.S. Reacts Coolly to Peace Initiative by Lopez Portillo in Central America," The New York Times, February 24, 1982, p. 6. "Mexican Peace Plan Gets U.S. Attention As Tensions Mount in Central America," The Wall Street Journal, March 17, 1982, p. 26. "Mexican Says Haig Has Ideas To Solve Caribbean Tension," The New York Times, March 15, 1981, p. 1. Philip Taubman, "Latin Policy: Out of Focus," The New York Times, March 17, 1982, p. 1. "Soviet Favors Mexico's Mediation Offer," The New York Times, March 18, 1982, p. 6.

207. "It's Mexico's Doorstep, Too," The New York Times, March 17, 1981, p. 26.

208. See Strategic Situation in Central America and the Caribbean, Current Policy No. 352, U.S. Department of State, Bureau of Public Affairs, Washington, DC, December 14, 1981.

209. "Text of President's Address on Aid Program for the Caribbean," The New York Times, February 25, 1982, p. 8. "Reagan Outlines Caribbean Basin Initiative," Latin American Index, Vol. X, No. 4, March 1, 1982, p. 13.

210. "Caribbean Vision and Nightmare," The New York Times, February 25, 1982, p. 24. "Reagan Urged by Aides

to Note Caribbean Peril," The New York Times, February 17, 1982.

211. "Central American Stability," The New York Times, February 26, 1982. "Common Market Plans to Increase Economic Aid to Central America," The New York Times, March 31, 1982, p. 6.

212. Alan Riding, "U.S. and Nicaragua Said to Agree to Hold Direct Talks on Dispute," The New York Times, March 24, 1982, p. 1. "Haig is Cautious About Any Accord with Nicaraguans," The New York Times, March 16, 1982, p. 1. "Nicaragua Accepts U.S. Plan for Talks on Reconciliation," The New York Times, April 15, 1982, p. 1.

213. Bagley, op. cit., p. 354.

214. "3 Nations Criticize France and Mexico," The New York Times, September 2, 1981, p. 4. And V Informe de Gobierno, op. cit., p. 26.

215. "5 rightist parties in El Salvador try to form coalition," The New York Times, March 31, 1982, p. 1.

216. V Informe de Gobierno, op. cit., p. 26.

217. "Mexico, Venezuela - Caribbean and Central American countries set regional oil supply plan," Energy Developments, V. XXIII, n. e273-8, July 15, 1980, pp. 53-54. Also, "Mexico and Venezuela Reap Harvest, and Share Some Wealth," Washington Report on the Hemisphere, Council on Hemispheric Affairs, Vol. 2, No. 4, November 17, 1981, p. 7.

218. Salvatore Bizzarro, "Mexico's oil boom," Current History, Vol. 82, No. 463, February 1981, p. 87.

219. "Se Prorroga por un año la Vigencia del Pacto de San José," Excelsior, August 5, 1981, p. 4-A.

220. Report of the Director General, op. cit., pp. 24-25. Also, "El Acuerdo de San José, paso hacia el Plan Mundial de Energía," Excelsior, August 4, 1980, p. 4-A.

221. Plan Global de Desarrollo, 1980-1982, op. cit., pp. 272-273.

222. "Plan de Nuevo Orden Mundial en la ONU; base, el de JLP," Excelsior, November 9, 1979, p. 1. And "Negociarán las potencias el proyecto energético de JLP," Excelsior, November 10, 1979, p. 1.

223. "La ONU reordenará el Mercado Mundial de Energía con base en el plan propuesto por López Portillo," Excelsior, September 1, 1980, p. 17-A.

224. "Se opone la OPEP al Plan Mundial de Energia," Excelsior, September 5, 1980, p. 1.

225. "Se Creará una Multinacional Petrolera Latinoamericana," Excelsior, April 9, 1981, p. 1.

226. "Canada quiere participar también en programas petroleros de ayuda a la región centroamericana," Uno mas Uno, August 7, 1980, p. 14.

227. "Giro radical Mexico-Brasil," Excelsior, July 27, 1980, pp. 1 & 22.

238

228. Washington Report on the Hemisphere, Council on
Hemispherc Affairs, Vol. 2, No. 4, November 17, 1981,
p. 2.
229. See Richard M. Harley, "Rich and Poor together
in Cancun," and Charles J. Harley, "Here are some of the
issues facing the summit," in St. Louis Globe-Democrat,
October 22, 1981, p. 17-A.
230. Bernard D. Nossiter, "Shift in Economic Order
to be the Focus at Cancun," The New York Times, October
21, 1981, p. 9. Alan Riding, "Reagan Supports Talks on
Poverty in Cancun Speech," The New York Times, October
23, 1981, pp. 1 & 8. "Negociacion Global 'Mutuamente
Aceptable' Plantea EU," Excelsior, October 23, 1981,
pp. 1 & 12. Also, "Excerpts from Reagan Speech on U.S.
Policy Toward Developing Nations," The New York Times,
October 16, 1981, p. 4.
231. "Cancun Summit Called a Success; Latin America
Leaders Oppose Reagan," Latin American Index, Vol. IX,
No. 18, November 1, 1981, p. 71.
232. Harley, op. cit. "Excerpts from Reagan Speech,"
op. cit. And, Alan Riding, "Cancun Talks End Without
Accord on Antipoverty Strategy," The New York Times,
October 24, 1981.
233. See Howell Raines, "President Asserts Meeting in
Cancun Was Constructive," The New York Times, October
25, 1981, p. 1.
234. V Informe de Gobierno, op. cit., p. 26.
235. See Luis Angeles, "La Politica petrolera de
Mexico" in El Petróleo Hoy (Supplement), Uno mas Uno,
March 18, 1981, p. 10.
236. Cited in Carlos Ramirez, "Revela la OPEP: crudo
Istmo en los mercados libres desde 1980," Proceso, Ano 5,
No. 244, July 6, 1981, pp. 6-8.
237. See, for example, Jose Luis Ceceña, "Razones
para la Incorporación," Excelsior, June 24, 1981, p. 7-A.
238. See, for example, "Mexico aplica tesis de la
OPEP," Excelsior, December 22, 1980, p. 1. "Ante Cepal,
Mexico rechaza estrategias petroleras como las de la
OPEP," Excelsior, April 27, 1979, p. 8-A.
239. "Role for Mexico in OPEC, is reported." The New
York Times, May 3, 1982, p. 27.
240. V Informe de Gobierno, op. cit., p. 26.
241. Ibid. Also, "Belize to face opposition in
U.N.," St. Louis Globe-Democrat, September 22, 1981,
p. 1.
242. See Christopher Dickey, "López Portillo Underlines Growing Rifts with U.S.," The Washington Post,
September 2, 1981, p. A-17.
243. See, for example, Robert Leiken, "Como ganar la
amistad de Mexico," in Vuelta, Vol. 5, No. 53, April
1981, pp. 26-28.
244. Bernard D. Nossiter, "Europe Allies Vex U.S. on
Salvador," The New York Times, November 25, 1981, p. 7.

245. V Informe de Gobierno, op. cit., p. 26.

8
Perspectives

FORCES AT WORK IN MEXICAN DEVELOPMENT

In the early 1980s, Mexico's process of development
appears to have reached a crucial juncture, propelled to
a great extent by its petroleum resources. A number of
factors qualify the situation.

It is clear by now that Mexico has ample oil and
natural gas reserves, which guarantee for the short and
middle ranges a steady expansion of its energy sector.
This fact represents a wide flexibility for governmental
policy, in regard to both the rate and modalities of
production of hydrocarbons, and the overall process of
development. But development remains unbalanced, and its
fruits unevenly distributed. Furthermore, the exports
sector of the Mexican economy relies overwhelmingly on
oil and its derived products, with the subsequent inflationary effects on the domestic market, and the danger
of "petrolization" of the economy.

Mexico remains today a dependent society, in economic, social and cultural terms, with its corresponding
political implications. This dependency takes place
primarily vis a vis the United States. However, Mexico
has also achieved by now a significant degree of national
integration. Nationalism is the most powerful political
force in Mexico. Historically, petroleum has been a
rallying point of Mexican nationalistic elan. Thus,
a growing dependency, linked to oil exploitation,
would exacerbate nationalism. On the other hand,
hydrocarbon reserves represent a possibility to promote
and consolidate an autonomous project of development.
The Mexican state is bound to play a critical role in
such a scenario, both as a promoter of, and benefactor
from nationalism.

Mexican nationalism is reinforced by a U.S. official
approach that borders on ethnocentrism. American official
and academic circles still, and inexcusably, tend too
often to see Mexico as just an extension of the American

model of development. This is, clearly, a biased perspective that does not engender good will among Mexican
decision makers and public opinion in general. There is
a need to approach Mexico, and Mexican domestic and
foreign policy, on their own terms, for what the country
is intrinsically as a society and a polity.

Likewise, the imperative and momentum of economic
growth cannot explain everything in Mexico. Due partly
to that same economic growth, stability and orderly
change are being constantly challenged by social and
political tensions. Ideology, whether in substance or
just rhetorically, plays a wider role in Mexico than in
the United States. All these factors, nationalism,
dependency, social and political forces at work towards
greater participation, ideology, must be taken into
account in order to better understand Mexico as a nation,
the import of its petroleum resources, and the configura-
tion of its foreign and domestic policy.

Most important, it is crucial to recognize that
solutions to these problems must originate in Mexico's
own reality, and in its historical and societal
processes. In this context, dependency represents a
source of stress for the system, since it undermines the
very basis of the nationalism which holds together
Mexican society. Mexico's stability and orderly development are directly related to whether its political system
can overcome the gnawings of domestic and international
flux, and whether it can be flexible enough to accom-
modate new groups and sectors of the population into an
inclusionary scheme. One of the keys to the viability
of the system will be the degree of success in achieving
a more just distribution of income during the 1980s.

The possibility of greater equilibrium for the
Mexican system is directly bound to the fact of dependency. To the degree that dependency increases, tensions
are likely to mount, too, out of a basic discord between
external influences and Mexico's unique characteristics.
The project of the Mexican state is geared to achieving
the stability of the polity under conditions of rapid
development, and a peaceful adjustment among its component groups. An abatement of dependency would give the
Mexican government more maneuvering room for implementing an appropriate and more equitable course of
development. In this context, the resources from hydrocarbon exploitation may propitiate a more acceptable
level of economic and political autonomy. However, this
objective emerges within a narrowing historical margin of
action, which is both the result of a confluence of
domestic and global trends, and the scenario for a
reappraisal of U.S.-Mexican relations.

PROSPECTS FOR U.S.-MEXICO RELATIONS

There appears to be a prevalent tendency in the
United States to equate increased Mexican oil production
with closer U.S.-Mexican relations and a healthier process of development in Mexico. This view, widely spread
among American official as well as academic circles, is
highly simplistic, and misses the general, complex dimension of the problem.
Representative of this position is Richard B.
Mancke. Mancke argues that rising oil production and
exports by Mexico would imply benefits for the United
States in strategic, economic and environmental terms.
Additionally, a deeper reliance on expanding Mexican oil
and gas production would mean that the United States
could postpone the costly search for alternative domestic
fuels, which require high-risk, long-term capital investments. On the other hand, an increase in petroleum output would foster economic growth and general prosperity
in Mexico, which in turn would help reduce the flow of
undocumented Mexican workers to the United States.
Mexico, says Mancke, unlike other oil-exporting countries
such as Saudi Arabia and Kuwait, has a sizable population
and a relatively developed infrastructure, which would
allow it to spend its oil earnings in acquiring foreign
goods and services.[1] Explains Mancke,

> In sum, since both Mexico and the United States
> would profit from a policy to expand production
> of Mexico's crude oil and national gas at the
> highest technical feasible rate, the crucial
> question becomes: what policies are available to
> each country for promoting achievement of this
> goal?.... The principal constraints slowing down
> the rate of long-term expansion are current short-
> ages of capital and technical expertise -resources
> of which the United States has an abundance.
> Since both countries would reap large gains from
> accelerating the rate of expansion, policies
> should be aimed at alleviating these constraints.[2]

Like so many arguments caught up in the fallacy of
the "growth paradigm," these views suffer from serious
shortcomings, and cannot stand the weight of evidence.
At first sight, the United States would seem to gain in
economic and strategic terms, from a rapidly expanding
Mexican oil production. But, on a middle and long range
basis, possible advantages are likely to be widely offset
by a series of potential dangers to the stability of
U.S.-Mexico relations.
The view that intensified oil exploitation would
redound in clear benefits for both the United States and
Mexico could be effectively challenged. The present

domestic situation would seem to lead to the conclusion
that if Mexico's economy and society become more petroleum-bound, dormant social and economic tensions might
reach a critical level, with the obvious negative political implications. Of course, it could be argued that
this would be the situation even more so without rapid
oil exploitation. But the point is that petroleum
could aggravate disequilibriums present in Mexican
society, and to become a mirage of apparently easy
solutions to deep-seated structural problems.

Looking at the strategic questions more carefully
from the previous perspective, it is clear that a rest-
less Mexico would be problematic for U.S. security and
strategic interests. In other words, the benefits accruing to the United States from a Mexico somewhat less formidable as an oil producer and exporter, but politically
stable, would seem to outweigh by far the ephemeral
benefits of a larger flow of petroleum, at the expense of
a politically volatile situation.

In this respect, a word of caution has already been
expressed by several critics of U.S.-Mexican relations.
In a 1977 article, Richard R. Fagen acknowledged that oil
represented a way out for Mexico from its immediate
social and economic problems, but also warned that

> Oil may allow Mexico to slip away from the IMF
> but not from history. Oil exports, the related
> relaxation of debt limits, and the easing of some
> aspects of the austerity program give breathing
> space, another chance for hard-pressed Mexican
> politicians. But oil by itself cannot respond
> to peasants' demands for land; nor can it create
> hundreds of thousands of new jobs each year; nor
> can it keep millions of Mexicans from crossing
> the border; nor make rapid inroads on redressing
> a distribution of income that is one of the most
> unequal in the world; nor reduce public and private
> corruption; nor deal with the human and social
> problems generated by a population that doubles in
> size every 20 years. All that oil can do -and
> this is not to be scoffed at- is soften and
> perhaps postpone for some years the sharpening of
> the contradictions that are inherent in the
> Mexican development model. It cannot solve them.[3]

More recently, David F. Rondfelt, Richard Nehring
and Arturo Gandara, in a study prepared for the Rand
Corporation, have warned that, under high production
levels, Mexican oil reserves might wane within fifteen
to twenty years. On a long range basis, for the United
States to see Mexican oil primarily as a cheap and convenient solution for its energy-related security
problems, might prove to be very costly. The danger

lies, say the authors, in the political and economic
instability that might result from an excessively rapid
development of the oil industry, and which might turn
Mexico from a secure to an insecure source of petroleum.[4]
    In this respect, Olga Pellicer has emphasized the
need for the United States to be aware of these ominous
possibilities and to contribute to prevent them. It is
a question, says Pellicer, for American political leadership to place the goal of balanced Mexican development
before certain American particular interests that favor
short-range capital expansion and fully irrestricted
trade. In the long-range, U.S. security will be better
protected by paying due attention to the requisites for
the peaceful, stable development of its southern neighbor.[5]
    It would seem that as Mexico consolidates itself
as an oil producer and exporter, its government will
continue to pursue an assertive and dynamic presence in
international affairs. Mexico's foreign policy, partly
because of a defensive reaction due to wariness of the
overwhelming U.S. proximity, and also because of its
nationalistic propelling force, will not acquiesce to
American overtures in Central America and the Caribbean.
And it is here that the greatest danger to the relations
between the two countries resides. Furthermore, the more
economically dependent Mexico is on the United States,
the greater its compensating efforts will be to implement an independent foreign policy, as a counterbalance
to the uneasy domestic cauldron.

A RECAPITULATION

    The Mexican government would seem to be caught in
the vicious circle of high levels of oil production,
recrudescence of socioeconomic shortcomings, and efforts
at compensation through still higher levels of oil production. This impasse will prove to be difficult to
overcome. In spite of the Energy Program and official
protestations in regard to a firm oil production and
exports platform, self-imposed levels of output are
likely to be surpassed. Increases in oil production and
exports are bound to take place because of the distortions in Mexico's process of development, and the need
to earn foreign currency to pay for domestic programs.
The fact is that Mexico's model of development remains
deeply unbalanced. Easy oil money is bound to underline
the negative aspects of the Mexican system. The challenge to Mexico's political leadership, is to create a
proper model of development, congruent with Mexico's
traditions, available means, and national goals.
    The Mexican state has been evolving since the reform
period in the 1850s. Petroleum wealth represents a big,

and probably the last, opportunity for the Mexican state
to give new sustenance, and justice, to the national
process of development, under its auspices. If it fails,
then the initiative will pass to private enterprise, or
to the military. The potential implications of either
course are grave: deep instability originating in
Mexico's nationalistic and leftist groups as the private
sector takes over the control levers of the economy, or
repression a la South America, with its impact on
Mexican migration to the United States.

These ominous possibilities should motivate the U.S.
government to devise and implement comprehensive policies
that take into account the entire scope of relations with
its southern neighbor, and promote the maintenance of a
moderately fluid interplay of political forces within
Mexico. At present, U.S. policies that encourage
increasingly higher levels of oil production in Mexico,
and at the same time thwart Mexican foreign policy initiatives, are myopic and counterproductive.

U.S.-Mexican rapprochement must tread, by necessity,
a path towards conciliation and compromise. This path
is located somewhere between Mexico's historical memory
and U.S. historical amnesia, between American attempts
to achieve total control of its sphere of influence, and
Mexico's need to uphold its sovereignty. A true partnership is required. As the stronger partner, the United
States must have, at the center of its foreign policy, a
special concern for the process of development in Mexico.
As Fagen asserts,

> At one level this means a frank recognition of
> the "specialness" of the U.S. relationship with
> Mexico by virtue of the 2,000-mile frontier, the
> weight of the U.S. presence in the Mexican economy,
> and the scale and importance of Mexico to the
> United States....an even greater challenge in the
> long run will be to find ways of supporting
> those aspects of Mexican development and political
> practice that promise to increase social justice
> ....to fail to understand that a Mexico in which
> the fruits of development are not more equitably
> shared is also a Mexico which cannot indefinitely
> continue to be a "good neighbor" is to misread
> history and to ignore geography.6

In any case, controversy over foreign policy matters
will continue to be a fact of life in U.S.-Mexico relations, at least in the short run. The challenge for both
countries is to keep confrontation within manageable
limits, and to set the basis for more amicable and
mutually satisfying relations in the long run. In this
context, U.S. energy needs must not blind Washington to

the increasingly complex scenario in Mexican domestic
politics, and its external reverberations.

Ultimately, Mexican nationalism does not need to be
incompatible with the national interest of the United
States, as long as the latter understands the nature of
ongoing changes in Mexico, and the need to go beyond
dependency towards a new form of interest association.
Mexico is trying to consolidate its political and economic autonomy, and to expand the range of its external
actions. A strong, self-reliant Mexico, and not a
dependent Mexico, is the best insurance for good, stable
bilateral relations.

On the other hand, Mexican initiatives in foreign
policy matters may pave the way for greater cooperation.
Under a more imaginative policy framework, the U.S.
government would encourage Mexico to play a greater role
in bringing peace and reconciliation between the warring
factions in El Salvador. Likewise, it could be argued
that American interests would be best served by improving
relations with Cuba, and thus reducing its reliance on
the Soviet Union, or by increasing economic and political
contacts with the Sandinista government in Nicaragua.
In both scenarios, Mexico would play an extremely useful
role as a mediator.

In any case, petroleum constitutes a watershed in
U.S.-Mexican relations. For the United States, it means a
change in its conduct and patterns of action towards
Mexico and, for the latter, a definition of its project
as a nation. This will require the demise of ethnocentric approaches on the part of the United States.
In the words of Michael and Nanneke Redclift:

> ...If Mexican policy is characterized by a
> search for greater economic independence, more
> attention to resource conservation, redistribu-
> tive policies at home, and an active foreign
> policy in Central America and the Caribbean,
> Washington should recognize that these policies
> are consistent with long-term U.S. interests.

If an association based on mutual interests and
benefits is to evolve, the U.S. government must understand and accept the changes that are taking place in
Mexico, and the emergence of the Mexican state as a
middle power with autonomous goals of its own. Under
other circumstances, the temptation of economic and
political interventionism may effectively obstruct this
unique opportunity.[8] The setting is thus ready for
closer friendship or escalating confrontation in the
relations between Mexico and the United States. In
this context, petroleum constitutes both a source of
confidence, and a quandary. It may turn out to be a
propelling force, or a quagmire. It corresponds to

decision makers in both nations to seize this historical challenge and turn it into a stepping stone for cooperation.

NOTES

1.   Richard B. Mancke, <u>Mexican Oil and Natural Gas</u> (New York: Praeger Publishers, 1979), pp. 4-13.

2.   <u>Ibid</u>., p. 12.

3.   Richard R. Fagen, "The Realities of U.S.-Mexican Relations," <u>Foreign Affairs</u>, Vol. 55, No. 4, July 1977, pp. 685-700.

4.   Cited in "E.U. no debe ver al petróleo mexicano como solución a sus problemas: Rand," <u>Excelsior</u>, June 20, 1980, p. 9-A.

5.   Olga Pellicer de Brody, "La Política de los E.U. hacia Mexico en la coyuntura actual: Una relación muy especial?" Working Paper No. 7, Colloquium, The Woodrow Wilson International Center for Scholars, April 1978, Washington, DC, pp. 14-15.

6.   Fagen, <u>op</u>. <u>cit</u>., pp. 699-700.

7.   Michael and Nanneke Redclift, "Unholy Alliance," <u>Foreign Policy</u>, No. 41, Winter 1980-1981, p. 133.

8.   See Óscar González, "Entenderán los Estados Unidos?" <u>Proceso</u>, No. 237, May 18, 1981, p. 30.

Bibliography

Books

Adams, Richard N. The Second Sowing: Power and Second-
    ary Development in Latin America. San Francisco:
    Chandler Publishing Co., 1967.
Adie, Robert F. and Guy E. Poitras. Latin America: The
    Politics of Immobility. New Jersey: Prentice Hall,
    Inc., 1974.
Aguilera Gomez, Manuel. La Desnacionalización de la
    Economía Mexicana. Mexico: Fondo de Cultura
    Económica, Archivo del Fondo 47, 1975.
Almond, Gabriel A. and G. Brigham Powell. Comparative
    Politics: A Developmental Approach. Boston:
    Little, Brown and Co., 1966.
Anderson, Charles W. Politics and Economic Change in
    Latin America. Princeton: D. Van Nostrand Co.,
    Inc., 1967.
Angeles, Luis. Crisis y Coyuntura de la Economía
    Mexicana. Mexico: Editorial El Caballito, 1979.
Barnet, Richard J. and Ronald E. Muller. Global Reach:
    The Power of the Multinational Corporation. New
    York: Simon and Schuster, 1974.
Bergsten, Fred C. and Lawrence B. Krause (eds.). World
    Politics and International Economics. Washington:
    The Brookings Institution, 1975.
Berle, Adolph. Latin America: Diplomacy and Reality.
    New York: Harper and Row, Inc., 1962.
Bermúdez, Antonio J. La Política Petrolera Mexicana.
    Mexico: Editorial Joaquín Mortiz, 1976.
Bhagwati, Jagdish (ed.). La Economia y el Orden Mundial
    en el Ano 2000. Mexico: Siglo XXI Editores, 1973.
Blake, David H. and Robert S. Walters. The Politics of
    Global Economic Relations. Englewood Cliffs, NJ:
    Prentice Hall, Inc., 1976.
Bueno, Gerardo. Opciones de Política Económica en
    Mexico después de la Devaluación. Mexico:
    Editorial Tecnos, 1977.
Burnett, Ben G. and Kenneth F. Johnson. Political Forces
    in Latin America: Dimensions of the Quest for
    Stability. Belmont, CA: Wadsworth Publishing
    Co., Inc., 1968.
Carmona, Fernando, et al. El Milagro Mexicano. Mexico:
    Editorial Nuestro Tiempo, 1970.
Cardoso, Fernando Henrique and Enzo Faletto. Dependencia
    y Desarrollo en América Latina. Mexico: Siglo XXI
    Editores, 1976.
Carrillo C., Alejandro. Las Empresas Públicas en
    Mexico. Mexico: Instituto Nacional de Administra-
    cion Publica, 1976.
Ceceña Luis, José. Mexico en la Orbita Imperial.
    Mexico: Ediciones El Caballito, 1970.

Chilcote, Ronald H. and Joel C. Edelstein. <u>Latin</u>
    <u>America: The Struggle with Dependency and Beyond</u>.
    New York: John Wiley and Sons, 1974.
Cline, Howard F. <u>The United States and Mexico</u>. New
    York: Atheneum, 1971.
Cockcroft, James, Andre Gunder Frank, and Dale L.
    Johnson. <u>Dependence and Underdevelopment: Latin</u>
    <u>America's Political Economy</u>. Garden City, NY:
    Doubleday, 1972.
<u>Continuidad y Cambio en la Política Exterior de Mexico:</u>
    <u>1977</u>. Mexico: El Colegio de Mexico, 1977.
Denison, Edward G. <u>Accounting for Slower Economic</u>
    <u>Growth: The United States in the 1970's</u>. Brookings
    Institution, 1979.
Frank, Andre Gunder. <u>Lumperburguesia: Lumpendesarrollo</u>.
    Mexico: Serie Popular Era, 1971.
_____. <u>Capitalism and Underdevelopment in Latin</u>
    <u>America</u>. New York: Monthly Review Press, 1967.
García Cantú, Gastón. <u>Las Invasiones Norteamericanas en</u>
    <u>Mexico</u>. Mexico: Ediciones Era, 1971.
Gettell, Raymond Garfield. <u>Political Science</u>. Boston:
    Ginn and Co., 1949.
Green, Rosario. <u>El Endeudamiento Público Externo de</u>
    <u>Mexico: 1940-1973</u>. Mexico: El Colegio de Mexico,
    1976.
Hansen, Roger D. <u>La Politica del Desarrollo Mexicano</u>.
    Mexico: Siglo XXI Editores, 1979.
Hartz, Louis. <u>The Founding of New Societies</u>. New York:
    Harcourt, Brace and World, Inc., 1964.
Hirschman, Albert O. <u>Journeys Toward Progress</u>. New
    York: Doubleday and Co., Inc., 1965.
Huntington, Samuel P. <u>Political Order in Changing</u>
    <u>Societies</u>. New York: Yale University Press, 1968.
Ianni, Octavio. <u>Imperialismo y Cultura de la Violencia</u>
    <u>en America Latina</u>. Mexico: Siglo XXI Editores,
    1976.
Jaguaribe, Helio. <u>La Dependencia Politico-Economica de</u>
    <u>America Latina</u>. Mexico: Siglo XXI Editores, 1971.
Katzenstein, Peter J. <u>Between Power and Plenty</u>.
    Madison: The University of Wisconsin Press, 1978.
Krauze, Enrique. <u>Historia de la Revolucion Mexicana,</u>
    <u>Volumen 10, Periodo 1924-1928: La Reconstruccion</u>
    <u>Economica</u>. Mexico: El Colegio de Mexico, 1977.
<u>Las Fronteras del Control del Estado Mexicano</u>. Mexico:
    El Colegio de Mexico, 1976.
<u>Las Perspectivas del Petróleo Mexicano</u>. Mexico: El
    Colegio de Mexico, 1979.
<u>Las Relaciones Mexico-Estados Unidos I</u>. Mexico, UNAM:
    Editorial Nueva Imagen, 1980.
<u>La Vida Política en Mexico: 1970-1973</u>. Mexico: El
    Colegio de Mexico, 1974.
Levinson, Jerome and Juan de Onis. <u>The Alliance that</u>
    <u>Lost its Way</u>. Chicago: Quadrangle Books, 1970.

Lieuwen, Edwin. Generals vs. Presidents. New York: Frederick A. Praeger, 1964.

López Portillo y Weber, José. El Petróleo de Mexico. Mexico: Editorial Fondo de Cultura Económica, 1975.

Lowenthal, Abraham F.. The Peruvian Experiment; continuity and change under military rule. Princeton, NJ: Princeton University Press, 1975.

Malloy, James M. (ed.). Authoritarianism and Corporatism in Latin America. Pittsburgh: University of Pittsburgh Press, 1977.

Mancke, Richard B. Mexican Oil and Natural Gas: Political, Strategic, and Economic Implications. New York: Praeger Publishers, 1979.

_____. The Failure of U.S. Energy Policy. New York: Columbia University Press, 1974.

Mander, John. The Unrevolutionary Society: The Power of Latin American Conservatism in a Changing World. New York: Knopf Publishers, 1969.

McBride, Robert H. (ed.). Mexico and the United States. Englewood Cliffs, NJ: Prentice Hall, Inc., 1981.

McEoin, Gary. Revolution Next Door. New York: Holt, Rinehart and Winston, 1971.

Mecham, John Lloyd. A Survey of U.S.-Latin American Relations. Boston: Houghton Mifflin Co., 1965.

Mejido, Manuel. Los Aventureros del Petróleo. Mexico: Editorial Grijalbo, 1980.

Meyer, Lorenzo. Mexico y Estados Unidos en el Conflicto Petrolero. Mexico: El Colegio de Mexico, 1968.

Mieres, Francisco. Crisis Capitalista y Crisis Energética. Mexico: Editorial Nuestro Tiempo, 1979.

Needler, Martin C. Political Development in Latin America: Instability, Violence and Evolutionary Change. New York: Random House, Inc., 1968.

_____. Politics and Society in Mexico. Albuquerque: University of New Mexico Press, 1971..

Noreng, Øystein. Oil Politics in the 1980's. New York: McGraw Hill, 1978.

O'Donnell, Guillermo. Modernization and Bureaucratic-Authoritarianism: Studies in South American Politics. Berkeley: University of California Press, 1973.

Ojeda, Mario. Alcances y Límites de la Política Exterior de Mexico. Mexico: El Colegio de Mexico, 1976.

Padilla Aragon, Enrique. Mexico: Desarrollo con Pobreza. Mexico: Siglo XXI Editores, 1979.

Paz, Octavio. El Laberinto de la Soledad. Mexico: Fondo de Cultura Economica, 1967.

_____. Posdata. Mexico: Siglo XXI Editores, 1974.

Pazos, Luis. Mitos y Realidades del Petróleo Mexicano. Mexico: Editorial Diana, 1979.

Pellicer de Brody, Olga and Esteban L. Mancilla.
    Historia de la Revolución Mexicana, Volumen 23,
    Periodo 1952-1960: El Entendimiento con los
    Estados Unidos y la gestación del Desarrollo
    Estabilizador. Mexico: El Colegio de Mexico, 1978.
Petras James and Maurice Zeitlin. Latin America: Reform
    of Revolution? New York: Fawcett Publications,
    Inc., 1968.
Pike, Frederick B. and Thomas Stritch (eds.). The New
    Corporatism. South Bend, IN: University of Notre
    Dame Press, 1974.
Powell, J. Richard. The Mexican Petroleum Industry:
    1938-1950. Berkeley: University of California
    Press, 1956.
Reyes, Alfonso. Mexico in a Nutshell. Berkeley: Uni-
    versity of California Press, 1964.
Riggs, Fred W. Administration in Developing Countries:
    the Theory of Prismatic Society. Boston: Houghton
    Mifflin Co., 1964.
Rippy, Merrill. Oil and the Mexican Revolution. Muncie,
    IN: Ball State University, 1972.
Robock, Stefan H. and Kenneth Simmons. International
    Business and Multinational Enterprises. Homewood,
    IL: Richard D. Irwin, Inc., 1973.
Rostow, Walt W. The Stages of Economic Development: A
    Non-communist manifesto. Cambridge: University
    Press, 1971.
Saxe-Fernández, John. Petróleo y Estrategia, Mexico y
    E.U. en el contexto de la política global. Mexico:
    Siglo XXI Editores, 1980.
Schmitt, Karl M. Mexico and the United States, 1821-
    1973: Conflict and Coexistence. New York: John
    Wiley and Sons, Inc., 1974.
Sepúlveda, Bernardo and Antonio Chumacero. La Inversión
    Extranjera en Mexico. Mexico: Fondo de Cultura
    Económica, 1973.
_____, et al. Las Empresas Transnacionales en
    Mexico. Mexico: El Colegio de Mexico, 1974.
Silvert, Kalman H. The Conflict Society: Reaction
    and Revolution in Latin America. New York:
    American Universities Field Staff, Inc., 1966.
Stein, Stanley J and Barbara H. La Herencia Colonial de
    America Latina. Mexico: Siglo XXI Editores, 1975.
Stepan, Alfred. The State and Society: Peru in Com-
    parative Perspective. Princeton: University Press,
    1978.
Sunkel, Osvaldo. El Subdesarrollo Latinoamericano y la
    Teoria del Desarrollo. Mexico: Siglo XXI Editores,
    1971.
Tannenbaum, Frank. Ten Keys to Latin America. New York:
    Random House, Inc., 1962.
Veliz, Claudio. Obstacles to Change in Latin America.
    London: Oxford University Press, 1965.

_____. The Politics of Conformity in Latin
America. London: Oxford University Press, 1967.
Vernon, Raymond. The Dilemma of Mexico's Development.
Cambridge: Harvard University Press, 1965.
_____. Sovereignty at Bay. New York: Basic
Books, Inc., 1971.
Wiarda, Howard J. and Harvey F. Kline. Latin American
Politics and Development. Boston: Houghton Mifflin
Co., 1979.
_____ (ed.). Politics and Social Change in Latin
America: the Distinct Tradition. Amherst, MA:
University of Massachusetts Press, 1974.
Williams, Edward J. The Rebirth of the Mexican Petroleum
Industry. Lexington, MA: D.C. Heath and Co., 1979.
Wionczek, Miguel. Inversión y Tecnología Extranjera en
América Latina. Mexico: Editorial Joaquin Mortiz,
1971.
_____ (ed.). La Sociedad Mexicana: Presente y
Futuro. Mexico: Fondo de Cultura Economica, 1974.
Zorrilla, Luis G. Historia de las Relaciones entre
Mexico y los Estados Unidos de America II. Mexico:
Editorial Porrua, 1966.

Documents (General)

Allub, Leopoldo and Marco A. Michel. Industria Petrolera
y Cambio Regional en Tabasco. Centro de Investiga-
ción para la Integración Social, Mexico, 1980.
America Latina y los Problemas Actuales de la Energía.
Comisión Económica para America Latina. Mexico:
Fondo de Cultura Económica, 1975.
Angelier, Jean Pierre. Producción y Reservas de Energía
en Mexico. CIDE, Mexico, December 1976.
Arauz, Luis (ed.). Legislación Petrolera Internacional.
Mexico: Siglo XXI Editores, 1978.
A Time to Choose: America's Energy Future, Final Report
by the Energy Policy Project of the Ford Foundation.
Cambridge, MA: Bellinger Publishing Co., 1974.
Different Fiscal Incentives and Comments to the Law of
Foreign Investments and Registry of Technology.
Mexico: Mexican Institute for Foreign Trade, 1975.
Domínguez, Jorge I. The Implications of Mexico's
Internal Affairs for its International Relations.
Center for International Affairs, Harvard Univer-
sity, April 18, 1980.
Fagen, Richard R. Mexican Gas: the Northern Connection.
Working Paper No. 15, Latin American Program,
Woodrow Wilson International Center for Scholars,
March 1978.
Fitzgerald, E.V.K. The Fiscal Deficit and Development
Finance: A Note on the Accumulation Balance in
Mexico. Working Paper No. 35, Center for Latin
American Studies, University of Cambridge, London.

Martínez Corbala, Gonzalo. "Lázaro Cárdenas y la
    Expropiación Petrolera." Conference given at the
    Workers' University on May 13, 1975. El Dia,
    Mexico, May 29, 1975.
Mexico 1980, Compendio de Datos y Estadísticas de Mexico.
    Cámara Nacional de Comercio de la Ciudad de Mexico,
    September 1980.
Mexico: La Política Económica del Nuevo Gobierno. Banco
    de Comercio Exterior, Mexico, 1971.
Nehring, Richard. Giant Oil Fields and World Oil
    Resources. Rand Corporation (R-2284-CIA), June 1978.
Pellicer de Brody, Olga. La Política de los Estados
    Unidos hacia Mexico en la Coyuntura Actual: Una
    Relación muy Especial? Working Paper No. 7,
    Latin American Program, Woodrow Wilson International
    Center for Scholars, April 1978.
Robinson, H.J. and T.G. Smith. The Impact of Foreign
    Private Investment on the Mexican Economy. The
    American Chamber of Commerce of Mexico, SRI,
    Stanford, 1976.
Speeches by the U.S. Ambassador to Mexico, Robert
    McBride, and the Mexican Secretary of Commerce,
    José Campillo Sainz, and subsequent discussion,
    during the meetings of the U.S.-Mexican Managerial
    Committee in Acapulco, on October 12, 1972.
    Comercio Exterior, Vol. XXII, No. 10, Mexico,
    October 1972.
Sterrett, Joseph Edmund and Joseph Stancliffe David.
    The Fiscal and Economic Condition of Mexico. Report
    submitted to the International Committee of Bankers
    on Mexico, May 1928.
Spinrad, B.I. and W. Sassin. Sustainable Energy Supplies
    for Our World. International Institute for Applied
    Systems Analysis, 1979.
Szulc, Tad. "An Interview with Mexico's President Jose
    Lopez Portillo." Parade, St. Louis Post-Dispatch,
    October 4, 1981.
Tomasek, Robert D. United States-Mexican Relations:
    Blowout of the Mexican Oil Well Ixtoc I. American
    Universities Field Staff Reports, No. 20, Hanover,
    NH, 1981.
Torres, Rodolfo. Perspectivas Energéticas de Mexico.
    Asociación de Tecnología Apropiada, A.C., Mexico,
    May 1980.
Williams, Edward J. Petroleum and Political Change in
    Mexico. Paper prepared for delivery at a Symposium
    on Mexican Politics, Harvard University, April 1980.
_____. Petroleum Policy and Mexican Domestic
    Politics: Left Opposition, Regional Dissidence, and
    Official Apostasy. Paper presented at the Annual
    Meeting of the Southern Economic Association,
    Washington, DC, November 1978.

Wilson, Carroll L. Workshop on Alternative Energy Strategies (WAES), Energy: Global Prospects 1985-2000. New York: McGraw Hill, 1977.

Wonder, Edward F. Mexico, Oil Supply and the Western Alliance. Paper presented at the Conference on Energy and the Atlantic Alliance, Committee on Atlantic Studies, Courmayeur, Italy, October 8-11, 1981.

World Energy Outlook. OECD, New York, 1977.

Yager, Joseph A. and Elear B. Steinberg. Energy and U.S. Foreign Policy. A Report by the Energy Policy Project of the Ford Foundation. Cambridge, MA: Bellinger Publishing Co., 1975.

Documents (United States Government)

Blowout of the Mexican Oil Well Ixtoc I. Hearings before the Committee on Merchant Marine and Fisheries and the Subcommittee on Water Resources of the Committee on Public Works and Transportation, House of Representatives, 96th Congress, 1st Session, on the Impact of the Blowout of the Mexican Oil Well Ixtoc I, and the resultant oil population on Texas and the Gulf of Mexico, Corpus Christi, TX, September 8-9, 1979. U.S. Government Printing Office, Washington, 1980.

Conant, Melvin and Fern R. Gold. Geopolitics of Energy. Committee on Interior and Insular Affairs. U.S. Senate. Energy Publications, No. 95-1, Washington, January 1977.

Hubbert, M.K. U.S. Energy Resources, A Review as of 1972. Document No. 93-40, U.S. Government Printing Office, Washington, 1974.

Mexico's Oil and Gas Policy: An Analysis. Document prepared for the Committee on Foreign Relations, U.S. Senate, and the Joint Economic Committee, Congress of U.S., by the Congressional REsearch Service, Library of Congress, 96th Congress, 2nd Session, U.S. Government Printing Office, Washington, 1979.

Newfarmer, Richard S. and Willard F. Muller. Multinational Corporations in Brazil and Mexico: Structural Sources of Economic and Noneconomic Power. Report to the Subcommittee on Multinational Corportations of the Committee on Foreign Relations, 94th Congress, 1st Session, U.S. Government Printing Office, Washington, 1975.

Recent Developments in Mexico and their economic implications for the United States. Hearings before the Subcommittee on Inter-American Economic Relations of the Joint Economic Committee, Congress of the United States, 95th Congress, January 17 and 24, 1977. U.S. Government Printing Office, Washington, 1977.

Remarks of the President in his Address to the Nation,
The Oval Office, The White House, Office of the
White House Press Secretary, July 15, 1979.
The International Energy Situation: Outlook to 1985.
Central Intelligence Agency, April 1977.
Text of the President's Energy Address to the Nation,
The White House, Office of the White House Press
Secretary, April 5, 1979.
U.S.-Mexican Joint Announcement, The White House, Office
of the White House Press Secretary, September 21,
1979.
U.S.-Mexico Relations and Potentials Regarding Energy,
Immigration, Scientific Cooperation and Technology
Transfer. Report prepared by the Subcommittee on
Science, Research, and Technology of the Committee
on Science and Technology, U.S. House of Representa-
tives, 96th Congress, 1st Session, July 1979. U.S.
Government Printing Office, Washington, 1979.

Documents (Department of Energy)

A New Start; The National Energy Act. DOE, Office of
Public Affairs, U.S. Government Printing Office,
Washington, 1979.
Importation of Mexican Natural Gas -1979. Order approv-
ing in part an application of Border Gas, Inc., to
import natural gas into the United States from
Mexico, DOE, Economic Regulatory Administration,
December 29, 1979.
DOE gives final clearance to import of natural gas from
Mexico. DOE News, December 29, 1979.
DOE receives application to import Mexican Natural Gas.
DOE News, Office of Public Affairs, November 21,
1979.
Mexico's Petroleum and U.S. Policy: Implications for the
1980's. Rand Corportation, R-2510-DOE, June 1980.
Natural Gas Policy Act of 1978. Public Law 95-621, 92
Stat. 3350, 95th Congress, DOE, November 9, 1978.
National Energy Plan II. A Report to the Congress
required by Title VIII of the Department of Energy
Organization Act, Public Law 95-91, DOE, May 1979.
Petroleum Supply Alternatives for the Northern Tier and
Inland States through the year 2000. DOE-RA-0042-1
& 2, DOE, Assistant Secretary for Resource Applica-
tion, Energy Supply Transportation Division,
Washington, October 31, 1979.
Response Plan: Reducing U.S. Impact on the World Oil
Market. DOE-IR-0048, DOE, April 1979.
Report to the President on the activities of Oil
Companies affecting Gasoline Supplies, DOE, July
24, 1979.

"Coal: The Dynamo of Energy Independence." An address
by John C. Sawhill, Deputy Secretary of the U.S.
Department of Energy, Johnstown, PA, April 14, 1980.
Secretary's Annual Report to Congress (DOE-S-0010-80).
DOE, U.S. Government Printing Office, Washington,
January 1980.

Documents (Mexican Government)

"Acto Conmemorativo de la Expropiación de la industria
petrolera." Discurso del Presidente José López
Portillo, Guadalajara, March 18, 1980.
"Conferencia de Prensa con corresponsales extranjeros,"
January 26, 1978. Cuadernos de Filosofía Política,
No. 3, "Política Petrolera," Secretaría de Programa-
ción y Presupuesto, Mexico, February 1980.
Constitución Política de los Estados Unidos Mexicanos.
Mexico: Editorial Porrua, 1971.
Cuarto Informe de Gobierno. Uno mas Uno, September 2,
1980.
"Decreto por el que se aprueba el Programa de Energía y
se ordena su ejecución." Diario Oficial, Mexico,
February 4, 1981.
Directorio de organismos descentralizados y empresas de
participacion estatal. Secretaría del Patrimonio
Nacional, Mexico, 1976.
"Discurso de Toma de Protesta como Presidente de la
Republica," de José López Portillo, December 1976.
Cuadernos de Filosofía Política, No. 9, Secretaría
de Programación y Presupuesto, Mexico, October 1978.
"En Torno a la visita del Presidente Carter a Mexico."
Cuadernos de Filosofía Política, No. 17, Secretaría
de Programación y Presupuesto, Mexico, March 1979.
"Ley de Ingresos y Presupuesto de Egresos de la Federa-
ción para 1981." Secretaría de Hacienda y Crédito
Público, Mexico, 1980.
"Ley para promover la inversión mexicana y regular la
inversión extranjera." in Fausto Zapata, Mexico:
Notas sobre el Sistema Político y la Inversion
Extranjera (Mexico: Publicidad y Offset, S.A.,
1974).
Plan Global de Desarrollo, 1980-1982. Secretaría de
Programación y Presupuesto, Mexico, 1980.
Primer Informe de Gobierno. Cuadernos de Filosofía
Política, No. 0. Secretaría de Programación y
Presupuesto, Mexico, February 1980.
Programa de Energía. Energéticos: Boletín Informativo
del Sector Energético, Comisión de Energéticos.
Secretaría de Patrimonio y Fomento Industrial,
Año 4, No. 11, Mexico, November 1980.
Quinto Informe de Gobierno. El Universal, September 3,
1981.

Segundo Informe de Gobierno. Excelsior, September 2, 1978.

Documents (Petroleos Mexicanos)

Chicontepec: Un Desafío...una Oportunidad. Pemex, Mexico, March 1979.
Ducto Troncal del Sistema Nacional de Gas. Pemex, Mexico, March 18, 1979.
El Petróleo. Pemex, Mexico, 1976.
Informe Anual del Director de Pemex. Pemex, Mexico, March 18, 1978.
Informe Anual del Director de Pemex. Pemex, Guadalajara, March 18, 1980.
Petróleos Mexicanos: Memoria de Labores, 1979. Pemex, Mexico, 1980.
Report of the Director General. Pemex, 1981.
Rescisión de los Contratos CIMA. Pemex, Mexico, 1969.
Tres Años de la Nueva Política Petrolera: 1977-1979. Pemex, Mexico, 1979.

ARTICLES FROM SPECIALIZED JOURNALS

Anderson, Earl V. "North American Trade Alliance Gains Support." Chemical and Engineering News, Vol. 58, No. 28, July 14, 1980.
Bath, Richard C. and Dilmus D. James. "Dependency Analysis of Latin America: Some criticisms, some suggestions." Latin American Research Review, Vol. XI, No. 3, 1976.
Behrman, J.N. "Sharing International Production through the Multinational Enterprise and Sectorial Integration." 4 Law and Policy in International Business 2, 1972.
Beltrán del Río, Abel. "El Síndrome del Petróleo Mexicano: Primeros Síntomas, Medidas Preventivas y Pronósticos." Comercio Exterior, Vol. 30, No. 6, June 1980.
Berkstein K., Samuel. "Mexico: Estrategia Petrolera y Politica Exterior." Foro Internacional, Vol. XXI, No. 1, El Colegio de Mexico, July-September 1980.
Bizzarro, Salvatore. "Mexico's Oil Boom." Current History, Vol. 82, No. 463, February 1981.
Briggs, Vernon M., Jr. "Mexican workers in the U.S. labour market." International Labor Review, Vol. 112, No. 5, November 1975.
Castañeda, Jorge. "Mexico y E.U.: El Próximo Decenio." Comercio Exterior, Vol. 30, No. 6, June 1980.
Chilcote, Ronald H. "A Question of Dependency." Latin American Research Review, Vol. XIII, No. 2, 1978.
D'Souza, Victor S. "La transformación de las sociedades: una perspectiva para las relaciones entre los

países desarrollados y los que estan en vías de
desarrollo." Social Action, Vol. 26, No. 2, New
Delhi, India, April-June 1976.

Finbenzhutz, Juan. "Panorama General de Energéticos en
Mexico." Comercio Exterior, Vol. 26, No. 4, 1976.

Fagen, Richard R. "The Realities of U.S.-Mexican Relations." Foreign Affairs, Vol. 55, No. 4, July
1977.

_____. "Studying Latin American Politics: Some
Implications of a Dependency Approach." Latin
American Research Review, Vol. XII, No. 2, 1977.

Franco, Alvaro. "Latin America's Petroleum Surge Gathers
Momentum." The Oil and Gas Journal, June 5, 1978.

_____. "New Reforma Finds Push Mexico to new Oil
Heights." The Oil and Gas Journal, May 17, 1976.

_____. "Recent Discoveries vault Mexico in new
position." The Oil and Gas Journal, October 21,
1974.

García-Colin Scherer, Leopoldo. "La Ciencia y la
Tecnología del Petróleo: Situación Actual y Per-
spectivas Futuras en Mexico." Foro Internacional,
Vol. XVIII, No. 4, El Colegio de Mexico, April-
June 1978.

Grayson, George. "Mexico's Opportunity, the Oil Boom."
Foreign Policy, December 1977.

_____. "Oil and Politics in Mexico." Current
History, December 1977.

Green, Rosario. "La deuda pública externa de Mexico,
1965-1976." Comercio Exterior, Vol. 27, No. 11,
November 1977.

Cribomont, C. and M. Rimez. "La Politica economica del
gobierno de Luis Echeverria (1971-1976): Un primer
ensayo de interpretacion." El Trimestre Economico,
Vol. XLIV (4), No. 176, October-December 1977.

Gutiérrez R, Roberto. "La balanza petrolera de Mexico,
1970-1982." Comercio Exterior, Vol. 29, No. 8,
August 1979.

Hafeler, Wolf. "La Demanda de Energía." Boletín Informativo del Sector Energético. Comisión de Energéticos, Año 2, No. 7, 1978.

Hodara, Joseph. "Hacia la finlandización de Mexico?"
Vuelta, Vol. 5, No. 51, February 1981.

Jaguaribe, Helio. "La Crisis de Petróleo y sus Alternativas Internacionales." El Trimestre Económico,
Vol. XLIV (3), No. 175, July-September 1977.

Kaplan, Marcos. "La concentración del poder político a
escala mundial." El Trimestre Económico, Vol. XLI
(1), No. 161, January-March 1974.

_____. "Petróleo y Desarrollo: el impacto
interno." Foro Internacional, Vol. XXI, No. 1,
El Colegio de Mexico, July-September 1980.

Latin American Petroleum Survey, Part I, Washington
Report on the Hemisphere, Vol. 2, No. 4. Council

on Hemispheric Affairs, November 17, 1981.

LeBlanc, Leonard. "The rising of an oil powerhouse." Offshore, Vol. 39, No. 51, May 1979.

Leighton, Marian. "Mexico, Cuba and the Soviet Union: Ferment in the U.S.' Backyard." Radio Liberty Research, RL 1/80, December 27, 1980.

Leiken, Robert. "Como ganar la amistad de Mexico." Vuelta, Vol. 5, No. 53, April 1981.

McNally, Rich. "Oil and gas prospects of deep offshore." Petroleum Engineer International, Vol. 52, No. 10, August 1980.

_____. "World instability spurs home drilling." Petroleum Engineer International, Vol. 51, No. 7, June 1979.

"Mexico and Venezuela Reap Harvest, and Share Some Wealth." Washington Report on the Hemisphere, Vol. 2, No. 4, Council on Hemispheric Affairs, November 17, 1981.

"Mexico, Venezuela-Caribbean and Central American countries set regional oil supply plan." Energy Developments, Vol. XXIII, No. e273-8, July 15, 1980.

Michel, Marco Antonio and Leopoldo Allub. "Petroleo y Cambio Social en el Sureste de Mexico." Foro Internacional, Vol. XVIII, No. 4, El Colegio de Mexico, April-June 1978.

Noreng, Øystein. "La Relacion entre la OPEP y los exportadores que no la integran." Comercio Exterior, Vol. 29, No. 8, August 1979.

O'Donnell, Guillermo. "Reflections on the pattern of change in the bureaucratic-authoriatarian state." Latin American Research Review, Vol. XIII, No. 1 (1978).

Ojeda, Mario. "El poder negociador del petróleo: el caso de Mexico." Foro Internacional, Vol. XXI, No. 1, El Colegio de Mexico, July-September 1980.

_____. "The Perils of Proximity to a Powerful Country: the Viewpoint of a Mexican." Typewritten.

Pellicer de Brody, Olga. "La Politica de Estados Unidos hacia Mexico: la nueva perspectiva." Foro Internacional, Vol. XIX, No. 2, El Colegio de Mexico, October-December 1978.

Peña Guerrero, Roberto. "Crisis: reajuste, hegemonía y dependencia." Relaciones Internacionales, Vol. VI, No. 21, CRI UNAM, April-June 1978.

Rham, B.A. "Peculiarities of a regional crisis." Petroleum Economist, Vol. XLVII, No. 3, March 1980.

Redclift, Michael and Naneke. "Unholy Alliance." Foreign Policy, No. 41, Winter 1980-1981.

Rondfelt, David R. and Caesar D. Sereseres. "Un nuevo marco político para las relaciones de Mexico con Estados Unidos." Foro Internacional, Vol. XIX, No. 2, El Colegio de Mexico, October-December 1978.

Rubin, Seymour J. "Multinational Enterprise and National
    Sovereignty: A skeptic's analysis." 3 Law and
    Policy in International Business 2, 1971.
Seaton, Earl. "U.S. pipeline system continues to grow."
    The Oil and Gas Journal, Vol. 78, No. 32, August 11,
    1980.
Stepan, Alfred. "The United States and Latin America:
    Vital Interests and the Instruments of Power."
    Foreign Affairs, Vol. 58, No. 3, 1980.
Stewart-Gordon, T.J. "Mexico: offshore is in the news."
    World Oil, Vol. 189, No. 3, August 15, 1979.
Turrent Díaz, Eduardo. "Petróleo y Economía: Costos y
    Beneficios a corto plazo." Foro Internacional,
    Vol. XVIII, No. 4, El Colegio de Mexico, April-June
    1978.
Vagt, Detev F. "The Global Corporations and Inter-
    national Law," 6 The Journal of International Law
    and Economics 249, 1972.
Vernon, Raymond. "The Multinational Corporation." 5
    Atlantic Community Quarterly 553, 1967-1968.
Villar, Samuel E. del. "El Sistema Mexicano de Regula-
    ción de la Inversión Extranjera; Elementos y
    deficiencias Generales." Foro Internacional,
    Vol. XV, No. 3, El Colegio de Mexico, January-
    March 1975.
"Western Energy Policy after Carter." Lloyd's Bank
    Review. London, January 1978.
Wiarda, Howard J. "Toward a Framework for the study of
    Political Change in the Iberic-Latin Tradition:
    the Corporative Model." World Politics, Vol. XXV,
    No. 2, January 1973.

Index